TRADITIONAL
CHRISTIAN
ETHICS

TRADITIONAL CHRISTIAN ETHICS

VOLUME ONE: AN INTRODUCTION AND INDEXES

DAVID W. T. BRATTSTON

WESTBOW·
PRESS
A DIVISION OF THOMAS NELSON
& ZONDERVAN

WestBow Press books may be ordered through booksellers or by contacting:

WestBow Press
A Division of Thomas Nelson & Zondervan
1663 Liberty Drive
Bloomington, IN 47403
www.westbowpress.com
1 (866) 928-1240

ISBN: 978-1-4908-2122-1 (sc)
ISBN: 978-1-4908-2121-4 (e)

Library of Congress Control Number: 2013923598

Printed in the United States of America.

WestBow Press rev. date: 07/01/2014

Dedication

To the interlibrary loan services of
the South Shore Public Libraries
Nova Scotia
Serving Lunenburg and Queens Counties

Contents

Volumes Two and Three:

List of Affirmative Commandments/Precepts

Volume Four:

List of Negative Commandments/Precepts or Prohibitions

Introduction

This book is a completely new work. It is not a revision or digest of previous works in the recent past. Nor do its most proximate precursors provide itemized alphabetical lists of ethical precepts, include a breakdown by author and book, systematically refer through citations to the relevant writings, discuss the place of tradition in transmitting the moral teaching of earliest Christianity, or give reasons why the period AD 249-251 should be the terminal date for the reliability of this tradition. This book is unique also in drawing from the canonical New Testament, accounts of martyrdoms, New Testament apocrypha, and church fathers in order to present early Christian ethics as comprehensively as possible, thus lessening the bias of individual writers, their geographic area or their church party/denomination.

The study that resulted in this book originated in my search for how I as a Christian am to behave in order to love God and my neighbour in action. As a lawyer and judge on minor tribunals, I learned that loving one's "neighbour" is not always clear nor does it follow a direct route, that there can be valid doubts and uncertainty as to which course of action best helps a "neighbour", and that perplexities can often arise within a well-meaning person as to which of two "neighbours" to favour or love more when their legitimate interests conflict. My first resort was to the Bible. All denominations and sects of Christianity appeal to the Scriptures as the cornerstone of Christian ethics. Most Protestants hold it to be an all-sufficient guide in matters of faith and practice. With the flourishing of Protestant fundamentalism and other forms of evangelicalism, this is becoming the most widely-accepted view.

In my own spiritual journey I have found the Bible to be insufficient, or at least unclear and subject to a myriad of interpretations, each claiming exclusive validity for itself. All or almost all hermeneutical methods I encountered require a certain amount of mental gymnastics, facile proof-texting, finessing or slurring of inconvenient passages, extension beyond what (I think) the text can reasonably bear, and reliance on verses whose applicability is not apparent to anyone except the already-convinced. I felt the Bible needed a supplement or method of interpretation that was unassailable on objective grounds.

Granted, there are denominations that assert that they possess a supplement to Scripture in the form of a tradition dating back to Jesus Christ and are the only inspired or authorized interpreters and teachers of the Bible and Christian ethics. Ecclesiastical bodies of this type include the Roman Catholic, Eastern Orthodox and Oriental Orthodox ("Monophysite") churches. Although resembling each other more than do the Protestant bodies, there is division among them which confuses the seeker after truth in his or her attempt to establish the ethical contents of the authentic original gospel and its demands on a believer's behaviour.

In addition, there are denominations that base their claims on latter-day revelation or direct inspiration that came to their founders in the nineteenth or twentieth century unconnected with preceding ecclesiastical organizations. There are many such religious bodies, some of them originating in schisms after the deaths of the original leaders or revelators. If it were not for the mutually-contradictory assertions about possessing the sole or complete truth and about exclusively continuing the unadulterated teachings of these founders, a bystander would think that divine inspiration had multiplied and that revelation had split into several parallel but never-commingling channels. The same is true of Islam, which claims to be the successor of authentic and primitive Christianity through divine revelations in the seventh century.

Dissatisfied with the confusion caused by contending claims and the lack of a means of objectively verifying them free of denominational presuppositions (no matter how inadvertent), I looked for a species of claim that could not be duplicated or fabricated. Anybody can claim a latter-day revelation, unique guidance by the Holy Spirit, or correct hermeneutics. Even descent through a line of ordinations stretching back to the apostles is suspect because there are conflicting allegations as to which modern-day denomination most closely reflects the collectivity of the ancient bishops and apostles, and the Roman Catholic Church does not recognize Anglican succession.[1] I wanted something unique, something that could not be invented or asserted by anyone unsupported by unassailable evidence.

At length it occurred to me to go back to the literature of the earliest age of Christianity, before medieval and modern differences arose as to the exact content of the gospel and as to the interpretation of the Scriptures' pronouncements on morality. Unlike claims to revelation, possession of the Holy Spirit, or faultless hermeneutics, this method cannot be duplicated or falsely raised because there is only one body of primitive Christian writings and, unlike modern pretensions to possession of divine guidance, cannot be contrived or asserted without being liable to falsification by a definite body of universally accepted data. Not even the most expert of exegetes or self-declared prophets can duplicate or fabricate data of this type.

Granted, lost ancient Christian documents come to light from time to time, but their authenticity is thoroughly checked by competent scholars. Where a text undiscovered until modern times is of doubtful authenticity, I exclude it from consideration. On the other hand, I include all truly ancient writings, not just those judged orthodox, because such inclusion (1) avoids applying suppositions as to what is true or authentic Christianity by the criteria of a later time or of a rival denomination within its own time, (2) provides a fuller view of the subject-matter, (3) avoids straight-jacketing the literature by my own—or my age's—unwitting assumptions or presuppositions, and (4) gives the consensus of the whole of the Christianity of its day instead of a single denomination or author.

The first chapter of this book sets the stage by considering the terminology and approaches to Christian ethics, especially the approach adopted in this book. The second chapter shows that the approach of the earliest Christians to morality was through a large body of specific injunctions and prohibitions. Chapter Three points out why the Scriptures in the commonly-received canon are insufficient to reveal the full body of such morality. Chapter Four outlines the benefits of following tradition in addition to the Bible or as a means of interpreting it and demonstrates that early Christians were thus guided by tradition; it also touches on criteria by which a teaching or practice is to be accepted as part of this tradition. Chapter Five explains why attestations of this tradition are not reliable after the middle of the third century, and thus why AD 249-251 is the terminal date of this study. The sixth chapter is an introduction to the lists following, and to methods of interpreting them. As stated in Chapter Six, various approaches can be taken in using the lists. I leave selection of the approach to my readers so that the finished work will not be cluttered by my subliminal or subjective predispositions.

I have deliberately kept my use of modern commentaries on early Christian literature to a minimum. This is to allow the original authors to speak for themselves more completely, to avoid any inclination toward one side or another among contending medieval or modern opinions, and to lessen anachronistic judgments. In addition, I was reacting against the practice of many twentieth-century scholars whose writings concentrate so heavily on modern commentaries and treatises that, to my way of thinking, the product is really about recent books rather than ancient ones.

A note on my use of the word "denomination": I employ this term to denote any group of Christians, both ancient and modern, that (1) maintains fellowships separate from those of other Christian groups, (2) holds to doctrines and practices, the totality of which is distinct from those of other such groups, (3) has its own teachers and leaders, (4) states or implies that it has a more correct or more acceptable approach to the Faith than do the others, (5) does not allow non-members to vote or hold office in the group, (6) interacts only voluntarily (or not at all) with other such groups, as opposed to being compelled by a common earthly authority, (7) holds its own assemblies for instruction, governance or public worship, and (8) usually does not automatically accept the decisions of other such groups but makes its own investigations and ratifies independently of them. In modern times and almost always in antiquity, a denomination has or had its own ecclesiastical organization. Because these characteristics of denominations in the sixteenth through twenty-first centuries were paralleled in the first three centuries, I believe this modern-day term can be justly used to denote a division within ancient Christianity. Professor Gregory J. Riley has thus employed the word "denomination", although guardedly, to describe ante-Nicene Christian groups and sects.[2]

I use the words "catholic" and "orthodox" to denote the majority group or Great Church within early Christianity because this is what its members called it in distinction from Gnostics, Montanists and other factions whose doctrines or practices it did not accept as accurate representations of true Christianity. The modern-day Roman Catholic Church is only one of the descendants of this catholic church and the present-day Eastern Orthodox and Oriental Orthodox do not constitute all descendants of the early orthodox church. I had considered using the words "universal" or "Great Church" instead of "orthodox" and "catholic" but the corresponding adjectives are more problematical than for the words I have used. For instance, "universalist" is in well-established use for an approach to spirituality that is quite different from early Christian orthodoxy or catholicism.

I have read enough modern commentaries to realize that in some cases there may be hazards in accepting the statements of ancient authors at face value. Four examples come immediately to mind. First, F. F. Bruce correctly describes the writings of Ignatius of Antioch as "exaggerated and passionate", possessed by "an *idée fixe*", and whose very vehemence shows that his view on church government "was far from being universally shared."[3] Professor Cross opines that "The psychiatrist might be disposed to pronounce him unbalanced or neurotic. But the reader of his letters will soon discover that he falls outside all conventional categories."[4] Second, the Greek original of Irenaeus' *Adversus haereses (Against Heresies)* has been lost and the translator who produced the extant text "was in every way inferior to the work that he undertook; independently of the barbarisms and solecisms with which his style abounds, he is frequently totally unable to catch the author's meaning."[5] Third, Hippolytus' statements against some practices of his opponents in the Great Church may have been motivated not only by pastoral and theological principles but also by rivalry for position and merely personal dislike.[6] Indeed, in commenting on one of Hippolytus' books, Assistant Professor Williams notes "we cannot be exactly certain whether the teaching presented here represents the instruction given in the Church at Rome or is the idiosyncratic views of one man."[7] Lastly, even the four canonical Gospels are suspect, for "each gospel-writer may have selected from/4/a vast store of genuine utterances of Jesus those sayings which suited his own purposes."[8] Rather than compensate through second-guessing based on a remove of seventeen to twenty centuries with its conjectures, age-related prejudices and partial knowledge of a later era, I believe my method compensates for ancient weaknesses by including as wide a range as possible of pre-Decian writers, letting all available voices be heard (whether orthodox or not by the standards of their or own or a later age), and using only texts or quotations from their own works instead of including the paraphrases and representations by their opponents. There is support for this method in Assistant Professor Williams' comments following upon the quotation from him above: when the particular book of Hippolytus is compared to other Christian works of the period, we can safely conclude that it "reflects the broader spectrum of Christian teaching".[9]

Chapter One

Terms, Values, and Approaches

Description

In this book, "Christian moral law" means the body of rules of morals or ethics to which a Christian's actions and attitudes must conform in order to live according to God's will. It prescribes the deeds and mental states a disciple must or must not perform and have in relation to God and other people in order to do and be what God considers good. It can be divided into two parts: the sort of person God wants an individual to be (character) and the sorts of actions God wants a Christian to perform or refrain from performing (acts). Christian moral law can be divided another two ways: how an individual Christian is to think and act, and how a congregation or other combination of Christians is to think and act. There is yet another twofold dimension: what God wants us to do (positive commandments, injunctions) and what God forbids (negatives, prohibitions). The present book is about the last-mentioned.

Christian moral law is rooted in what God considers good and is based on criteria given by Him. It does not vary with a person's wishes, emotions, or desire for gain. It is not a means by which a human being is to manipulate God or another person. What is "moral" is what God wants; thus, the word is not properly used in the sentence "The moral thing for you to do is ..." when the speaker really means "I want you to do something for my benefit without me incurring an obligation or taking responsibility for any adverse results." Nor should calling something "moral" or "immoral" be used as a method of arguing that the hearer do something to please the speaker when the speaker otherwise has no leg to stand on, either in the law of the land or on any other basis.

A Christian obeys the moral law out of his love and commitment to God and in order to fulfill God's commands and do what God knows is good. Such obedience flows from faith and is possible only with God's continuing grace.

1

David W. T. Brattston

Christian Law or Christian Ethics?

The term "Christian law" is disagreeable to many twenty-first-century disciples of Jesus, especially some Protestants; when they wish to express something akin to it, they say "Christian ethics". All Christians like to regard themselves as ethical but few like to admit that they are subject to religious "law".

For our present purposes, there is no meaningful difference between "ethics" and "law".[10] In common parlance, "ethics" is the systematic study of morals (the rules of conduct as an abstraction) while "law" is a body of rules which a community recognizes as binding, with punishment for those who break them. Properly speaking, the subject of the present book may be categorized as "moral theology" but the subject matter of this term is usually dealt with in the imprecise language of today as "morals" or "ethics". I submit that if the Christian community recognizes a rule of morality or of moral theology to be binding on its members, then it is a law.

In everyday speech, ethics is often the equivalent of law. In the professions, "ethics" are as binding as the general law of the land except that the means of enforcement do not include imprisonment or the death penalty. For a violation of its code of ethics, a professional regulatory body can suspend or expel one of its members from practice, exclude him/her from the profession, fine him/her, and deprive him/her of her/his livelihood. In contrast with these sanctions, the comparatively minor fines and other punishments for lesser violations of a highway traffic statute or the amounts recoverable through small claims courts are trifling. In the same manner as a profession or trade union, the church can suspend or expel a member from the Eucharist, and exclude him from its fellowship—the equivalent of the old legal penalty of banishment and exile. Subject to the restraints of secular law on private persons depriving others of life and bodily liberty, ethics are just as much law for a member of a church, profession or other organization.

For the purposes of the present book and its lists, the word "law" is more appropriate than "ethics" or "morality" because the lists cover all rules of Christian behaviour, including many which some people might consider to be outside the scope of pure ethics.

Some twentieth-century authors employed other expressions for the concept that the present book subsumes under the word "law". In expostulating that the Mosaic Law no longer binds Christians *as law*, particularly in the thought of the Apostle Paul, some of these writers held that it remains in force as "instruction", "ethical principle", "commandment", God's standard and judgment, norm of Christian life, aid to life, "Scripture", "promise", or requirement of character and conduct.[11]

Common Approaches to Christian Ethical Decision-Making

Seven approaches to the moral life are widely practised by Christians in the Western world at the beginning of the twenty-first century:

1) adoption of the behavioural norms and practices of the surrounding secular community,

2) self-interest, tempered only by secular law and the desire not to fall into disrepute among persons of the same or a higher socio-economic class,

3) sincere conscience,

4) acceptance, sometimes with reservations, of the teachings of a person's religious denomination,

5) application—as the situation arises—of broad, general moral principles, such as love of neighbour, without more specific criteria,

6) the practical application of Bible principles, and

7) compliance with a sizable number of predetermined rules of moral law.

These are not textbook methodologies formulated by professional ethicists or other academics but are the ones I have observed to be in most widespread use among the general community. Let us consider these seven:

(1) and (2): The behavioural norms of the surrounding secular community, or self-interest tempered by secular law and the desire not to fall into disrepute among persons whose approval is sought.

These first two are simply not Christian but depend upon a source of authority other than God's revelation. They fluctuate from place to place and time to time, sometimes within a few years or months. They are frequently disseminated or even created by the secular media or other opinion-makers. Unlike God, they are inconstant and changeable. Neither honours the commandment to love God or one's neighbour in its own right. Nor are standards uniform throughout communities: in contrast to the willing compliance of most segments of the community to help law enforcement, some classes or associations within Western societies regard it immoral or as a breach of honour to tell the police or the courts anything about the criminal behaviour of their friends or associates. Being based on community standards and legally-permitted egocentrism, these community-based ethical values derive their validity from purely human fashion.

On the contrary, as noted by Carl F. Henry, "The Christian ethic is a specially revealed morality—not merely religious ethics. It gains its reality in and through supernatural disclosure."[12] Further, as noted by the prominent Christian ethicist, James M. Gustafson, "the ethics of Christians is and must be exclusively Christian because the community is called to absolute obedience to Jesus as Lord; all the moral actions of the community must be determined by his lordship."[13] Moreover, such lordship is determinative for every aspect of a Christian's life, including ethics.[14] A greater authority, the Bible itself, opts for this view: Romans 12.1 appeals to Christians to present their bodies—the totality of themselves—as a continuing sacrifice to God rather than dividing themselves between God and the surrounding secular world and its values; the next verse amplifies this by saying "Do not be conformed to this world, but be transformed by the renewal of your mind."

3

(3) Sincere conscience:

Conscience is susceptible to the limitations and frailties that limit all human minds, to a greater or lesser extent. Besides unreliability due to innate physical imperfections of the brain, the conscience can be impaired by poor formation in childhood or traumatic experiences at any time of life. Most people would grant that the mind and conscience of the severely mentally or emotionally ill is undependable, but there is no cut-off point on the continuum between these and the hypothetically perfect healthy mind. To take one example, many schizophrenics sincerely believe that God tells them what to do through a voice or voices that only they can hear. Another example: a psychopath has no conscience at all. Indeed, the perfect human brain does not exist. Even if it did, we are not all geniuses. Mental differences being a matter of degree, with a long continuum between the most superior and the most impaired, the ability to develop a conscience is variable or lacking and hence unreliable. To a greater or lesser degree, even a "normal" mind is heir to such impairments as self-delusion,[15] self-interest, emotions, family interest, confusion, rationalizing the unjustified, ignorance of fact, and ignorance of God's will. Conscience can be misled or corrupted.[16] Nor is sincerity a moral guide: sincerity is no guarantee of correctness, as witness the number of well-intentioned but mistaken people over the centuries who have created havoc through the best of intentions (e.g. the Apostle Paul before his conversion). Neither sincerity nor unaided conscience guards a person from becoming self-righteous, fanatical, or so deluded that he believes that whatever he wants God wants also. "Conscience...needs education and development. The difference between right and wrong does actually exist outside us. What is inside us needs to be taught about that reality."[17] True, the phrase "for conscience's sake" does occur in the New Testament[18], but even there it "never implies that conscience is the voice of God demanding obedience."[19] Rules of morality "are one of the main mechanisms that we have for challenging our own consciences, for erecting barriers against the self-deception and callousness to which we are all prone."[20]

(4) Acceptance, sometimes with reservations, of the teachings of one's religious denomination:

Like Stanley Hauerwas, the position of Bruce C. Birch and Larry L. Rasmussen in *Bible & Ethics in the Christian Life*[21] is that a Christian should accept the moral teachings of one's religious denomination. Ethics are to be developed within the church. A very developed treatment of the local church as a community of moral discourse and deliberation, especially through the exegesis and application of Scripture, can be found in Part One of Associate Professor Allen Verhey's *Remembering Jesus: Christian Community, Scripture, and the Moral Life*[22] However, none of these authors answer the all-important question "Which church?" Although the best-known example of a Christian organization that provides comprehensive moral guidance is the Roman Catholic Church, many smaller denominations also lay down precise regulations about how their members are to behave. In many instances, minority sects which legislate behaviour and attitudes destroy the faithful's capacity to make independent moral judgments, a situation which has led to mass suicides, gun battles with the police, and surrendering all property and women to a charismatic leader. At the other extreme, a large number of Roman Catholics consider some papal pronouncements on morals so burdensome or out-of-keeping with their desires[23] that they rationalize them away, sometimes on the premise that while the pronouncements are the official teaching of the Church they are nevertheless not *ex cathedra*.

Adherence to denominational moral directives is declining in our ecumenical age, largely because they are fewer and members have less opportunity to know what they are. This is due in large part to the phenomenon that the method most mainline denominations give effect to Jesus' prayer in John 17.11, 21-22 is by diminishing the characteristics which distinguish them from each other. A common method of downplaying sectarian identity is by decreasing the number and obligatory nature of ethical standards and by increasing members' personal responsibility for moral decision-making. One of the purposes of the present book is to help the church members discharge that responsibility in an informed manner. What few ethical issues mainline Protestant churches do address are proposals for reform of their own national governments or, much more frequently, criticisms of foreign regimes—neither of which an individual Christian has much power to influence. The paraenesis directed to those who are least likely to heed it or even know of its existence. Mainstream Protestantism offers less and less official guidance on practical issues of day-to-day morality that confront the ordinary Christian.

Even when a denomination as a whole does try to offer or formulate moral guidance, the process is so time-consuming, cumbersome, and prone to procedural delays as proposals wend their ways through committees and various levels of solemn assemblies that a number of months or years pass between the emergence of the issue and the church's pronouncement on it. Such a source of guidance is of no practical use when an individual Christian must make a quick moral decision within a shorter time span. In the meantime, guidance for the parishioner is uncertain or lacking.

Although it offers the advantages of safety in numbers and opportunities to exchange judgments and considerations and to fine-tune and to deliberate what are the relevant ethical principles and precepts, such an approach has the inherent weakness of exacerbating a common accusation against some individual Christians which is often extrapolated against Christians in general. In addition to the protracted delays and the propensity to introduce irrelevant (often political) considerations into making decisions for a church at the national or international level, there is an inherent weakness even when moral decision-making takes place at the local (congregational) level, a weakness that by the very structure of the process adds fuel to this criticism against believers, and by extension against the belief-system itself. The accusation and criticism is that many Christians (usually those outside one's own group) are merely "Sunday Christians"—pious, loving and Christlike on the day of worship but devoid of love of neighbour and of consideration for other people on the six other days of the week, such a Christian reputedly being motivated on workdays solely by self-interest and materialistic values, with no regard for the well-being of those whom his/her words and actions affect. Although congregations meet far more frequently than do regional or national bodies, the fact that congregations gather on only one or two days of the week means that even a local church is a viable community for moral exhortation and deliberation only on the day of worship. Even in the shrinking number of congregations where a midweek prayer meeting or Bible study is still held, these activities are attended only by a fraction of the membership, thus so diminishing the pool of local Christians who can contribute to working out moral decisions and principles that the Sunday Service and social hour are the only frequent opportunities for reflection upon and discussion of practical ethics. What little moral teaching is available to the overwhelming majority of Protestants on a frequent basis is confined to the Lord's Day, leaving them abandoned to their own doubts, lack of knowledge, and devices from Monday through Saturday. There is inadequate or no guidance in moral dilemmas emerging on weekdays. To prevent us from being mere "Sunday Christians", any practical system of or approach to ethics integrated into weekday life must provide the tools and resources for individual believers to make and apply moral decisions during the time when the church is not in session, i.e. during the six days of the week and the twenty-two or twenty-three hours of the seventh that no ecclesiastical assembly is available for moral exploration and deliberation.

At least for mainline denominations, it may well be sheer idealism to suggest that a member take his or her moral quandary to his/her local church community for discussion. As Allen Verhey found,[24] the very idea of consulting a member of one's congregation would be met with indications that a conversation on moral problems would be considered out-of-place or not welcome at their church or that they prefer not to be even minimally involved. Church members would not even dare to try, for fear that their local church would think less of them or be judgmental or not open-minded enough for a fruitful discussion. Moreover, such is the nature of the church as currently constituted that some members who are willing to discuss their moral dilemmas with other people, outside the church, would not do so with members of their Christian community. They do not trust their congregation with their problems and choices or to care enough about them in their predicaments or to refrain from acting negatively to the fact that they even have a problem. According to Verhey, such distrust is often well founded, for sometimes[25]

> the churches are not worthy of such trust, pretending a perfection that does not allow hard choices, inhospitable to suffering, ready to despise or condemn those who find themselves suddenly on the margins of congregational life. Sometimes churches would simply prefer to avoid hard conversations about hard choices

In any event, consulting one's local congregation only begs the question of what problem-solving method(s) its members should use. Even if a congregation were to possess plenty of receptive, open-minded, accepting and sympathetic members worthy of trust, there remains the question of how well-versed they are in Christian ethics. What basis or bases would they use in exploring and discussing a moral problem in a specific, concrete case, and by what criterion or criteria would they produce a solution? Short of an official pronouncement in the same or a closely related field of ethics by a supra-congregational body, these members would have to proceed on one or more of the six approaches examined in this section, optimally (in my opinion) with the last: compliance with a sizeable number of predetermined rules of moral law.

Granted, the major (or at least most publicized) moral teachings of most Christian denominations are well-known to their members, but a huge host of precepts and principles remain unknown to the individual in his or her workaday world, as does knowledge or guidelines for deciding (1) where to draw the dividing-line when two or more rules or principles might seem to compete, or (2) which is the most applicable in a given situation.

Denominational moral teachings are usually circumscribed in time and place. The official social and moral teachings of any given denomination have varied significantly since the Reformation or even earlier in the twentieth century. What is Christian truth in one period is error in another. Birch and Rasmussen's standard is a non-uniform and variable "standard" and thus no standard at all. It similarly varies from one part of the world to another, depending on the local Christians' perception and evaluation of the issues.

(5) Application as the situation arises of broad, general moral principles, such as love of neighbour, without more specific criteria:

There are numerous drawbacks to using general principles instead of a particularized body of concrete rules. These include (a) how to eliminate extraneous motives, (b) the mental agility required to start from fundamental premises and balance competing principles each time a moral decision is being made, and (c) the assumption in Fletcher's situationism and analogous systems that the actor has plenty of time in which to decide. Not everybody has the ability to perform the second and very few possess the luxury of the third. Moreover, "we are not always certain what the 'loving' act is. We need instruction—sometimes even boundaries—to help us determine what it means to love."[26] Other defects of situation ethics are that it refuses "to allow any predefinitions for the nature and content of love",[27] "utterly disregards human egotism, stupidity, and cruelty",[28] fails to account for the common fact that the same action may be loving to one person but harmful to another or to society,[29] and does not include parameters wherein decisions are to be made:[30]

> Calculating consequences is a hazardous business with little certainty and with the additional problems of knowing when to cease the calculation. Is the sum of the most loving thing judged at the end of this year, next year, or in thirty years time? The answers may very well be different according to when and where to draw the line.

Moreover, the Bible does not say that love is the paramount consideration for Christian behaviour, and some New Testament authors do not give it any special status. "Nowhere in Mark's Gospel does Jesus teach or command his disciples to love…. If Mark were the only Gospel in the New Testament canon, it would be very difficult to make a case for love as a major motif in Christian ethics."[31] Mark does not portray Jesus' exorcisms, healings and other miracles so much as signs of love "as signs of the power of God's inbreaking kingdom."[32] There are few references to love in the Epistle to the Hebrews and the Revelation of John; whenever they mention love, it is closely linked to good works. "[O]nly in Revelation 2:4 is there a hint that love is anything more than a conventional description for good behavior."[33] More strikingly, the word "love" nowhere appears in the Lukan Acts; its summaries of apostolic preaching contain no references to love and "neither commends love nor exhorts readers to experience or practice it."[34] Nor does the commandment to love God appear in any of the writings of Paul or his circle or in the Epistle of James.[35]

A common variation or restatement of this approach to behavioural decision-making is "do as you would be done by". Besides the flaws mentioned above, it fails (at least in principle) to take into account that different people want different things: not everyone wants to have the same things done to them. If I am suicidal, it is my Christian duty to kill other people because this is how I want others to treat me. A homosexual would like to be sexually fondled by another man, but this is not the desire of a heterosexual; yet a sexual approach is, in the circumstances, merely the gay doing to another person what he would like done to him. These examples also illustrate another great failing of this approach: it is overly broad. Adherents of "do as you would be done by" do not realize this until specific moral situations are posed to them. For example, I would like other people to give me all their money, therefore it follows that other Christians should give me all theirs and also that I should denude myself of my life's savings by giving them to another, perhaps to the first person who asks. This would leave me unable to accommodate other people who want money from me, including my dependants and creditors. By doing to one person as I would be done by, I would be put into a position to confer less love in a material way to persons other than the first. These examples of the suicidal, the gay, and giving away money are extreme but they follow logically and ineluctably from the broad rule. When similar hard examples are posed to them, people who claim to be guided by this approach quickly produce reasons why such extreme acts are not to be performed, however inexorably these acts follow from this logically-flawless approach. Such people create exceptions. They insert parameters. They enunciate qualifications. They make the principle less general. They introduce restrictions based on common sense or on Bible principles or on a general Christian morality that comes from a source other than "do as you would be done by". At the end of the discussion or the decision-making process, these exceptions, qualifications, restrictions, etc. begin to resemble or be a mass of particularized and concrete rules. As a result, all institutions have precepts that are as specific as feasible. Families have set rules. Most churches have rules, even if they consist only of their constitutions, administrative by-laws, and qualifications for membership. The Scriptures do not provide definitions of "good", "moral", "ethical", "righteous" or "love" but lay down specific commandments or patterns of behaviour.

The other frailties inherent in living a Christian moral life through non-specific generalizations are illustrated below under the problems that a Christian moral law helps to solve.

(6) The practical application of Bible principles:

Although it often aims at the same type of structuring as a body of specific religious laws, the ad hoc application of Bible principles usually proves deficient, or at least inferior. There is great disagreement as to the scope and content of "Bible principles" and how to formulate them. Even if the undisputed Scriptures spoke for themselves, they do not select themselves nor organize themselves into a widely-accepted paraenesis. A further weakness in this approach is demonstrated by the plethora of sects, each formulating and applying its own "Bible principles"—with each sect's methods and interpretations inconsistent with the others'. From time to time, major conflicts arise within a denomination when some members "have attached absolute authority to some single commandment and so have come into conflict with persons who make some other injunction absolute".[36]

Consciously or unconsciously, too many Christians find their "Bible principles" to be whatever they want them to be and justify them in doing whatever they want to do, especially make money for themselves or their church. Saying they govern themselves by the "spirit" of the Scriptures as distinct from its otherwise-clear specific commandments of fair play, too many of them dismiss the legal rights and interests of others as mere "technicalities" or "legalism", and instead distil from the Bible any principles they think will advance themselves or their cause. Such Christians act so freely and are so nebulous as to formulate ethical principles or paraenesis from the Bible that they can never be pinned down as to what is objectively or eternally right or wrong—other than their own self-interest—and cannot be convinced that the Scriptures contain provisions that would protect their victims. So self-deluded are they in their self-serving ethical methodology that they cannot see that their victims have rights worth being protected or even that they are victims. They can acknowledge neither that they are sinning nor that they need to repent of their actions, being thoroughly self-justified in following their own "Bible principles". Although quite vocal in their criticisms of the deeds of persons outside their own circle, they are mentally blind to the legitimacy of their victims' rights and interests, which they airily dismiss as obstacles to the implementation of the spirit of the Scriptures as they want to conceive it. I am not saying that they always realize they have this serious shortcoming, but that this approach too frequently opens the door to it in even those who believe themselves to be honest and sincere.

A subsidiary of this approach holds that all problems in practical ethics can be solved by asking oneself "What would Jesus do in this situation?" and doing what the answer indicates. This is no solution because the Jesus of the four Gospels lived a life far removed from ours: He taught and slept in the open air, which is not possible in winter in Canada and many other Christian countries,[37] He was not burdened with family responsibilities,[38] nor did he maintain a home,[39] and He could work miracles. There is no record or even a hint in the present Scriptures as to how He conducted Himself in gainful employment, in which most of us are engaged to stay alive; the four Gospels mention nothing of how He dealt with people as a carpenter and thus how Christian carpenters and other workers today should relate to them. Keeping in mind how Jesus behaved at funerals, what should a Christian do at one: take the widow by the hand and murmur condolences or take the corpse by the hand and exclaim "Rise up and live!"? The Bible records that Jesus did the latter on at least three occasions,[40] but never the former.

The earliest records of Christian teaching do not regard Jesus to be a complete model for the behaviour of individual believers. For instance, He was circumcised.[41] Yet the New Testament is clear that this does not set a compulsory or even advisable pattern: the Apostle Paul went to great length in saying that circumcision is not mandatory for Christian males, and sometimes even should be avoided.[42] All the apostles agreed that it is unnecessary for the practice of Christianity.[43] Being of Jewish background, all of them were themselves circumcised,[44] yet they did not consider it as something believers should do because of the example of Jesus and His first male followers. The point of the present paragraph is not so much the law of Christ or His teachings and examples setting aside those of Moses or the symbolic ramifications of circumcision but that Christ's first followers, those closest to Him and who absorbed His first-hand teaching and recorded it before there was time for it to be corrupted, did not consider what He had done or would do to be criteria for Christian behaviour.

(7) Compliance with a sizable number of predetermined rules of moral law:

Definitive laws of behaviour are necessary for the Christian because it is often hard to decide which of a number of alternative acts will best manifest love toward God and/or one's neighbour, and there is the issue of whether love can be properly manifested by a deed that is contrary to other Christian moral norms or to what another Christian believes to be desirable. There is also the question of whether an act that promotes the welfare only of one's neighbour must be preferred to one that benefits both the "neighbour" and the actor. What if helping one's neighbour harms another neighbour? In cases where their legitimate interests conflict, which neighbour am I to love more? Must a Christian accommodate as many people as possible? Once a person starts formulating answers to these questions, he is beginning to create moral law, for s/he is constructing specific criteria by which to act. Given this tendency or necessity to make laws for ourselves, God did not act contrary to grace by providing Christians with a detailed moral law.

A code of rules for regulating a Christian's attitudes and conduct promotes the welfare both of the particular Christian himself and of other people (the "neighbour" of the Gospels). It does this by: (1) teaching him/her how to conduct himself/herself, (2) reducing his/her problems in ethical decision-making, (3) cementing her/his relationship with God, and (4) enabling him/her to perform his/her actions in a totally loving manner toward other people both as individuals and as groups by introducing structure and consistency:

1) the particularized moral law teaches a Christian how to conduct himself because it:

- protects a Christian from being manipulated by untrue allegations that it is his/her moral duty to perform a particular act
- enables decisions to be made quickly, without the need to return to first principles and "reinvent the wheel" when making a moral decision
- states with precision what moral behaviour is acceptable to God
- provides the safety of numbers from a great cloud of witnesses who lived closest to Jesus in time, culture, outlook and geography
- teaches the breadth and limits of moral duties
- gives confidence in making ethical judgments
- facilitates the application in daily life of a disciple's loving response to God

- provides a steadier foundation on which to base daily conduct
- renders moral situations less debatable
- provides standards and points of reference for personal behaviour
- makes concrete the way we are to manifest the love Jesus commanded us to have for God, our neighbours and ourselves
- contributes specific data from which to develop "an outlook on life, which leads us beyond petty rules to far-reaching and fundamental principles"[45]
- teaches clearly what is important and significant in life
- orders priorities of values in accordance with those of God
- teaches the standards of Christian judgment
- within a church, enables a person to predict with reasonable certainty how matters will be conducted, and therefore how to act in anticipation
- gives specific examples and parameters of what "love" is
- provides consistency and stability in moral decision-making
- brings to ethical situations the demands and meaning of a Christian response to God's love
- provides a less debatable source of moral guidance
- provides illustrations as to how people of good character act
- helps prevent the inflating of trivialities or self-interest into ethical issues
- decreases or eliminates myopic absorption ("navel-gazing") in ethical theory in favour of acting
- significantly simplifies moral choices
- discourages solitary self-righteousness
- gives structure and guidelines in which to formulate answers to new moral questions
- minimizes the confusing of self-interest with God's will.

2) a particularized code of Christian law solves numerous problems in moral decision-making by equipping a Christian to:

- distinguish genuine moral issues from spurious or pretended ones
- distinguish genuine moral imperatives from spurious or pretended ones
- distinguish genuine moral imperatives from mere custom and etiquette
- weed out incorrect ethical ideas and theories
- diminish mental conflicts in making decisions
- reduce the influence of emotion in moral decision-making
- protect himself/herself from the moral confusion inherent in pluralistic societies
- reduce the number of conflicting moral claims
- choose between "neighbours" when their interests conflict

- remove moral blind spots
- diminish over-scrupulousness and lack of assertiveness
- lessen one-sided, self-centred or chauvinistic misunderstandings of God's will
- obtain particulars and details as to what acts and attitudes manifest Christian love as God wants them to be
- share in a "fund of practical experience available to help people make their moral decisions"[46]
- assess situations as to how best apply the principle of love.

Christian moral law performs (1) and (2) by providing objective, clear and predetermined commandments and prohibitions in place of making deductions from general principles (such as "love your neighbour") for every moral decision. Obeying the predetermined and definitive mandates of God's law eliminates the confusion and uncertainty attendant upon guidance by community standards, self-interest, denominational pronouncements and overbroad general principles. It does this by reducing the probabilities of irrelevant or selfish considerations entering the decision-making process. Some kinds of schizophrenics are particularly assisted because they can rest assured that God expresses God's will for them by means of specific mandates transmitted to them from external sources rather than by voices in their heads which they sincerely believe is God telling them what to do. As for (2) alone, it also assists many post-Vatican II Roman Catholic moral theologians in determining which acts are norms that are always and intrinsically good and which acts are always and intrinsically evil.

3) A detailed Christian law draws a person closer to God by:

- informing her/him what is good in God's sight
- warning what kinds of thoughts and behaviour God will reward or punish
- showing how to express gratitude to God for giving and sustaining life
- teaching what is appropriate for someone who has responded to Jesus' call and accepted His love
- informing her/him precisely what God expects
- leading a Christian deeper and more confidently into "the mind of Christ" (1 Corinthians 2.16)
- giving specific information as to how to live in integrity and loyalty towards God[47]
- giving her or him specific details on how to imitate the Apostle Paul in the same way that he imitated Christ (1 Corinthians 11.1)[48]
- telling him what are "the fruits of righteousness" (Philippians 1.11)
- instructing her/him how his manner of life can be worthy of the Christian gospel (Philippians 1.27)
- telling him/her how to "lead a life worthy of the Lord, fully pleasing to him, bearing fruit in every good work" (Colossians 1.10).

4) Christian moral law benefits people who are affected by a disciple's conduct (the "neighbours"), either as an individual or as part of a church. By providing steady patterns of behaviour without variability or rationalizing escapes from duty, Christian law:

- ensures that a Christian will take due account of the rights and needs of other people and the equality of their rights and needs with his/her own
- ensures that he will recognize the humanity of other people
- fosters consistent behaviour so that other people will have a general idea of what to expect from him/her and plan their own actions accordingly
- guards a church from falling into disrepute through a key member applying (or inventing) principles of morality in a dubious, non-traditional or self-serving way
- in a church setting, provides sufficient direction in procedure to maximize the probability that affairs will be conducted decently and in order (1 Corinthians 14.40)
- alerts the Christian to some of the sensitivities of "weaker" Christians' consciences so that he or she can avoid being a stumbling block to them (1 Corinthians 8.9-11,14)
- enables a church or other people to distinguish a false prophet or false disciple from a true one by providing particulars of the fruits that are brought forth by a person claiming to be a true prophet or disciple (Matthew 7.15-23)[49]
- helps to determine when a person, especially a stranger, is sanctified and living in integrity and loyalty towards God[50]
- provides data which communities and the advanced student of ethics, especially of "character ethics", can analyze to draw out what Professor Lisa Sowle Cahill calls "general values, principles or virtues that reflect God's self-disclosure in Christ."[51]

For rule-agapists and others who wish to follow general rules or principles, a compilation of specific precepts is valuable for determining what "loving acts" are, which acts promote love and righteousness and justice, and provides bases on which to formulate such rules and principles. We learn and formulate moral principles only through knowing what God has specifically commanded.[52] The above also provide the wherewithal to formulate moral principles and provide a means for educating conscience.

The Other View Considered

A number of objections have been raised against the concept of an itemized collection of moral rules in contrast to broad principles. These arguments are based on either (1) history, (2) doctrine or (3) Scripture.

(1) History:

Among others, J. L. Houlden contends[53] that the foremost concern of the primitive church was the proclamation and preparation for God's approaching Kingdom, with prime emphasis on preserving and increasing the cohesion of those who anticipated this Kingdom. Ethics were a secondary concern until after Christians concluded that the Second Coming would not be until many years in the future. According to Houlden, it was in this second phase that Christians sought and formulated moral standards for the community. The theme of Chilton and MacDonald's *Jesus and the Ethics of the Kingdom*[54] is that the coming Kingdom was a paramount preoccupation in earliest Christianity, with little concern for love or ethics. This proposition is regarded as established fact in Wolfgang Schrage's *The Ethics of the New Testament*.[55]

On the other hand, not all scholars believe that expectations of an early Second Coming displaced a concern for ethics. Bishop Eduard Lohse, formerly a professor of New Testament, sees eschatology and ethics as having been bound together and forming a unity in early Christianity.[56] Instruction in rules of ethical conduct existed from the very beginning in Christianity. He denies that there are clear statements in the New Testament in favour of the idea that there were no Christian ethics in the period when an imminent parousia was still expected. "Eschatology and ethics are by no means mutually exclusive—as already Jesus' call to repentance shows".[57] He also denies that ethics and eschatology are unrelated. He further goes on to say that "The eschatological hope thus does not make ethical instruction superfluous, but rather makes it the more urgent."[58]

Houlden[59] and Freyne[60] state that Jesus never laid down a definite code of moral teaching. Nevertheless, Jesus did condemn some acts and attitudes, commend others and inculcate morality through parables, sayings and miracles.[61] Matthew portrays Him as a new lawgiver while John speaks of his teachings as "commandments".[62] "Jesus multiplied ethical demands in the synoptic gospels by specifying what the law—a law of love—required."[63] Jesus was also a perfect example of obedience to the Father and a role model for believers. He submitted to the Law of Moses and disregarded the rules invented by the Pharisees that contravened or mutilated it. Moreover, in the period after Christians realized that Christ would not reappear in the near future, the Apostle Paul or his circle delivered many brief collections of binding moral precepts to his congregations: Romans 1.29-31, 12.9-19, 13.5-10, 1 Corinthians 4.11f, 5.12-15, Galatians 5.19-23, Ephesians 4.25-32, 5.18-22, 6.1-4, and Colossians 3.5-23. Another apostle did the same in Chapters 2 to 4 of 1 Peter. More replete collections of ancient Christian law are found in such early documents as the *Didache*, the *Epistle of Barnabas*, the *Didascalia* and the *Sentences of Sextus*. The fact that such commandments and collections were written down, circulated and preserved indicates that early Christians valued such moral directives, particularly in a comprehensive form. Indeed, the history of salvation as contained in the Hebrew Scriptures reveals a God who requires His people to conform to stated patterns of behaviour.

Christians in the twenty-first century are in the same position as their early post-apostolic brethren, with the Second Advent consigned to the remote future and direct two-way access to the Supreme Lawgiver no longer available. Our only sources of learning what God requires are the moral precepts recorded by Paul, other New Testament writers, and the authors of the *Didache* and other early Christian writings.

(2) Doctrine:

The doctrine of justification by faith is alleged to be the crucial theological objection to a Christian moral law that spells out duties and prohibitions. The reasoning is that because salvation is by faith alone, a law of Christian conduct is at best superfluous while at worst it fosters the delusion that a person can earn or maintain his or her salvation by her or his own efforts and legal observance instead of on God's grace alone. However, for the regenerated, ethically upright conduct:

- is commanded by God
- will be remembered by God (Matthew 25.34-40, 46; John 5.29; Romans 2.6, 10)
- evidences a true and living faith (James 2.18, 22)
- glorifies God (John 15.8; Philippians 1.9-11; 1 Peter 22.9, 12)
- is an inherent result of conversion and the new life in Christ (Romans 7.6; Colossians 1.10)
- inspires and encourages other Christians (Matthew 5.16; 2 Corinthians 9.1f)
- assures a Christian of his/her salvation (1 John 2.3-5
- shows a disciple's gratitude to God (Psalm 116.12-14)
- helps refute opponents of Christianity (1 Peter 2.15; 1 Timothy 6.1)
- instructs a Christian and gives her/him details on how to accomplish the foregoing (Galatians 5.18-25; Ephesians 2,10; 1 Thessalonians 4.1; Titus 2.11-15; 1 John 2.15).

(3) Arguments to the contrary from Scripture:
   a) love is the only law (Romans 13.8-10). However, moral law teaches in detail exactly how God wants love to be manifested.
   b) "the law is not laid down for the just, but for the lawless and disobedient" (1 Timothy 1.9). However, because we are all sinners, everyone is "lawless and disobedient". Even if Christian law does not apply to a just person, s/he is no longer just after s/he violates it. One of the benefits of a comprehensive collection of Christian moral rules is that it tells an individual how to be just and alerts him/her when s/he starts to be lawless and disobedient. Indeed, this verse is followed by a list of activities that Christians are instructed to avoid (verses 9f).
   c) "To the pure all things are pure" (Titus 1.15). However, because we are all sinners, everyone is "impure". Even if Christian law does not apply to a pure person, s/he is no longer pure after s/he violates it. One of the benefits of a comprehensive collection of moral laws is that it tells an individual how to be pure and alerts him/her when s/he begins to be impure. Indeed, this verse is followed by a list of activities that are commanded or forbidden to church leaders (1.16-2.10).
   d) "we are not under law but under grace" (Romans 6.14). The context of this clause is an exhortation to obey God's revealed will, avoid sexual sins and do good works (Romans 6.12f; 6.15-20). The thrust of the entire sixth chapter of Romans is that readers must

avoid sin. Unless specific acts can be identified as sin, then the sixth chapter of Romans is meaningless, for the reader would not know what acts and mental states to avoid. Christian law informs us how to give effect to the author's exhortation. God gives us grace to observe His law. Moreover, Christians were created to perform good works (Ephesians 2.10).

e) "all things are lawful" (1 Corinthians 6.12 and 10.23). However, in 6.12 this clause is followed by "but not all things are helpful" and stands in the midst of a number of moral precepts that Paul wants his readers to follow. In 10.23 it is modified, again by "not all things are helpful", and by "not all things build up" and is also preceded and followed by directives relating to moral behaviour. The terms "helpful" and "build up" indicate what God wants and expects of His people. Christian law is like a motor traffic statute which provides the structure for directing vehicles along their way and increasing public welfare by minimizing the number and severity of collisions; the purpose of the criminal penalty for violation is to promote these ends and is not designed as a means of finding people to punish. Highway traffic laws seek to be helpful to people on or near the road and to build up conditions of safety for the community; similarly, Christian moral law seeks to be helpful to the Christian community and to build them up spiritually.

f) "the written code kills, but the Spirit gives life" (2 Corinthians 3.6) This verse has no application to a collection of Christian law because (i) like the New Testament itself, Christian rules of conduct had not been reduced to writing before this Epistle was written around A.D. 55, (ii) if a document is objectionable because it is in written form, the same objection applies to the four Gospels and all other parts of the (written) Bible, and (iii) the only reference to law in this chapter is to the Law of Moses, not to a moral code originating within Christianity.

g) Through His crucifixion Jesus freed us from law (Romans 3.20, 3.30, 4.14; Galatians 2.16-3.29; Ephesians 2.15; Colossians 2.13-23). The general answer to this ground of opposition is that, taken with the literalness and isolation often found in such methods of argument, these passages would teach that a Christian is free to do whatever s/he wants, including acts which were classified as sins under the Law of Moses and even those punishable by secular laws. Such a conclusion is contrary to moral behaviour as it has always been known, especially in the earliest times. Joseph Michael Winger's *By What Law?*[64] suggests a more likely (but not the only) interpretation is that when Paul said "law" he almost always meant Jewish law. C. H. Dodd's "Ennomos Khristou"[65] convincingly demonstrates that when Paul contrasted "the law of Christ" with what he spurned as "the law", the latter means Jewish law. Moreover, the Apostle's injunctions and prohibitions, some of which coincide with Jewish regulations and others not, support the interpretation that Jesus freed Christians from Hebrew laws unrelated to ethics but expected His disciples to obey Christian moral law. Indeed, Paul himself remarked "I delight in the law of God in my inmost self." (Romans 7.22).

More specifically, Galatians 2.16-3.29 when read in context does not teach that Christians are exempt from all religious law. From Paul's two quotations from Deuteronomy and one from Leviticus, and his statement that the law of which he speaks was handed down four hundred and thirty years after Abraham, there can be no doubt that the Apostle is referring only to the Mosaic legislation and not to a Christian parallel of it. The mention of circumcision and frequent references to breaking down barriers between Jews and Gentiles in the text surrounding Ephesians 2.15 indicate that the law that Christ abolished was that of Moses. Although Colossians 2.13-23 strongly warns its recipients not to submit to the regulatory system described there, its author was not referring to the moral law generally recognized by Christians as binding on themselves but to sectarian ordinances; some aspects of the objectionable precepts were those of Judaizers who wished to introduce elements of Jewish law into Christianity while other precepts were those of Gnostics. It was to counter the latter that the author followed this section by thirty-one verses on Christian duties for his readers to fulfill.

Chapter Two

Evidence for the Existence of an Early Christian Law

Of course, the mere desirability of something does not prove its existence. This is especially true when the evidence for its existence lies in a period long before living memory. It must be proved affirmatively. The present chapter will seek for indications among the earliest Christians that a detailed moral law was a part of their religion.

The First Century - The Gospels

In the synoptic gospels, ethical demands are multiplied in order to specify what Christ's law of love requires.[66] As mentioned in Chapter 1, Matthew's Gospel connects discipleship very closely with obeying "commandments".[67] To some extent, it depicts Jesus as a new lawgiver.[68] In John 13.34, 14.15, 14.21 and 15.10 Christ spoke of His teachings as commandments and urged obedience to them.[69]

As the Presbyterian William Lillie points out about the Gospels and our next writer,[70]

> What Jesus and St Paul said about right conduct is not mere pious exhortation; it is *law*, and the requirement of law as such is that it cannot be violated with impunity. This may explain the emphasis in the New Testament on rewards and punishment in unquenchable fire….

Jesus' teaching, e.g. that in Matthew 5, contains commandments and is in the imperative. A listener or reader can only conclude that, if they are to be taken at face value, what Christ phrased as commands He intended to be commands. Indeed, in Matthew 5.20 He indicates that He is enjoining a fresh or amplified law or righteousness when He tells us that "unless

18

your righteousness exceeds that of the scribes and Pharisees, you will never enter the kingdom of heaven."[71]

The First Century - The Letters of Paul and His Circle

In Romans, Paul specifically set out what sorts of acts a Christian is to do or not to do, that is, what sort of fruit we are to bear and how we are to serve "in the new life of the Spirit" (Romans 7.6). Romans 1.29-31 contains twenty-one prohibitions; 2.8f contain three. Romans 6.13 mentions one act forbidden to believers and one commanded to them, as does 12.3. Romans 12.9 to 19 has twenty-one affirmative commands, 13.5-8 three. There are six prohibitions in 13.13, and 14.1, while 15.2 and 15.7 lay down one precept each. These rules are so specific that it is difficult to believe that the moral lives of Christians in the apostolic age were governed by ad hoc interpretation of general ethical principles or accepted the moral standards of the people around them.

Similarly with 1 Corinthians: 5.9-6.10 list sixteen things Christians are to do or not to do. Chapter 11.6 to 12 and 14.33f contain rules particularly applicable to females while 7.1-5, 8-13, 17f and 27f set out Christian matrimonial law in detail, as does 2 Corinthians 6.14.

The other letters attributed to Paul also provide detailed particulars of conduct and attitudes which constitute "a life worthy of the Lord", the fruit Christians are to bear, what is in the category of "every good work" (Colossians 1.10), and "how you ought to live and to please God" (1 Thessalonians 4.1). To spare readers the boredom and distraction of long lists of citations, future lists of references are in footnotes.[72] Suffice it to say that, with some inevitable overlap, the ten Pauline epistles contain two hundred and fifty-nine specific mandates for Christians, and the Pastorals one hundred and five. It strains credibility to maintain that the author(s) itemized Christian duties and prohibitions this many times and in such detail if he/they did not intend them to be accepted as binding rules.

Moreover, the writer(s) of these letters made explicit statements that there was a distinctively Christian law. Paul asserted at Romans 3.31: "We uphold the law"; at Romans 7.12: "the law is holy, and the commandment is holy and just and good"; at Romans 8.2 he refers to "the law of the Spirit of life in Christ Jesus". At 1 Corinthians 9.21 he states that although he is free from the Law of Moses he is "under the law of Christ", while at Galatians 6.2 he mentions that "the law of Christ" is in force.

Indicative of the writer's/writers' belief that the Two Great Commandments do not comprise the whole of Christian law nor even displace specific duties and prohibitions is that the more general commandment to love God nowhere appears in the entire Pauline corpus.[73] Nor does it appear in our next author.[74]

The First Century - James

The letter ascribed to James is almost completely a compilation of particularized rules for personal and community spiritual law, including morality. At 1.25 the author calls the

Christian moral code "the perfect law, the law of liberty" and stresses concrete action. The high regard in which this law was held by contemporary Christians is indicated at 4.11f: "He that speaks evil against a brother or judges his brother speaks evil against the law and judges the law. But if you judge the law, you are not a doer of the law but a judge." Here, Christian law is the criterion for conduct. The rest of this letter enunciates that law or part of it in express detail.

James 2.8-13 is noteworthy because in a discussion of Christian law the passage begins with one of the Two Great Commandments and then gives two commandments from the Decalogue of Moses as examples. This writer appears to have regarded at least a couple of the Ten Commandments as definite ways in which one of the Two is to be put into action.

The First Century - Peter

The First Letter of Peter spells out fifty-two directives for attitudes and actions. They are organized into three collections, one each in Chapters 2, 3 and 4.[75] The first collection is interrupted or amplified by the exhortation "Live as free men, yet without using your freedom as a pretext for evil; but live as servants of God."[76] There are two interjections into the third such collection: one refers to living in the Spirit[77] and the other contrasts Christians with "those who do not obey the gospel of God".[78] It would appear that obeying, like a servant or subject, is part of living in the Spirit. The large number of rules related by Peter and his interspersing these three thoughts among them indicate that he is giving details of how to live in the Spirit as free men but in the manner of servants obeying the Gospel.

From their position among so many specific commands, it is inconceivable that the more general descriptions of the new life in Christ were intended to replace detailed rules by such broad summaries. Indeed, Peter's first readers would not have known the meaning of the term "evil" in 2.16 except from precisely-delineated Christian moral directives, either from prior acquaintance or from 1 Peter itself.

The First Century - The Letters of John

First John 3.4 teaches: "Everyone who commits sin is guilty of lawlessness; sin is lawlessness." Lawlessness presupposes a law. For the first readers of this Letter to understand the author, they must have been familiar with a Christian law. Conversely, to make himself understood by readers, John would have used terms and concepts with which he believed them to have already been familiar. If this were not so, he would not have defined "sin" by reference to lawlessness and, by implication, to a Christian law. His use of these terms and concepts indicate that his first readers were already familiar with the idea of a Christian law.

The First Century - *1 Clement*

The First Letter of Clement to the Corinthians was written between A.D. 70 and 97 to the church at Corinth by the church at Rome, reputedly by Clement, its bishop-pastor.[79] This letter was written while in the church at Rome "there were many still remaining who had received instructions from the apostles."[80] Indeed, Clement himself "had seen the blessed apostles, and had been conversant with them" and had their preaching echoing in his head.[81]

Although "the commandments of God" cited in Chapters 1 of *1 Clement*[82] and "His holy commandments" in Chapter 37[83] could conceivably refer only to the Two Great Commandments, Chapter 2 refers to "[t]he commandments and ordinances of the Lord."[84] Mention of "the commandments" in the plural indicates that the church (or at least the author writing on its behalf) recognized at least two; mention of "the ordinances" in the plural similarly indicates that it or he accepted a minimum of two, for a total minimum of four, thus indicating that ancient Christian moral law was not confined to loving God and one's neighbour with no particularized guide on how they were to be implemented. Indeed, Chapters 16, 21 and 30 quote twelve such commandments and/or ordinances as part of Christian law.

The Transition to the Early Second Century - The *Didache*

The Teaching of the Twelve Apostles, usually called the *Didache*, is a manual of church law compiled in Syria. With a certain amount of disagreement among modern authorities as to the exact date of its composition, it is dated in the period between A.D. 50 and 150. According to Professor Bebis of the Greek Orthodox Church; "it is the first written document after the books of the New Testament" and dates from "the end of the first century A.D. or in the first quarter of the second century".[85] The Dominican Servais Pinckaers[86] and the Protestant university professors Daniel H. Williams[87] and Richard B. Hays[88] assign it a similar date. In his monumental study of more than a thousand pages, Aaron Milavec works on the basis, at points giving reasons, that it was probably composed between A.D. 50 and 70, before the Gospel of Matthew.[89]

The first six chapters relate to ethics, reciting one precise moral commandment after another, like a modern-day compendium of secular law. Chapters 7 to 10 give instructions for public and private devotions while 11 to 15 set out the procedures for church organization.[90] As a whole, the *Didache* constitutes a manual of Christian law for all occasions.

Didache 6.2 reveals that Christian moral law was already of such complexity and detail that not everyone could perform all of it easily—perhaps no-one could perform it in its entirety: "if thou art able to bear all the yoke of the Lord, thou wilt be perfect; but if thou art not able, what thou art able that do."[91]

That the *Didache* was produced at all indicates that one or more Christians perceived a need for a collection of Christian law extracted from the New Testament and other sources, just as its being copied, distributed and preserved indicate that many other believers found great value in it. The itemized and detailed lists, especially those in the first six chapters, and the great of volume of this paraenesis indicate that Christians of this early period were guided by something more concrete and precise than mere conscience or applying a few general principles to ethical situations.

The Early Second Century - Ignatius

Shortly before his martyrdom in A.D. 107, Ignatius, bishop-pastor of Antioch in Syria, wrote letters to churches in Rome and the Aegean basin, and one to the pastor-bishop of Smyrna (modern Izmir). These letters contain two hundred and twenty-four positive and negative injunctions or exhortations to piety and action that he considered necessary in order for his readers to live in accord with the will of God.[92] Indeed, he stated "those that profess themselves to be Christians shall be recognized by their conduct."[93] In the letter to the Trallians he spoke of "the enactments of the apostles",[94] thus intimating that the Christian's life was regulated by mandates in addition to the Two Love Commandments.

The Early Second Century - Polycarp

There is a division in opinion whether Polycarp's *Letter to the Philippians* was contemporary with those of Ignatius or was written around A.D. 135, or is a combination of an earlier with a later letter. In any event, its author belonged to the first generation after Jesus, a generation that personally knew the apostles. Indeed, Polycarp had associated with John and his companions after the Apostle settled in the Ephesus area, not far from Smyrna.

Most notable about this letter is the use of the singular in Chapter 5: "Knowing then, that God is not mocked, we ought to walk worthy of His commandment and glory."[95] Either one of the Two Dominical Commandments had been deleted from Christian ethics or the singular was used collectively or generically, i.e. as incorporating all Christian mandates. The latter is more probable because in the preceding chapter Polycarp mentioned four activities which believers are to avoid, and Chapters 5, 6, 10, 11 and 12 enunciate forty-one duties of Christians, some of which are paraphrases or quotations from the New Testament. We therefore have one instance of the singular of the word "commandment" being used generically.

The Early Second Century - *Barnabas*

There is more uncertainty over the date of the *Letter of Barnabas* but there is general agreement that it dates from no later than the third decade of the second century. In ancient times it possessed great authority and was even included in some editions of the New Testament. It is believed to have been written in Syria or Egypt.

Like the *Didache*, Chapters 10, 19 and 20 recite one moral precept after another. Chapter 19 lists sixty-four commandments, including those to love God and one's neighbour. Chapters 10 and 20 set out fifty-four acts or states of mind Christians are to avoid. While some are repeated in other chapters and/or mirror prohibitions expressed elsewhere, the text clearly indicates that Chapters 19 and 20 were intended as a codification of Christian moral law.

As in the case of 1 Peter and of the letters of Paul and his circle, it is hard to believe that anyone would include such a collection of laws in a letter to Christians if the concept of a body of binding rules were alien or repugnant to its intended readers. On the contrary, its very existence, preservation, distribution, and being accorded canonical status indicate that Christians of the time conducted—or at least wished to conduct—their lives by a large number of specific rules.

The Early Second Century - Papias

Papias, bishop-pastor of Hierapolis in Phrygia in the first half of the second century, was the first antiquarian of Christianity and collector of what is now called "oral history". His motives included legal research in the religious sense. A fragment of his *Exposition of the Oracles of the Lord* describes his methods:[96]

> But I shall not be unwilling to put down, along with my interpretations, whatsoever instructions I received with care at any time from the elders.... For I did not, like the multitude, take pleasure in those who spoke much, but in those who taught the truth; not in those who related strange commandments, but in those who rehearsed the commandments given by the Lord to faith, and proceeding from the truth itself. If, then, any one who had attended on the elders came, I asked minutely after their sayings,--what Andrew or Peter said, or what was said by Philip, or by Thomas, or by James, or by John, or by Matthew, or any other of the Lord's disciples....

Apparently there were facets of Christian morality which had not yet been written down by Papias' time and which were numerous enough for the dedicated scholar of Christian belief and practice to make inquiries about. It also appears that heretics had concocted spurious rules which needed to be separated from the genuine. Both these phenomena disclose that there was a sizeable body of Christian ethical law that had only partly been recorded in writing.

The Middle of the Second Century - Aristides

The Apology of Aristides the Philosopher was addressed to the Roman Emperor Hadrian in A.D. 125 in an attempt to persuade him to end government persecution of Christians. In it, the Christian philosopher Aristides describes Christian beliefs and behavioural norms to show that disciples posed no threat to the government. In portraying the conduct of Christians, Chapter 15 states that because of their beliefs they did not commit adultery or fornication, bear false witness, embezzle what had been entrusted to them or covet, but rather they honoured their parents, showed kindness to their neighbours and, when they held judicial office, were honest judges. That Aristides could point to definite norms of conduct as characterizing Christians as a group reveals that disciples followed a religious law which consisted of detailed, obligatory provisions.

The Middle of the Second Century - Ptolemy the Gnostic

Dating from before A.D. 150, Ptolemy's *Letter to Flora* contains an in-depth lengthy exposition of the relationship between the Mosaic Law and Christian law and contrasts the two. The discussion discloses that both orthodox Christians and Ptolemy's denomination of Gnostics agreed that the Law of Moses was different from "the law of God" as far as Christians were concerned, and hence that they both regarded themselves as bound by a "Christian law".

Ptolemy's analysis demonstrates the existence of a well-developed legal system and of prior discussions among Christians about the source and organization of the rules of conduct. His dissertation is too advanced to be meaningful in a religious organization that based its moral life on community standards, self-interest, ad hoc deductions from general ethical principles or on no system at all. That such a thesis was produced so early in Christian history indicates that disciples were quite accustomed to shaping their moral lives in accordance with a what was explicitly called "law" and which contained specific precepts binding on believers.

The Middle of the Second Century - Hermas

Dating from the first half or middle of the second century, *The Shepherd of Hermas* was held in such high regard that many early churches included it in their New Testaments, and it was popular and much used by those that did not.[97] *The Shepherd* is a set of visions, commandments and parables on the theme of repentance from sins committed after conversion. They were given to a Christian layman in Italy named Hermas. In Vision 5 an angel orders him to write down and practise the commandments he was about to give him. There follow twenty-five chapters of moral instructions, grouped into twelve categories of commandments. I will spare you a statistical breakdown. Hermas was bidden to communicate them to the elders of the church at Rome. The contents of *The Shepherd* show that a Christian author in the early or mid-second century felt free to produce twenty-five chapters of itemized rules for ethical living. This and the fact that his labour was widely received for centuries in the church indicate that the concept of a user-friendly compendium of detailed Christian rules was acceptable or desirable. *The Shepherd* did at Rome what the *Didache* had done in Syria and *The Letter of Barnabas* in Syria or Egypt.

Hermas' division of commandments into twelve instead of Moses' ten or Jesus' two indicates that no exact number was regarded as definite or unalterable. He also resembled Ptolemy in attempting to construct the rudiments of a classification scheme for Christian law.

The Middle of the Second Century — Justin Martyr

Justin was a Gentile of Roman origin from Samaria. Well-educated, he travelled the eastern half of the Empire in order to discover the truest or best philosophy, which he eventually found in Christianity. Sometime between A.D. 155 and 160 he wrote his *Dialogue with Trypho*, a depiction of a friendly debate between a Christian and a Jew in which the main issue was whether the Old Testament was misunderstood by Jews and could be correctly interpreted only by Christians. Justin referred to Christ or God as "the Lawgiver"[98] or "the new Lawgiver".[99] Justin argued that this "Lawgiver" is correctly or fully obeyed only by Christians. From this it would appear that Christians possessed their own law, an institution that Justin unequivocally terms "law" rather that "advice" or "persuasive example".

Although Justin stated that the new law and new covenant of the Christians abrogated that of Moses and are to be universally followed, he explained that this "new law" is Christ, the eternal and final law, after whom there shall be no new commandments.[100] He similarly called Jesus "the everlasting law and the everlasting covenant".[101] That Christ is the law is a maxim to which all Christians will agree, but this does not mean that a Christian's life is unregulated. As with the Apostle Paul's use of the word *nomos*[102] and the multitude of meanings of *logos* throughout early Christian literature, it must be recognized that Justin also used the word "law" in two or more ways:

The first meaning is "law in the abstract", connoting the ultimate authority or embodiment of power. For Christians, this means God and His wishes regarding our thoughts and actions. In this collective and generic sense, *nomos* is more accurately translated as "legal system" or "legal authority". By this interpretation, Jesus is the font or embodiment of law. It is in this sense that we say in a secular context: "you will be in trouble with the law".

The second meaning of "law" is narrower and more specific. In this sense, "a law" or "law" is a component unit, just one of the many thousands of statutes, regulations and ordinances which constitute a secular legal system. It is only one of the many parts of the general body of rules, judicial precedents, regulations, constitutions, decrees, local ordinances, and by-laws.[103]

This accords with the fact that the word "commandment" had two principal uses in the Old Testament of the first Christians: "In the plural in the Septuagint it normally describes the totality of legal ordinances, while the singular can convey either a precept or the whole Law."[104]

Justin recognized this distinction by saying that adultery, fornication and murder are sinful (specifically prohibited by God) and that "our Lord and Saviour Jesus Christ spoke well when he summed up all righteousness and piety in two commandments" and then repeating the Two Love Commandments.[105] Thus, there was a law in addition to the Law. Note also that Justin regarded the Two as a mere summary of Christian ethics, not as an exhaustive statement or replacement of them.

Examples of these two meanings of law can be found in reference to dictators and autocratic monarchs. Although embodiments of the law, they rule by means of individual decrees, orders and commands. Some tyrants may have asserted that they were the law itself, but they did not attempt to displace the entire corpus of specific statutes and customary law. They leave undisturbed all "laws" (in the second sense) except those that limit their power. For instance, despots very seldom alter contract law, legislation on wills and succession upon death, or conditional sales registration statutes unless and until they affect their own interests.

In his *First Apology* Justin provided further information on the concept of Christ as the Law who expects His disciples to obey specific laws: "He accepts only those who imitate the excellencies which reside in Him, temperance, and justice, and philanthropy, and as many virtues as are peculiar to a God who is called by no proper name."[106] So also in the *Dialogue with Trypho*: "we cultivate piety, righteousness, philanthropy, faith and hope, which we have from the Father Himself through Him who was crucified".[107] This shows that Christian law was more detailed than general principles or a vague commandment to do the most loving action in the circumstances.

Justin's scanty description of the commandments governing Christians may sound not so much like precise rules than as broad principles to be interpreted as each situation requires, but they do show that there were restrictions on how vaguely the Two Commandments could be interpreted.

Through Justin Martyr we are reminded of an important feature of Christian moral law. This law does not exist for its own sake. Jesus is the embodiment of how Christians are to believe and behave. The individual precepts, rules and ordinances are only a means of making us more like Him. The purpose of precise laws is to describe Christlike behaviour so that Christians can imitate Him: the more detail, the better enabled we are to emulate His example.

The Middle of the Second Century - *Theophilus to Autolycus*

Theophilus became bishop-pastor of Antioch in Syria in A.D. 168. The most trustworthy dating of his *Letter to Autolycus* is the third quarter of the second century. It states that Christians had their own law and Theophilus calls it "law": "For God has given as a law and holy commandments; and every one who keeps these can be saved".[108] He reinforces this with:[109]

> And we [Christians] have learned a holy law; but we have as lawgiver Him who is really God, who teaches us to act righteously, and to be pious, and to do good. And concerning piety He says....

followed by the Ten Commandments, except the one about the Sabbath. Then there continues as if among the Ten:[110]

> Thou shall not wrest the judgment of the poor in his cause. From every unjust action keep thee far. The innocent and righteous thou shalt not slay; thou shall not justify the wicked; and thou shall not take a gift [i.e. bribe]

Then Chapters 12 to 15 of the same Book are given over to particularized details of Christian moral obligations.

Theophilus thus provides another example that a code of the specific and concrete rules that governed ancient Christians. More complete than Aristides', it was also composed to acquaint pagans with the character of the Christian faith and thus equally implies that new converts were expected to absorb a sizeable body of ethical teachings.

The Late Second Century – Irenaeus

Irenaeus was acquainted with Polycarp at an early age and received his Christian training from him. Irenaeus later left the Aegean area and relocated at Lyons in southern France, becoming its pastor-bishop for many years. In the A.D. 180s he composed *Against Heresies*, a multi-volume collection of rebuttals of false ideas about Christianity.

In arguing that the deity who handed down the Law of Moses was the same one who gave the Gospel, Irenaeus stated that both the Law and the gospel enjoin the Two Great Commandments and that "the precepts of an absolutely perfect life" are the same in both Old and New Testaments but that God "has promulgated particular laws adapted for each".[111] The Two had their practical manifestation through the Ten and the Levitical legislation. It would similarly appear to that under the New Covenant the love commandments have their practical manifestations through similarly specific duties and prohibitions.

In the same vein, Irenaeus wrote:[112]

> For to yield assent to God, and to follow His Word, and to love Him above all, and one's neighbour as one's self (now man is neighbour to man), and to abstain from every evil deed, and all other things of a like nature which are common to both [covenants], do reveal one and the same God.

Note that Irenaeus did not regard love of God and one's neighbour as the whole of what God requires; Christians must also abstain from specific kinds of acts and do "all other things of a like nature".

Like Clement of Alexandria a decade later, Irenaeus believed that Jesus did not do away with the law but fulfilled, extended and widened it among His followers.[113] Like other Christian authors of the period, Irenaeus cited many of its provisions.[114]

The Late Second Century - Clement of Alexandria

Like Justin Martyr, Clement of Alexandria was born a pagan and had travelled the eastern Mediterranean in search of the true philosophy and found it in Christianity. His writings date from the decade beginning in A.D. 192, while he was president or dean of the most prominent Christian educational institution of the time.

Clement's writings abound with rules for disciples to follow, although only his *Stromata* refers to Christian law as an entity in itself. He writes as if it was already well established that believers are governed by a multitude of individual regulations. Book 2 Chapter 7 outlines the benefits of Christian law:[115]

> the law given to us enjoins us to shun what are in reality bad things—adultery, uncleanness, paederasty, ignorance, wickedness, soul-disease, death (not that which severs the soul from the body, but that which severs the soul from truth).

and ends the chapter with a quotation from *Letter of Barnabas* as an authoritative work of apostolic authority.

Contrary to some opinions on religious law which have been prominent since the Protestant Reformation, Book 1 Chapter 27 begins:[116]

> Let no one, then, run down law, as if, on account of the penalty, it were not beautiful and good. For shall he who drives away bodily disease appear a benefactor; and shall not he who attempts to deliver the soul from iniquity, as much more appear a friend, as the soul is a more precious thing than the body?

> • • •

> For the law, in its solicitude for those who obey, trains up to piety, and prescribes what is to be done, and restrains each one from sins, imposing penalties even on lesser sins.

Here Clement declares not only the desirability of a Christian law but also its necessity and the fact of its existence.

In dealing with the Christian attitude toward marriage, Clement touched on a question that later became perennial among Lutherans: the relationship between law and gospel. After presenting pagan matrimonial legislation and excerpts from pagan poets, he quoted Matthew 5.32 and 19.9 on divorce and asked: "What, then, is the law?" He alluded to the Law of Moses and stated: "And the law is not at variance with the Gospel, but agrees with it. How should it be otherwise, one Lord being the author of both?"[117] Clement saw no contradiction between law and gospel.

Another work of Clement, *Who is the Rich Man that Shall be Saved?*, contains a clearer indication that Christians were governed by a set of laws: he followed his statement that "And he loves Christ Jesus who does His will and keeps his commandments" by quotations from Matthew 7.1, Luke 6.46 and Matthew 13.16f, which emphasize the spiritual necessity on obeying injunctions which Jesus expressly prescribed.[118]

The Late Second Century - *The Sentences of Sextus*

Dating in its present form from before the end of the second century, *The Sentences of Sextus* are a collection of four hundred and fifty-one sayings and exhortations on Christian moral life. Organized along Greek philosophical lines instead of Jewish ones, the format and arrangement bear no relation to the Law of Moses, a change which is to be expected for a religion which is completing transition from the Jewish to the Gentile world and to accommodation to Greek philosophy. This is evidence that, despite the change in culture, Christian moral law remained a body of precisely-expressed ethical injunctions. *The Sentences* were well received by Christian communities, with many copies surviving in Greek, Latin, Coptic, Syriac, Armenian and Georgian. They were quoted with respect as early as the A.D. 240s.[119]

Transition to the Third Century

To this point we have examined writings from the first two centuries A.D. and established that they provide evidence that Christians of the period followed an ethical/religious law which consisted of a large number of specific injunctions and prohibitions in addition to the commandments to love God and one's neighbour. The first half of the third century likewise produced authors who left writings on the subject. Moreover, this later period also generated a voluminous literary output from Tertullian and Origen, two authors who provided much evidence of the existence of an early Christian law and of its contents. We have so extensive a sample of their writings that we can check whether they modified or negated in one book a statement they had made elsewhere.

Tertullian was the first major Christian author to write in the Latin language. He wrote more works in that language than any Christian prior to the great Augustine over a century and a half later. Origen produced his first works in Egypt and later ones in Palestine, and from both bases he travelled abroad as a theological consultant and was thus exposed to Christian thought in various geographical regions. He was the most prolific Christian author in any language until Martin Luther over twelve centuries later.

The Early Third Century: Tertullian

After a distinguished legal career, Tertullian converted to Christianity and authored presentations of the Faith to non-Christians, works on theology, on divisions within Christianity, and on the Christian life. His many years at the Bar gave him the highest qualifications for making distinctions and analyzing the methodology of behavioural decision-making. Although a person tends to relate what he learns later to earlier training and experience, Tertullian's works in no way resemble a law book. They recite far fewer rules and are less compendious than those of Paul the Apostle, the *Letter of Barnabas*, the *Didache* or the *Sentences of Sextus*. On the contrary, Tertullian appears at times to use the word "discipline" where other early Christian authors would use a word with stronger legal connotations. Because the present book seeks indisputable evidence of a Christian moral law instead of relying on inferences that are open to more than one conclusion, I shall not cite the abundance of passages where Tertullian used "discipline" in contexts in which it is debatable whether it is a synonym for "law".

The site of Tertullian's literary production was Carthage, in what is now Tunisia. It began around A.D. 197 and continued for over two decades. Almost all of his works were directed to a Christian readership. He composed many of them as arguments against the positions held by particular groups of Christians, some with whom he shared communion and others of different denominations. To make points more effectively, Tertullian sought for common ground accepted by both sides and then tried to show that his opponents were wrong on the basis of doctrines and practices they themselves accepted. This method of argument proves invaluable to us in the early twenty-first century because Tertullian's presentations thus preserve evidence of what most Christians of the early third century held in common, including the concept that they were governed by a religious law.

Tertullian: *De oratione*

On Prayer consists of a commentary on the Lord's Prayer, with a description of some customs accompanying Christian prayer in Tertullian's day, and his objections to some of them. One such custom was of female virgins praying bareheaded, which had met with a mixed reaction among Christians. (Members of the order of "virgins" were like the later nuns except that they could own private property, live where they wished and resign their vows more easily.) The virgins who refused to veil contended that, because they had never engaged in sex, they did not fit into the category "women" in 1 Corinthians 11.1 to 16. The virgins argued that Paul's instruction that women cover their heads did not apply to them because he had directed only "women" to cover their heads and did not extend the rule to persons who were female but not sexually experienced. They said that their status was closer to that of prepubescent girls, whom many Christians in Tertullian's day regarded as not within the scope of the Apostle's directions. Tertullian disagreed. He replied, *inter alia*, that Paul addressed his admonition to all female Christians in general, and Tertullian then raised the arguments of nature, honour and custom, and then stated that there is only one law ("discipline") concerning covering the head, a law which extends even to prepubescent females. Tertullian added that even if some Jews do not observe the Mosaic Law about headgear, "*our* Law" (i.e. Christian law) is an "amplified and supplemented" one which reinforces the precept and extends the obligation to virgins also.[120]

The words "law", "discipline" and "our Law" point to the existence of a law peculiar to Christians and regarded by them as authoritative. It was so well accepted in Tertullian's time that different parties in the church used it as a common ground in debate. It is not clear in *De oratione* to what extent "law" was a synonym for "discipline" or whether "our Law" was uniquely Christian or a revision of the Law of Moses, partly shared by Jews. In any event, Christian law was distinct from Jewish law and Christians regarded it as binding on Jesus' followers.

Tertullian: *De virginibus velandis*

The debate over headcovering resumed a few years later. This time Tertullian fell back on his experience as a barrister: his presentation technique in *De virginibus velandis* (*On the Veiling of Virgins*) is not essentially different from the one used today for a lawyer's brief or factum to a court. As is to be expected in such documents, Tertullian referred to the applicable law as recognized by both the judge (the reader) and the opposing party, then argued his case by interpreting that law in the way most favourable to his own position. It appears from Chapter 4 that the opposition also cited Christian law: in summarizing their argument Tertullian quotes the adversaries of compulsory headgear for virgins as saying that female virgins "are not comprised in the law of veiling the head, as not being named in this law"[121] (i.e. 1 Corinthians 11.1 to 16). It is not clear whether "law" in this quotation means "law in the abstract" or "one of many statutes, by-laws and ordinances" as distinguished above under Justin Martyr, but in the present context the difference is immaterial.

Tertullian exegeted 1 Corinthians 11.5 to 16 and analyzed the characteristics which place a person into Paul's categories of "man" and "woman", and then directly addressed a contrary argument from another religious custom which was accepted by all Christians. This other custom was that sexually inexperienced adult males were considered to be in the category "men" and thus prayed bareheaded. Tertullian stated that the proper distinction in Christian law was not between virgins and non-virgins but between males and females. He emphasized that there were "two laws, mutually distinctive": a law for females and a law for males.[122] Here "law" is used in the sense of "one of many statutes, by-laws and ordinances" and carries the more general meaning, thus indicating that Christians were governed by a broad corpus of legislation consisting of many individual rules.

At Chapter 16 Tertullian makes a reference to "law" which can mean only a distinctively Christian law:[123]

> Herein consists the defence of our opinion, in accordance with Scripture, in accordance with Nature, in accordance with Discipline. Scripture founds the law; Nature joins to attest to it; Discipline exacts it.

Tertullian: *De poenitentia*

Tertullian began his *On Repentance* by discussing the effects, motives and benefits of repentance, and then wrote:[124]

> Well, since, God as Judge presides over the exacting and maintaining of justice, which to Him is most dear; and since it is with an eye to justice that He appoints all the sum of His discipline, is there room for doubting that, just as in all our acts universally, so also in the case of repentance, justice must be rendered to God?

Use of the words "rule", "justice" and "judge" suggest a legal system, while the word "discipline" in this context suggests a body of binding rules given by the Father to aid the development of His children.

Tertullian: *Adversus Marcionem*

Marcion was a Christian who believed that the Creator, the God of Moses and of the Old Testament, was not the God of Jesus and the New Testament. He believed that they were two different gods and actually warred with each other. Jesus came to liberate humanity from the Creator deity. In his *Antitheses*, Marcion condemned the Hebrew Scriptures as the work of the evil divinity and advocated that Christians use only the Gospel of Luke and ten letters of Paul, as edited by himself. Part of Tertullian's purpose in writing *Against Marcion* was to reconcile the Old Testament with the New and to demonstrate that it was the same God in both.

Book 4 Chapter 9 is somewhat confusing because it speaks of a "new law" for Christians while upholding the Law of Moses as still binding on Christ's disciples:[125]

> We have indeed already laid it down, in opposition to his *Antitheses*, that the position of Marcion derives no advantage from the diversity which he supposes to exist between the Law and the Gospel, inasmuch as even this was ordained by the Creator, and indeed predicted in the promise of the new Law, the new Word, and the new Testament.
>
> • • •
>
> The Lord, therefore, wishing that the law should be more profoundly understood as signifying spiritual truth by carnal facts—and thus not destroying, but rather building up, that *law* which He wanted to have more earnestly acknowledged....

It should not be surprising that Christian law resembles Mosaic Law, whether this is because the Christian discipline is a revision or extension of the Sinai Code or they are independent formulations: both as a deity who loves His people and as a lawgiver, God gives them what is best for them; the law of the Israelites and the law of the Christians naturally resemble each other because they were the best He could devise in their respective circumstances,

Although stating that he partly agreed with Marcion's doctrines, Tertullian wrote the following while commenting on Luke 10.27:[126]

> the Lord, being Himself the same, and introducing no precept other than that which relates above all others to (man's) entire salvation ... places before him the very essence of the law—that he should in every possible way love the Lord his God.

Note that Tertullian said "essence of the law". He did not state that one of the Two Great Commandments is the entire law for Christians. There is more law besides. In the original Latin, the word Tertullian used here for "essence" was *caput*, i.e. "head". The head does not comprise the entire body (see 1 Corinthians 12.12 to 21). In any living organism the existence of a "head" necessarily implies that there are other parts of the body. If the commandment to love God is the essence or head (*caput*) of the law, there must be a larger body (or *corpus*) of the law.

Elsewhere in *Against Marcion*, Tertullian placed the commandment to love God in an equal relationship with other precepts and practical examples of Christian law. In commenting on Luke 11.45 to 52 Tertullian argued that Christ did not abolish the Law of Moses and asked the rhetorical question:[127]

> For how could He have felt aversion to the law, who used with so much earnestness to upbraid them for passing over its weightier matters, alms-giving, hospitality, and the love of God?

Tertullian: *Scorpiace*

Tertullian wrote *Antidote for the Scorpion's Sting* in opposition the tenets of the Valentinian denomination of Gnostics. They believed that it was permissible for a Christian to deny his/ her faith in order to escape persecution. This was in an era when professing Christianity was a capital offence under Roman law.

Tertullian discoursed on the Old Testament martyrs and turned to whether their example was pertinent to Christians:[128]

> It remains for us, lest ancient times may perhaps have had the sacrament [i.e. martyrdom] (exclusively) their own, to review the modern Christian system, as though, being also from God, it might be different *from what preceded*, and besides, therefore, opposed thereto in its code of rules.

Here Tertullian indicated; (1) Christianity had its own "code of rules", and (2) Christian law was so similar to that of Moses that effort was needed to distinguish them on the less everyday provisions.

Tertullian: *Ad Uxorem*

In form, *To His Wife* was not written as part of a controversy with a different group of Christians but was addressed to Tertullian's spouse to persuade her not to remarry after his death or, if she did, to marry only another Christian. He buttressed his argument by appealing to four supreme principles as governing Christians: faith, holiness, the discipline of the church and the "prescription of the apostle" thus indicating the authorities that he and his wife shared as believers.[129]

Besides the spiritual peril of any remarriage, Tertullian mentioned that matrimony with a non-Christian incurred strong sanction by the church. He discussed 1 Corinthians 7.6 to 8 and 12 to 14,[130] and reminded her that the Christian partner is "excluded from all communication with the brotherhood in accordance with the letter of the apostle, who says that 'with persons of that kind there is to be no taking of food even.'"[131] This is evidence of a mandatory rule, of New Testament origin, and enforced by the church by the equivalent of banishment from the community when exile was still a common secular penalty for certain criminal offences. It has all the characteristics of a law.

Tertullian: *De Pudicitia*

Half-way through his writing years, Tertullian parted company with the catholic/Great Church and joined the Montanists, a Christian denomination which took a hard line on post-baptismal sin. At issue in his treatise *On Modesty* was the jurisdiction and willingness of the catholic church to grant forgiveness to persons who had committed adultery or fornication after baptism. Tertullian the Montanist dealt at great length with the catholics' many arguments, assessed them, and set forth the Montanist position that no church could pardon these great sins.

His long and comprehensive treatment of catholics' arguments reveals that they relied on the Old Testament as well as the New to contend that their denomination could forgive such sins. In referring to the Law of Moses, he agreed with them that "The law of piety, sanctity, humanity, truth, chastity, justice, mercy, benevolence, modesty, remains in its entirety"[132] and rhetorically asked "whether the law of not committing adultery be still in force".[133] Immediately continuing his argument, he sought to win over catholics by stating that "an additional law has been reared, condemning the origin even of sins"[134] in a context that appears to indicate that it was common ground between Montanists and the Great Church that Jesus had added to the Mosaic Law or introduced one of His own. Tertullian then said that this new law did not contain the same provisions as that of Moses for the forgiveness of sexual offenders.

It is unclear from *On Modesty* whether Christian moral law as accepted by both denominations was a revised continuation of the Sinai Code or a completely new creation, but this treatise leaves little doubt that both parties of Christians considered themselves bound by a law consisting of a number of specific rules.

Tertullian: *De idolatria*

In *On Idolatry* also, Tertullian touched on the abrogation or modification of the Mosaic Law and the existence of a distinctively Christian law—distinctive because it was separate from the Sinai Code and because it marked out Christian behaviour among the pagans. Making a reference to the Lukan Acts 15, he stated in the final chapter of this treatise:[135]

> The reason why the Holy Spirit did, when the apostles at that time were consulting, relax the bond and yoke for us,[136] was that we might be free to devote ourselves to the shunning of idolatry. This shall be our Law, the more fully to be administered the more ready it is to hand; (a Law) peculiar to Christians, by means whereof we are recognised and examined by the heathens. This Law might be set before such as approach unto the Faith, and inculcated on such as are entering it; that, in approaching, they may deliberate; observing it, may persevere; not observing it, may renounce their name.[137]

In sum, we have overwhelming evidence from the very early third century that Christians regarded themselves as subject to a well-defined law which was not a mere reiteration of the Sinai Code. This evidence was furnished by a professional whose personal qualifications both at the Bar and in the church equipped him to recognize law(s) and the nature, essentials, consequences and effects of law on both sides of disputes over permitted or desirable behaviour in a community.

The Early Third Century - *Didascalia apostolorum*

Dating from the first three decades of the third Christian century, the *Didascalia* is a law code in the full sense of the term: an exhaustive collection of the rules of behaviour on related subjects, systematically arranged and subdivided by topic, e.g. men, women, backsliders, deacons, heretics. One exception is that the many provisions on bishops-pastors are not in a single sequence but are interspersed throughout the whole text at the various subject matters to which each pertains. It is an ample and extensive code: commandment follows precept follows rule follows ordinance follows mandate for approximately a hundred and forty pages. In this respect, it is better organized than the Mosaic Law in the Old Testament. The *Didascalia* even provides for a system of Christian courts with their own rules of procedure.[138] Such tribunals adjudicated both offences against Christian law like a modern criminal court and also disputes between Christian and Christian over debts and property like a modern civil court. Indeed, such judicial bodies probably existed in New Testament times.[139] The *Didascalia* probably originated in Syria.

Although the *Didascalia* opposes Sabbath-keeping, it draws relationships between Christian law and the Law of Moses. Like Irenaeus[140] and Ptolemy's *Letter to Flora*, it connects Christian law with that given at Sinai and maintains that Jesus modified only parts of the earlier law and abolished only Pharisaic additions and corruptions.

The compilers of the *Didascalia* often expressed great concern that Christians should not follow "the Second Legislation".[141] Bishops were to warn their congregations against it and all Christians must be careful to distinguish it from the real law of God for Christians. It is uncertain from the *Didascalia* what this "Second Legislation" was, whether it was human accretions dating from near the time of Moses, or the Book of Deuteronomy (literally: "second law"), or the practices fossilized in the intertestamental period and by the Pharisees, or popular customs which interfered with or burdened full obedience to God's will in Christ. As a man of training and skill, it was the bishop who was to take the lead in making the distinctions between the true law and the "Second Legislation". He did this both in his capacity as pastor and also as judge in church courts, just as the judge in any court is the chief and final interpreter of the law. The references to the "Second Legislation" also indicate that Christian moral law was already voluminous and complex enough that many ordinary lay believers could mistakenly include unrelated rules as part of it. Whatever the uncertainty about details, the *Didascalia* demonstrates that by the early third century some Christian communities possessed an organized compendium of precise and detailed laws which governed their acts, attitudes and emotions.

Origen Adamantius

Origen Adamantius was a native of Egypt who in A.D. 202 succeeded Clement as head of the theological school at Alexandria. In A.D. 230 he established his own school at Caesarea in Palestine, where he lived and taught for the remaining twenty-odd years of his life, except when invited by churches abroad to help with their problems. In addition to teaching in his institute, he also preached hundreds of sermons to nearby congregations. He was one of the most prominent Christian scholars of his day. He wrote and preached until imprisoned and tortured in the Decian Persecution of A.D 249-251, and died soon afterward.

Origen: *De Principiis*

In *De Principiis* Origen was concerned with doctrine and the spiritual interpretation of Scripture rather than practical applications of Christianity. Nevertheless, this work reveals that there was in his day a corpus of Christian law which governed interpersonal behaviour. He mentioned that among the duties of the Apostle Paul was that he "enacts law for the Churches".[142]

Origen: *Homilies on Exodus*

Origen spoke of Christian law as being in a highly developed state. In his comparison of "studies of the divine Law" to a liberal education or other secular discipline, he cited the examples of books, tutors and other substantial expenses for secular studies and stated that the same dedication and effort are necessary for "a divine education" as for "a human education."[143]

The financial aspects of Origen's comparison should not be overdrawn. We know from other sources that Christians offered instruction free of charge and that a person was at liberty to extend his study of the Faith over many years instead of the comparatively few for secular disciplines. Even with this reservation, *Homilies on Exodus* corroborates the *Didascalia* that Christian law was not something that could be mastered in a few weeks, let alone put into practice after learning a few simple principles. These two sources show that even at this early time it was of such volume and complexity that a long period of dedicated study was required.

Origen: *Homilies on Joshua*

Origen further referred to a law within Christianity in his *Homilies on Joshua*. There he mentioned "the law of the Spirit" and "the law of the Gospel".[144] He counselled listeners not to separate from the gospel "the mystic precepts of the law."[145] As in his *Homilies of Exodus*, he indicated that it requires much study and dedication to acquire a knowledge of Christian law.[146] With some repetition, he indicated many prohibitions of this law, most noticeably in Homily 1.6f, 7.1f, 7.4, 7.6, 9.2, 9.9 and 10.3.

Homily 9 contains one of Origen's few sustained treatments of the subject of Christian law as an entity. Section 3 mentions the expression "the Second Law" but it appears to be different from that referred to in the *Didascalia*. Origen stated that the "Second Law" was the one handed down by Jesus after the original Law of Moses was rendered void. It was the provisions of the Second Law, not that of Moses, which Jesus instituted in the Sermon on the Mount.[147] Later in Section 3, Origen advised that when Christians see pagans turn to God and perform the works of the law, Christians should say that that the Second Law is written on these Gentiles' hearts.

While it is unclear how much and exactly what parts of Jewish law applied to Christians in Origen's time and how much and what parts of it had been annulled or replaced, his *Homilies on Joshua* leaves no doubt that early Christians possessed a system of moral law of some complexity and volume.

Origen: *Contra Celsum*

In *Against Celsus* Origen referred to Christians as those people "to whom has come the doctrine of a pure and holy worship, and who have obtained new laws, in harmony with the established constitution of all countries."[148] He further stated that God had "enacted laws which ensure happiness to those who live according to them"[149] and[150]

> We Christians, then, who have come to the knowledge of the law which is by nature "king of all things," and which is the same with the law of God, endeavour to regulate our lives by its prescriptions, having bidden a long farewell to those of an unholy kind.

Origen indicated that Christian law or Christian ethics consisted of more than the Two Great Commandments: "it is evident that he who keeps the law honours God, and that the worshipper of God is he whose life is regulated by the principles and precepts of the divine word".[151] As in the case of *1 Clement*, the pluralization of synonymous terms indicates that ancient Christian law consisted of more than the Two Love Commandments: "principles" in plural indicates that there were at least two principles while "precepts" in the plural indicates that there were at least two precepts, and that there were thus a minimum of four commandments binding on early Christians.

Origen recognized that the law of Christ obliged disciples to follow very definite precepts. With some repetition of content, eleven passages in *Against Celsus* remind the reader that the divine law specifically forbids killing, bearing arms, taking vengeance, drunkenness, anger, desecration of human corpses, pursuit of human glory, and reviling pagan idols, while commanding non-resistance and obeying secular laws which are not contrary to those of God.[152] Even with little ethical content, *Against Celsus* provides abundant evidence that ancient Christian law did not consist of only a few principles.

Origen: *Homilies on Leviticus*

In *Homilies on Leviticus*, Origen used the expressions "spiritual law",[153] "the laws of the Gospel",[154] "precept of the Gospel",[155] "laws of the New Testament",[156] and "the law of Christ",[157] and gave examples of the last-mentioned. In Homily 10 the phrases "the precept of the Gospel" and "the laws of the Gospel" are used in the context of instructions about fasts, after which Origen states that the Saviour "commands" the provisions of Matthew 6.17 for all believers.[158] Origen exhorted his congregation to memorize enough to "fulfill the divine precepts"[159] and warned them that they would be afflicted if they did not keep God's law nor observe His commandments.[160] Despite his spiritualising of the Mosaic Law, Origen in the seventh homily employed the term "the divine law" in an unmistakably Christian context[161] and taught that the prohibition in Leviticus 10.9 (against overindulgence in alcohol before officiating at public worship) was one of the Mosaic precepts still in force among Christians.[162]

Origen: *Homilies on Judges*

Christ told His apostles that if persecuted in one town they should flee to another.[163] Origen described this statement as being in "the laws of Christ",[164] presumably applicable to all Christians notwithstanding that it was spoken only to a special group in Matthew's Gospel and is not deducible from more universal principles.

Origen: *Homilies on Luke*

Origen alluded to a distinctively Christian law in Homily 16 when he mentioned that he applied the same exegetical method to the old law as to the new.[165] The existence of a body of commandments and prohibitions binding on Christians also emerges in Homily 34.[166] In the same sermon he stated that Christ retained those commandments of the Mosaic Code which lead to eternal life and that Jesus gave the Two Great Commandments as "only a sort of abridgement".[167]

Origen: *Commentary on the Letter to the Romans*

In his *Commentary on the Letter to the Romans* Origen gave extended treatment to Paul's use of the word "law". He demonstrated that "law" has different meanings and nuances in the Scriptures and that even these differ from passage to passage. Sometimes, wrote Origen, more than one sense occurs in the same passage, and cited Romans and Galatians as examples.[168] The exegete, he cautioned, must pay careful attention to ascertain the correct shade of meaning wherever "law" appears in the holy writings.[169]

In this *Commentary* Origen mentioned about a dozen meanings of "law" in Paul's letter to the Romans.[170] Even so short a fragment of Cairo Museum Papyrus 88748 refers to (1) the Mosaic Law, (2) a pre-Mosaic law written on the hearts of Adam, Eve, the casualties in the Noachian Flood, the inhabitants of Sodom and other people before Moses, (3) the law of nature, (4) a law of right reason, (5) the law in the prophetic texts, and (6) secular human law.[171] In her analysis of part of it Marguerite Harl made a sixfold distinction.[172] Whatever the exact number, such analyses support Michael Joseph Winger and C. H. Dodd to the effect that when Paul condemned obedience to "the law" he did not mean Christian law.[173]

Origen: *Commentaries on the Psalms*

Origen's comment on "Teach me to do thy will" in Psalm 143.10 was "This saying shows that practical ethics is not as clear as some people imagine",[174] an allusion to the complexity and amount of study required to know Christian law. In a similar vein, the lesson he drew from "hide not thy commandments from me" in Psalm 119.19 was that it is not simple to know all God's commandments.[175]

The Gospel of Mary

This and all other Gnostic texts in the Nag Hammadi library are almost completely devoid of law, rules, and other moral or interpersonal guidance. This is not surprising, for many Gnostics believed that what God desired of Christians was illumination and esoteric knowledge rather than ethical living. Dating from the early third century A.D., *The Gospel of Mary* nevertheless tacitly admits that Christ did indeed give His disciples their own law. There Jesus is represented as saying to His disciples after His resurrection: "Do not lay down any rules beyond what I appointed for you, and do not give a law like the lawgiver lest you be constrained by it."[176]

The fact that a Gnostic writer acknowledged, contrary to his or her denominational distinctives, that there were binding rules or laws in Christianity can only mean that the evidence for their existence was too overwhelming to be denied. To overcome this unpalatable fact and avoid recognizing the whole of Christian law handed down from the apostles, the author of *The Gospel of Mary* put into Jesus' mouth a prohibition against making rules. Here again is an admission that there was already a distinctively Christian law of some volume.

Cyprian of Carthage

Although 1 Timothy 3.5 deprecates a recent convert being made a bishop, Thascius Cyprianus Caecilius became pastor-bishop of Carthage (the city where Tertullian wrote) within four years of his conversion. He held that post from A.D. 248 or 249 until his death in 258. His writings are more fully discussed in Chapter Five below. Relevant to our present purposes are his remarks that indicate that early Christians possessed a law beyond a few general principles.

Cyprian intimated that the teachings of the Great Church were not simple or immediately deducible from the Scriptures when he opined that catholic clergy should teach their faith to converts from heresies and schisms by means of all "the evangelical and apostolical precepts"[177]. The fact that converts from within Christianity had to go through such instruction in the Faith in addition to what they had learned in their previous denominations indicates that "the evangelical and apostolical precepts" entailed a not inconsiderable body of knowledge. The same is shown in one of Cyprian's letters to Christians incarcerated during the Decian Persecution of A.D. 249 to 251. After reminding them how they had confessed and maintained their faith with bravery and devotion to God, he exhorted them to "also maintain the law and discipline of the Lord"[178] and pointed out how they were to do so in ways additional to what the presbyters and deacons had taught them about "the law of the Gospel".[179]

So highly did Cyprian and his readers value "the evangelical law" or "the law of the Gospel" that in another letter he included it—as apparently signifying equality—in the same phrase as "the order arranged by God" and "the unity of the catholic institution".[180]

De centesima, sexagesima, tricesima/Incipit centesima de martyribus

The last early Christian writing we will consider has two titles: *Hundredfold, Sixtyfold, Thirtyfold* and *The Hundredfold of Martyrs*.[181] Anonymous, it most likely dates from the early third century A.D., although estimates have ranged between the second and early fourth century. In keeping with the practice of the present book, I regard as determinative the latest date supported by scholarly opinion. Like the *Didache*,[182] this treatise postulates at Chapter 14 that not everyone can perform all of God's law, so it counsels a Christian to perform as much as she/he can; if he or she is unable to follow all the Lord's precepts, says Chapter 14, he or she should at least obey the Two Great Commandments. Such a statement in two sources indicates that Christian law was extensive to the point of burdensome. Indeed, Chapter 44 states that "the law of the Lord is hard and bitter".[183]

Chapter 15 continues the thought, after referring to the Two Love Commandments: "everything is included in the Two...so that, believing in the divine kingdom and precept, we may act with care."[184] Chapters 1, 16, 24, 42 and 46 condemn various specifically-named sins and exhort obedience to the Two Love Commandments. It appears that this document teaches that the Two do not contain the whole of the law which governs Christians but merely put a person on the right road so that he can eventually do God's will in its entirety, or at least obey as many of its rules as s/he can.

An Opposite View

Bishop Eduard Lohse seems to deny that in early Christianity there was an itemized or coherent body of moral rules or moral law free from complication:[185]

> Early Christianity included within itself different groups, with different opinions and schools of thought. In many places contrasting understandings of the Christian life emerged, which gave disparate answers to the problems of Christian ethics, and consequently resulted in varying patterns of conduct. How should Christians shape their lives in order to live in accordance with the gospel and so as not to hinder people's coming to accept it in faith? This question was raised again and again, and had to be resolved over and over in view of the conflicts it evoked.

and[186]

> From the writings of the New Testament no "early Christian ethic" can be
> derived in the sense of a system of universally valid general truths, for ethics
> had its place in the context of preaching and teaching within the churches. That
> Christians had to do what is good and right was a matter of instruction given
> along the way. But the question of just what this "good and right" in fact was,
> had to be raised and decided time and again in careful searching for the will
> of God and in circumspect probing of traditional teaching.

However, Lohse does not say that there was antinomianism or moral anarchy. He merely
says that our sources of this ethical law came down on a piecemeal basis and with no central
unifying authority to standardize it or to legislate for the whole church. He gives the example
of the church at Corinth, where local Christians tolerated gross immoralities. In response
to this, the Apostle Paul spoke for God by instructing them how Christians were to behave
in the circumstances. The present book agrees with Lohse's idea that there was no central
authority but says that the law, or at least the principles of it, came entire from Christ and only
its transmission was piecemeal. Like Paul, many apostles, bishops, presbyters, teachers and
perhaps laypeople preached and taught, as occasion arose, what they believed to be God's will
on particular matters of ethics. Lohse admits that[187]

> The earliest Christian community gathered, preserved, handed on, and
> interpreted the preaching of Jesus under the guidance of the leading question
> of the relevance of this message for Christian conduct. By so doing, they sought
> to provide a Christological foundation for ethical instruction.

Nor does Lohse deny that there are paraenetic compilations in the New Testament
letters of Peter, James and Paul. Confining his book to the New Testament, Lohse does
not draw on the ancient Christian witnesses (such as the *Didache*, *Barnabas*, and the
Sentences of Sextus) which reveal that the New Testament is part of a Christian context
that was very concerned with an ethical law, although the said paraenetic compilations in
the New Testament should have given him an inkling of it. Like the present book itself,
the present chapter draws on the entire body of earliest Christian writings, both inside and
outside the New Testament, to ascertain the context and mind-set of its first readers in order
to determine whether and to what extent they shared an attitude amenable to or against a
detailed moral law.

Bishop Lohse also differs from me in a fundamental matter of approach to the subject.
As is common for Continentals, his concern is with theory and theology. I follow my training
and experience in the legal system of the British Commonwealth and the United States by
looking at what actually happened, consulting as many relevant instances as possible, and
then formulating principles and judgments from the evidence of actual instances to produce
a working model rather than starting with a general theory and then deductively reasoning

from it. Nor did Lohse have the benefit of seeing long lists showing the surprisingly close correspondences and similarities among New Testament authors such as are contained in the present book.

How to deal with what Lohse terms "contrasting", "disparate" and "varying patterns", in the few instances where they exist, is considered in my Chapter Six under the heading "The Contrary View" and the first paragraph under the heading "Considerations as to Authorities".

All the above equally applies to Willi Marxsen's *New Testament Foundation for Christian Ethics*. In one place Marxsen stated: "I begin rather with the uncontestable observation that the authors of the New Testament writings present not only different ethics but also in part ethics that can be brought into agreement only with difficulty."[188] Elsewhere[189] he states this proposition as "obvious". But throughout his book Marxsen presented few or no instances of conflict in particular precepts but grossly exaggerated differences in Christology among the various New Testament authors (which to my mind are more differences in emphasis in treatment). His thesis as to differences in ethics flows from his vigorous straining to find differences in Christology and then blithely assuming that differences in Christology resulted in different ethics. Christology is beyond the scope of the present book, but Marxsen's method does lead the reader to be skeptical of the conclusion following from his assumption (which he calls an "observation"), an assumption he did not substantiate from solid data, and on which he constructed his entire edifice.

Conclusion

In practice, even if not in speech, "law" and "ethics" are synonymous terms within religious institutions. I have therefore used the more straightforward and less confusing word "law" as a more accurate representation of Christian system of compulsory behavioural norms, particularly the ancient ones. I have also done so because the subject-matter of this book is broader than what is usually considered to be "ethics". The letters of the New Testament and other Christian literature written before A.D. 250 reveal that the church of Christ possessed a law consisting of specific commandments and precise prohibitions; 1 Corinthians 6.1-6 and the *Didascalia* reveal that, like any legal system, it also had a judiciary to decide when the law had been broken and that all Christians were obliged in conscience to obey. Although some passages in the Pauline epistles, 1 Peter and Justin Martyr may at first sight appear to contradict this thesis, analysis of these passages in context indicates that this is not the case. Nor was the phenomenon merely local: Syria, Egypt, France, Tunisia, Phrygia (in western Turkey), the Roman Province of Asia (a bit farther to the west in Turkey), Greece, central Italy, and Palestine furnish a great host of witnesses that a distinctively Christian law governed believers, as do the "Catholic Epistles" in the New Testament which are directed to Christians everywhere. The evidence agrees with the observation of J. Patout Burns that "the Christian church used purity codes which it could readily verify—standards defined by actions or behaviors rather than by intentions."[190] Our remaining task is how to ascertain the content of this law.

Chapter Three

The Place of Scripture in the Christian Life[191]

Scripture by itself is insufficient to inform us of all aspects of Christian moral law within a tolerable degree of certainty, i.e. the Bible is an incomplete guide to upright living. This is partly because the contents of the Bible are themselves uncertain and incomplete, partly because of cultural gaps between its writers and our own day, and partly because it is subject to a host of conflicting interpretations.

The Bible Confesses Its Own Incompleteness

The Bible does not purport to contain all the message and teachings of Jesus. John 21.25 hyperbolically opines that the world itself does not have enough room to house the records of all His acts and words. John confesses at 20.31 that he had confined himself to writing only enough for people to obtain a saving knowledge of Him. The object of the Gospel of John is no more than to convert people to Christianity; it does not attempt to provide all that is necessary for Christian life and ethics. If John's Gospel were sufficient for all purposes, why do we accept and use those of Matthew, Mark and Luke?

Some of God's word has not been recorded in Scripture. At Revelation 10.9 John was instructed not to record what was said to him by the seven thunders. If it is possible to discover what they said, we can find it only outside the present Bible.

Not all of Jesus' teachings are contained in the four Gospels. Many are found in other ancient Christian literature. Probably the most quoted in Egypt and Syria was "Be ye skilful moneychangers", which was regarded as divinely inspired and attributed to Christ or Paul by Clement of Alexandria,[192] Origen,[193] the *Didascalia*,[194] a bishop of Alexandria writing in A.D. 257,[195] the *Clementine Homilies* of the next century,[196] Athanasius,[197] and the *Apostolic Constitutions* of the late fourth century.[198] (A relic of Jewish Christianity from Syria, the *Clementine Homilies* purport to narrate the acts of the Apostle Peter and Clement of Rome, who flourished in the second half of the first century. Famous for leading the struggle against the Arians, Athanasius was chief bishop of Egypt (with interruptions) from A.D. 328 to 373. As noted in Chapter 2, *The Didascalia* is a Syrian church manual compiled in the first half of the third century; most of it was later incorporated into the *Apostolic Constitutions*, another Syrian compilation.)

Some of the Apostle Paul's writings may also be lacking. At 1 Corinthians 5.9 he says "I wrote to you in my letter..." but 1 Corinthians is the first letter to the Corinthian church in the present New Testament. Some scholars suggest that 2 Corinthians 6.14 to 7.1 is the missing letter taken from its original place and appended to another epistle. Even if this transposition hypothesis is correct and we thus have a complete collection of Paul's letters to this church, it appears that the text has been tampered with. Moreover, Colossians 4.16 mentions an epistle to the Laodiceans but no document with this name appears in the present Bible.

The Old Testament bears witness in itself that it is incomplete, no matter which ancient or modern canon one accepts. According to 1 Kings 4.32, Solomon uttered 3,000 proverbs and 1,005 songs, yet even the most inclusive canons contain only a few hundred proverbs and perhaps only one song.

No Generally-Accepted Canon in the Early Church

In early Christian times, a multitude of writings competed for status as authoritative scripture. A representative sampling are translated or referred to in Werner Foerster's *Gnosis: A Selection of Gnostic Texts*,[199] Montague R. James and James K. Elliott's *Apocryphal New Testament*,[200] William Schneemelcher's *New Testament Apocrypha*,[201] and James M. Robinson's *The Nag Hammadi Library in English*.[202] The earliest Christians did not know or were in doubt as to which writings were part of Holy Writ. In some instances they experienced great difficulty in ascertaining which books belonged in the Bible. In the latter half of the second century Melito, the bishop-pastor of Sardis, reported to a correspondent in response to the latter's question that he had to travel much and perform a substantial amount of research in order to find which books constituted the Old Testament.[203] Even so, the list he produced omitted the Book of Esther. That the bishop was obliged to go to so much trouble indicates that there was material disagreement or indifference or lack of ready knowledge as to the exact boundaries of the canon. A generation later the bishop of Antioch discovered that a congregation fifty kilometres from his city was reading the *Gospel of Peter* as canonical during public worship. Although the bishop of a leading centre of Christianity he had never encountered it before. Only after studying the text and consulting with other churchpersons did he comment on its canonicity.[204]

Moreover, the first generations of Christians after the apostles felt free to differ over which books or parts of books to accept as Scripture. For instance the correspondence of Origen with his former student Julius Africanus in the second quarter of the third century records a debate between two well-informed Christians, both writing in good faith, on whether the story of Susannah properly belonged in the Book of Daniel and hence in the Old Testament.

They felt at liberty to discuss the inclusion or exclusion of a work from Scripture without one regarding the other as religiously or intellectually deficient.[205] Another example is the debate over the *Book of Enoch*: in the early third century Tertullian recorded a difference among Christians over a writing represented to be by this grandfather of Noah.[206] Origen's *Commentary on the Gospel of Matthew* indicates similar disputes over the *Ascension of Isaiah* and the *Shepherd of Hermas*.[207] Furthermore, his *Commentary on the Gospel of John* refers to a debate over whether 2 and 3 John should be accorded the status of Scripture,[208] and addressed the contention that the Lukan Acts and the letters of the apostles do not possess the same authority as the four Gospels.[209] As for the general situation, my investigations in this field accord with the following statement by a Professor of Ancient Christian History at Yale University:[210]

> Early Christian scriptures, then, sometimes presented messages or points of view that conflicted with one another. This is not surprising, for in the first three centuries there was only sporadic coordination among the various Christian groups and certainly no centralized uniformity. It was therefore only natural that in one group a particular book might be shown the respect due authoritative scripture, while another group elsewhere might accept it with less respect or even reject it.

Some ancient Christians accepted as scripture certain books that are not in the present sixty-six-book Bible. As shown by the length of Bruce M. Metzger's *The Canon of the New Testament: Its Origins Development and Significance*[211] and its fourteen-page bibliography,[212] a full exposition would be unduly long for the present chapter so I will select only three examples:

(1) The Roman Catholic Old Testament contains a few books not accepted by most Protestants. One or more of them are referred to as divinely inspired or spiritually authoritative in Irenaeus of Lyons' *Demonstration of the Apostolic Preaching*,[213] his *Against Heresies*,[214] (both A.D. 180s), repeatedly by Clement of Alexandria,[215] and in Tertullian's *On Fasting*[216] and *Scorpiace*.[217] They are similarly treated by Hippolytus of Rome in early third century.[218] In addition to his *Letter to Africanus*,[219] Origen cited them in at least nine of his works.[220] Similar treatment was accorded these "Old Testament Apocrypha" by one Bishop Barsabas of Jerusalem (2d or 3rd century),[221] by Bishop Alexander of Alexandria around A.D. 318,[222] and by a number of Latin Christian authors in the third century.[223]

(2) *The Book of Enoch* was a pre-Christian work which was very popular among ancient Christians and Jews but which today is considered Scripture only by the Church of Ethiopia. It was cited as authoritative in Jude 14f, Irenaeus' *Against Heresies*,[224] his *Demonstration of the Apostolic Preaching*,[225] the *Letter of Barnabas*,[226] and Clement of Alexandria's *Eclogae propheticae*.[227] Both Tertullian and Origen regarded *Enoch*

as scripture[228] but admitted that it was not accepted by all Christians.[229] In A.D. 277 a bishop of Laodicea considered it authoritative, at least as to Jewish practice.[230]

(3) *The Shepherd of Hermas* was written by a Christian before the middle of the second century. It was quoted as "scripture" in Irenaeus' *Against Heresies*[231] and eight times in Clement's *Stromata*.[232] Origen repeatedly treated it as accepted by some catholic Christians[233] and himself regarded it as divinely inspired.[234] When Athanasius in A.D. 367 drafted what eventually came into use as the present list of New Testament books he excluded Hermas but added that "from the time of the fathers"[235] the church recommended that it be read by or to recent converts to instruct them in religious truth. Although setting it off from the canonical books, Athanasius also distinguished it from the spurious books used by heretics.[236] Athanasius' *Easter Letter* of 367 by no means ended the uncertainty and differences in belief as to the contents of the canon. Other church fathers[237] and regional councils[238] after him in the fourth century continued to draw up their own independent lists of books of Scripture. A generation after him, there remained so little consensus on the issue within the established catholic denomination that the great Augustine felt it necessary to formulate a four-step method by which his readers could determine for themselves which books were canonical, a method which included even consulting other catholic churches overseas.[239] Unlike these fathers[240] and councils, but like Melito of Sardis, Athanasius omitted the Book of Esther from his list.[241] *The Easter Letter* was not very important even to Athanasius himself, for he continued to utilize as scriptural evidence in his creative theological writings various books that he had not included in it.[242]

The Late Date of Attempts to Define a Canon

These attempts to draft a list of what books and no others are contained in Christian holy scripture occurred between the mid-fourth century and the early fifth century—comparatively late in church history, inexplicably late if ante-Nicene Christians sought guidance only from the Bible as the sole and exhaustive resource for faith and practice with no authoritative supplement or interpreter. If the Bible or New Testament had been regarded—or meant to be regarded—as the exhaustive guide, one would expect its canon to have been defined by the apostles, or by the first generation after the apostles at the latest. On the contrary, as even Lee M. McDonald, a Baptist pastor and seminary president, observes:[243]

> There was, however, no fixed biblical canon handed over by Jesus to the apostles or by the apostles to the Christians. Those who claim that there was must first show references to one in the earliest writings of the Christians and then account for how the church, if it had such a sacred collection, could have lost it.

If the canon had existed in apostolic times, one is hard-pressed to explain the attempts by later churchmen to draft ones on their own as if no generally-accepted one had previously existed. One is also hard-pressed to explain why the canons produced by these later churchmen differed from each other, thus gainsaying the concept of an earlier, common, origin.

Reverend Doctor McDonald disputes that there were any attempts at all before the early fourth century to produce an exhaustive and complete list of the books of the New Testament. He believes that the canon lists attributed to earlier authors in Eusebius' *History of the Church* were that author's retrojecting into the past a concept that did not exist until his own time.[244] McDonald also states: "Eusebius in the beginning of the fourth century was the first church father to produce a list of NT scriptures and…there is considerable vagueness in regard to seven of the NT books in his list."[245] As for the canon list in Origen's *Homilies on Joshua* 7.1 (AD 249/250), McDonald agrees with Everett Kalin[246] that the text we now have of these homilies is not pristine but comes from a translation made around AD 400, the original text having since been lost. McDonald and Kalin believe that the translator altered the text to make it accord with his own time, including the fourth/fifth century idea of a fixed and exhaustive canon.[247] As will be seen in the present book under the heading "Tradition in Origen and His Circle" in Chapter Four, they are not the only twentieth-century scholars to believe that such translations do not faithfully represent Origen's thought. I am not sure that I can agree with McDonald and Kalin on this point, but even if Homily 7.1 was unaltered it was produced at a very late date—two centuries after the first New Testament writings and bordering on the cut-off date of the present book.

Nor might Marcion have been an exception to the comparatively late date of persons attempting to set out an exclusive canon. In paraphrasing Geoffrey M. Hahneman's *The Muratorian Fragment and the Development of the Canon,*[248] Rev. Dr. McDonald states:[249]

> G. M. Hahneman has shown that the later Marcionite communities were not limited to the so-called canon of Marcion and that Marcion himself may have not rejected other Christian scriptures so much as he edited them. …. Marcion does not present a closed biblical canon or, perhaps, a biblical canon at all. The writings in Marcion's collection no doubt functioned as scripture in his communities, but it was not an inviolable fixed catalog of scriptures to which nothing could be added or taken away.

Readers well versed in Christian antiquities may cite the "Muratorian Canon" as an objection to the thesis that formulating an exhaustive and exclusive New Testament canon did not begin until the fourth century. Also called the "Muratorian Fragment", it was found in a seventh- or eighth-century codex. It lists the books that the author believed to be the only ones that were or should be read publicly in church services. Some scholars believe it was originally compiled in the mid- or late-second century, but McDonald gives eleven pages of reasons[250] why he and Hahneman believe it to be fourth century. Despite a substantial body of scholarly opinion that it is second century, I must accept the opinion of McDonald and Hahneman because throughout the present book I rely only on documents which the scholarly world without substantial objection dates before the middle of the third century.

Whatever the date of the Muratorian Fragment, it does not purport to be exclusive, exhaustive or definitive, for it mentions that there was a difference in opinion whether a particular book (the *Revelation of Peter*) ought to be read during public worship. Nor does the Fragment refer to a letter or letters of Peter, the first of which was received by all or almost all early Christian authors. The Letter of James is also absent. It includes the *Wisdom of Solomon*, which no ancient writer except perhaps Clement of Alexandria[251] considered to be in the New Testament. Moreover, as McDonald points out, [252]

> If von Campenhausen and others are correct about the early dating of this document, it had no effect on the rest of the church for almost 150 years and is not referred to anywhere in the ancient church. As a late second-century document, the Muratorian Fragment's impact on the churches of that time is completely negligible and therefore cannot be of any consequence in piecing together the rather complicated puzzle of the formation of the Christian Bible.

To my way of thinking, the approaches of Melito and Irenaeus towards what might be called a canon do not favour the position that they were compiling a fixed, exhaustive or closed list of Christian scriptures or that such a collection was crucial in church life. Melito's list[253] pertains only to the Old Testament and thus omits the most significant part of the canon for Christians. Melito confined himself to the Hebrew Scriptures because they were the only part of the Bible about which he was asked. Four facts indicate that the exact parameters of the canon were not as important or as pressing in his day as they were in the fourth or fifth centuries or to some people in our day: (1) neither Melito nor his correspondent knew the contents of the Old Testament before Melito engaged in his research, which indicates that this knowledge was not commonly regarded as all-important for the Christian life, (2) Melito had to travel and do research, which means that the facts were not ascertainable locally, (3) he proceeded at a leisurely pace, which indicates that he did not regard the matter as pressingly important to himself or to the person who had asked him, and (4) he worked as an individual rather than in conjunction with intercongregational councils or other clergy, which means that the exact contents of the canon were of interest to only two or a few people. The lack of importance and absence of binding authority of his list are illustrated by the additional fact that nobody before Eusebius referred to or mentioned it. Yet the Christian life continued throughout the Roman Empire and beyond with the precise contents of the Bible being a matter of merely individual enterprise.

If it had existed, a complete and exclusive list of books of the New Testament handed down by dominical or apostolic authority would have been invaluable to Irenaeus of Lyons, who flourished at the same time as Melito. Irenaeus had to contend with Gnostics, who advanced their beliefs partly on the basis of writings which they asserted had come down as inspired scripture from the apostles, or at least from apostolic times. Instead, he had to devise ingenious arguments to advance his opinion that there were four gospels and only four gospels. We today would find his arguments specious and unconvincing, e.g. that there must be four gospels because there were four faces on every cherub, "four zones of the world" and "four principal winds".[254] As additional—and to him superior—arguments that the true Christian teaching was that of the catholic or Great Church, Irenaeus relied on "the rule of faith" and other facets of tradition coming down from the apostles and being reduced to writing gradually from the time of Jesus.

Even when inter-congregational councils and leading churchpersons finally did turn their attention to establishing canons in the fourth to sixth centuries, there were wide variations in the books they included.[255] Even at this late date, "what the Bible says" differed from place to place and writer to writer, leaving some differences that persist to the twenty-first century.

At a more grassroots and experiential level, early copies of the New Testament, such as those used weekly in public worship, varied considerably as to which books they contained. Only rarely were the books in any two manuscript Bibles the same. Moreover, in this inconsistency from one New Testament to another we find books not in the present twenty-seven-book canon standing proudly alongside those that are, while others of the twenty-seven were omitted.[256] Through necessity or not considering the written New Testament to be of dominant importance, its earliest copyists and users put more stock in some other source of religious truth.

The fact that it was not until comparatively late that Christians began to draft a New Testament canon as containing certain books and no others indicates that the Bible was not as central or as all-important to the church as Jesus founded it as it is to modern Fundamentalists.

No Generally-Accepted Canon in the Twenty-First Century

Even today there is no agreement among Christians as to which books or parts of books constitute the complete collection of inspired scripture. As Professor James Barr of Oxford points out: "Books do not necessarily say whether they are divinely inspired or not, and many books that do in some fashion claim divine inspiration were not accepted as canonical."[257] There is an exception to this: alone of the books in the twenty-seven books of the commonly-accepted New Testament, the Revelation of John makes claims for itself[258] that purport that it is a book of inspired scripture from God: "this is the only book in the NT that claims to be a revelation from God."[259] However, similar claims might possibly be found in New Testament apocrypha not in the present canon; the Koran certainly claims to be inspired scripture and a direct revelation from the Almighty.

The canon accepted by most Protestants contains an Old Testament of thirty-nine books with the Hebrew-language Masoretic text as the preferred textual authority; for some, it is the only authority. In 1546 the Council of Trent decreed that for Roman Catholics the Old Testament consists of seven more than the "Protestant" canon and of additions to some books recognized by Protestants. The Council also held that the Latin Vulgate was definitive. This decree was reaffirmed by the First Vatican Council.[260] The Eastern Orthodox churches are divided among themselves as to which books are in the Old Testament: they include the "Roman Catholic" additions, but have more besides.[261] The Old Testament text for the Orthodox is the Septuagint, a Greek-language version dating from pre-Christian times.[262]

They accept it even where it differs from the Hebrew original, in the belief that the translators' alterations were inspired by the Holy Spirit as part of continuing divine revelation.[263]

Due to its dedicated missionary efforts, the Nestorian Church was once the world's largest Christian denomination in geographic extent. Then and today it uses a New Testament which omits 2 Peter, 2 and 3 John, Jude and the Revelation of John.[264] The venerable Ethiopian Orthodox Church possesses a canon or canons of eighty-one books but there is incomplete agreement as to which books constitute the eighty-one. In the "Narrower Canon", the New Testament consists of the usual twenty-seven books. The "Broader Canon" contains eight more. The Old Testament lists correspondingly vary but both include the seven books of the "Roman Catholic" Bible.[265]

There is a letter titled *3 Corinthians* in the New Testament of the Armenian Church, and probably was also in that of the early Syrian church.[266] In fact, the Armenian canon even includes two more items of Corinthian correspondence.[267]

Lutherans possess no defined canon of Scripture except for territorial and national churches that have incorporated one into their constitutions or other subordinate standards. Unlike the Anglican *Thirty-Nine Articles*, the *Belgic Confession* of the Netherlands Reformed churches, the decrees of the Council of Trent and the Presbyterian *Westminster Confession*, the Lutheran doctrinal standards in the *Book of Concord* nowhere list the books of the Bible.[268] Unless the omission is supplied by a branch of Lutheranism in its subsidiary standards, it is without an authoritative list as to which books are Holy Writ. This is the situation of the Evangelical Lutheran Church of Canada, which has no officially-defined canon.[269]

As Helmut Koester of Harvard University has correctly summarized the situation, "A definitive decision about the exact content of the Bible, Old and New Testaments together, has never been made by the Christian church as a whole."[270]

Compounding this confusion are Gayle Riplinger and other Fundamentalists who accept the sixty-six book canon but maintain that the only authoritative text is that of the Authorized (King James) Version of 1611.[271]

A person may well wonder whether Pentecostals and other Protestant charismatics really regard the canon of divine inspiration as closed, complete and sufficient in the present Bible. If so, why do they seek guidance in prophecies that come to them in their worship services today, to which they also attribute divine inspiration?[272]

With all these uncertainties, it is no wonder that since the 1980s a growing number of scholars have questioned the viability of the biblical canon and have called for redefinition of it and changes to its contents.[273]

The Problem of Forgery

A further difficulty arises from the fact that texts of the New Testament and other early Christian documents have been subjected to forgery, either by words or passages being inserted or deleted from genuine texts or by complete fabrications being produced and passed off as the works of a prominent person of God. The Apostle Paul or his circle deemed it necessary to take measures against this practice. He railed against his Christian opponents who corrupted the gospel. Second Thessalonians 2.2 complains that perverse doctrines were being communicated "by letter purporting to come from us." Ironically, a substantial number of scholars believe that 2 Thessalonians is itself pseudonymous.[274] To overcome the problem of forged apostolic epistles he or the person writing in his name departed from the custom of leaving all facets of a letter to a secretary after dictating it: he signed 2 Thessalonians and four other letters[275] and added enough of his handwriting to permit comparison and identification. Additional evidence of the common occurrence of forgery of sacred texts is that John considered it advisable to lay a curse on anyone who tampered with the Revelation.[276] Rational people do not utter threats to prevent what is unlikely to happen.

About a century after Paul's death, the pastor-bishop of Corinth complained that his adversaries in the church were making unauthorized changes to his letters. He was not surprised at such tampering because, as he stated, the same people interpolated forgeries into the books of Scripture.[277] A few years later the bishop of Antioch mentioned that writings falsely ascribed to the apostles were in circulation. He believed that one of them, called *The Gospel of Peter*, contained genuine teachings of Jesus but that heretics had inserted spurious passages.[278] A little later, Hippolytus in Italy noted that certain heretics who had set out to "correct" Biblical manuscripts produced many more manuscripts, which were further corrupted and not even consistent with each other.[279] About the same time, Tertullian also accused heretics of making insertions into or deletions from the text of the Scriptures.[280]

The *Clementine Homilies* posit a more massive corruption.[281] When narrating Saint Peter's preparations for a debate with the heretic Simon Magus, the *Homilies* outline the apostle's alleged attitude toward the spurious passages in the Old Testament:[282]

> Simon, therefore as I learn, intends to come into public, and to speak of those chapters against God that are added to the Scriptures, for the sake of temptation, that he may seduce as many wretched ones as he can from the love of God. For we do not wish to say in public that these chapters are added to the Bible, since we should thereby perplex the unlearned multitudes, and so accomplish the purpose of this wicked Simon. For they not having yet the power of discerning, would flee from us as impious; or, as if not only the blasphemous chapters were false, they would even withdraw from the word. Wherefore we are under a necessity of assenting to the false chapters, and putting questions in return to him concerning them, to draw him into a strait, and to give in private an explanation of the chapters that are spoken against God to the well-disposed after a trial of their faith....

In short, some forgeries were so longstanding and so strongly entrenched that the apostles themselves were thought to have been constrained to treat them as genuine during in the first proclamation of the gospel in a locality.

Indeed, a book with the self-explanatory title of *The Orthodox Corruption of Scripture: The Effect of Early Christological Controversies on the Text of the New Testament* devotes three hundred and eighty pages to showing that one denomination in the second and third centuries altered the wording of the New Testament in order to advance its position on one point of doctrine.[283]

Other Alterations

Soon after the middle of the second century a Syrian Christian named Tatian combined the four Gospels with that of Peter to produce a single integrated account of Jesus' life called *The Diatessaron*. It was used as the standard Gospel by the Syrian church for centuries afterward. That he produced such a work and that the church accepted it show that the New Testament was not regarded as possessing a definite form nor that its wording was unalterable.

Cultural Differences

With the exception of some events connected with the Apostle Paul, the setting and the orientation of the twenty-seven-book New Testament were in Palestine with almost all the participants being Jews. Even Paul was Jewish and may have spent his childhood and youth in Jerusalem instead of growing up in a Gentile environment outside the Holy Land.[284] What little mention the commonly-received Scriptures make of regions outside the Land of Israel is only in relation to a religion at that time dominated by and largely confined to Palestine Jews. To find an early Christianity and its law that were not culture-bound to a small group of people in a small geographic area, we must look outside these twenty-seven books.

Moreover, the present New Testament is mostly occupied with the church on the mission field or within the first few years in the life of congregations while the later literature depicts a more settled and longer established Christianity, more like the church which functions in the West today.

The modern reader is somewhat at a loss in understanding or even knowing the ideas of Christians with whom Paul or his circle disagreed in the epistles attributed to him. The only knowledge in the twenty-seven-book New Testament a reader would have of these non-Pauline Christians has been lost except for the partial information that can be gleaned from the epistles' criticism of them---admittedly an indirect and hostile source. In the epistles, Paul or his circle assumed that the addressees/first readers shared with the author information about them by which they could fully appreciate what was being said about Paul's opponents.[285] This information is not contained in the present New Testament, so we must go outside it for the background, including information on the culture and Christian subculture that would give us the full meaning of what is written in the twenty-seven-book New Testament.

Chronic Problems in Interpretation

Scripture does not interpret itself. It does not indicate which passages are to be interpreted literally and which figuratively. Nor does it say which, if any, of its ethical mandates take priority over others. Christians themselves prove time and again that the Bible is an inadequate guide in faith or morals. Christendom has repeatedly witnessed the birth and proliferation of one or another religious denomination founded on a new interpretation of the Bible that its followers alleged to be more correct than all previous ones. Assertions to more correct interpretation are based on better exegesis of particular passages, or the entire method of interpretation, and/or emphasis on one verse or passage over another. Even denominations that are based on some other source of authority (e.g. the revelations to Joseph Smith among the Latter-day Saints) always try to create or invent interpretations of the Bible to support their unique theological positions.

With some degree of plausibility, every school of thought finds support for its distinctive position in the New Testament.[286] As Vincent of Lérins observed over fifteen centuries ago, Bible passages can be and are interpreted in so many different ways that there are as many interpretations as there are individuals trying to interpret them.[287] More recently, the Dominican Yves Congar has pointed out that:[288]

> The fact that all authors of new doctrines appeal to the Bible and yet fail to agree among themselves proves that the preservation of the faith is not governed simply by the individual's reading of Scripture; even presupposing the interior guidance of the Holy Spirit....

As has been often remarked, the circumstance that almost all Christian denominations have long formal statements or summaries as to what each believes to be the most important teachings of the Bible is evidence in itself that it is not completely sufficient;[289] this circumstance also impliedly admits that such teachings are not readily apparent to moderately advanced Bible students. The ongoing practice of resorting to ecclesiastical assemblies and conferences to give a definitive pronouncement on its message on a particular point for their contemporaries is further proof that most interpreters cannot discover or readily agree on such points. Indeed, the more frequent and more universal practice of clergypersons preaching sermons every week to convey the Bible's teachings to their congregations abundantly indicates that most Christians are unable—or unwilling to make the effort—to ascertain its meaning for themselves.

The actions and denominational affiliations of ordinary Christians indicates that many of them throughout the ages realize that the Bible is inadequate. For centuries they have sought out and embraced a supplement or replacement for it. They seek such additional guidance in later revelations, such as those of Mohammed, Joseph Smith Jr. and Emmanuel Swedenborg, or in a divinely-inspired interpreter, such as the bishop of Rome or Ellen G. White.

Conclusion

From the very beginning of Christianity there have been differences and uncertainty as to which books belonged in the Bible and whether—and how much—extraneous material has been inserted into them. Only a small fraction of ancient Christian writings is contained in the sixty-six-book Bible or even the "Roman Catholic" or "Eastern Orthodox" one. By their own admission not even these Bibles purport to contain the fullness of God's message. Moreover, some of the contents of the present Bible might be later forgeries instead of the divinely-inspired original. In addition to shortcomings related to its text, the Bible is limited by the culture gap between the era of its writing and the twenty-first century. Its interpretation is perennially problematic even apart from the uncertainty of its contents. The fact that it was not until comparatively late in church history that Christians began to draft lists of which books and no others are in the canon indicates that the Bible was not central or all-important to the church as Jesus founded it, or at least not as central or all-important as it is to some people in our day.

Because of these defects, many present-day Christians might be resting their faith and moral conduct on what is really "another gospel" within the meaning of 2 Corinthians 11.4 and Galatians 1.6-9.

Opposing Views Considered

Bible-stressing Protestant readers might wonder how God could allow there to be so much uncertainty about His book. The more extreme ones might reject the above well-established facts out of hand because their theological presuppositions do not allow God the freedom to permit such uncertainty and from this they reason that therefore He did not permit it, just as some Protestant Fundamentalists ignore the fact that there are variant readings and therefore uncertainties in the manuscripts of whatever Bible we now have. My reply is that Jesus never wrote a book nor commanded His disciples to write one. "When he sent the apostles to plant the Church, he did not say: Go and write; he said: Go into the whole world, preach the Gospel to every creature."[290] Remember that Romans 10.17 says "faith cometh by hearing" (KJV) rather than "faith cometh by reading". The written New Testament and early tradition flow from this oral preaching, products of the same source. Writing a Book is only part of preaching the gospel. The idea of exclusive reliance on the Bible alone did not appear in Christianity until well over a millennium later. As touched on in this chapter and more fully elaborated in the next, the earliest Christians—those who were the first to communicate or receive Jesus' message and had the best opportunities to understand it fully—did not regard the Bible as the sole and exhaustive resource for faith and practice nor its exact contents to be very important.

The more intransigent might proclaim "the Bible is the Bible, and any Bible I have seen contains the same sixty-six books as every other, but none of the other writings you mention! These Nestorian and Ethiopian Bibles are far away and have absolutely no influence on my life in the Western world." In reality, editions of the Bible including the "Roman Catholic additions" have been published for centuries. Beginning in the late twentieth century, these "additions" have also been included in editions printed for the ecumenical or nondenominational markets.

For example, as of 31 December 2006 such longer Bibles have been published in forty-seven of the sixty-one European versions in which the usual Bible has been printed in translation.[291] An English translation of the Septuagint, including Eastern Orthodox books, appeared in 1851 and has been reprinted a number of times in our day and is available on the Internet.[292] While the present book was being typed in the summer of 2007, there were two groups of scholars working independently of each other to produce two new translations, both including the Orthodox books, translations that were projected to be printed not long afterwards by different publishing houses.

Even Evangelical and other Protestant missions and scripture ministries print and distribute Scriptures they themselves consider to be incomplete. As of 31 December 2006, 989 languages or dialects of the world[293] possessed only part of the Scriptures printed in their tongue but not a complete New Testament, still less a complete sixty-six-book Bible. This is a relatively high number in that the complete Bible has been published in only 429, and complete New Testaments in only 1144.[294] Of the 2562 languages and dialects[295] for which translation has begun, only 429 or 17% possess the full sixty-six books while fewer than 45% possess a complete New Testament.[296] Speakers of these minor languages and dialects can equally assert that Bibles with more books are far away and not available in a form they can read.

The same people might also assert that because "the word of the Lord abides forever"[297] the Bibles we commonly possess today in its present selection and arrangement must have been the Scriptures they hypothesize Christ gave to the church. This view clearly contradicts the unassailable evidence of the centuries and solid manuscript data, as well as the experience of a better informed and larger number of people than those that have seen only sixty-six-book English translations.

Some might also try to mount an argument extending the inspiration and inerrancy of Scripture. They assert that because the writers of the New Testament had been acquainted with Christ in the flesh and had received the Holy Spirit from Him, what they wrote was as equally inspired and infallible as He and hence was unalterable. Then these Fundamentalists go a step further to arguing that such inspiration, inerrancy and inalterability must equally apply to the sixty-six canon or list of books of Scripture, so that the canon they now recognize is as inherently as inspired, infallible and inalterable as Jesus Himself. However, as one Baptist seminary president points out: "Those who argue for the infallibility or the inerrancy of Scripture logically should also claim the same infallibility for the churches of the fourth and fifth centuries, whose decisions and historical circumstances have left us with our present Bible."[298] We might also observe that they must logically make the same claim of infallibility and inerrancy for publishers and binderies of modern times, who are the ones directly responsible for the format and content of our printed Bibles. Can they be free from error when they contradict each other? As noted four paragraphs ago, it is fairly common for the "Roman Catholic" books to be included in the same cover as the "Protestant" ones, and the Latter-Day Saints have long since taken to binding the *Book of Mormon* with the sixty-six books in a single volume.

Fundamentalists and their likeminded might say that the above is an attack on the Bible. It is not. It is an attack on their misuse and distortion of the Holy Scriptures and their place in Christian life.

Chapter Four

The Apostolic Tradition on Ethics

<u>Introduction</u>

Because of the inadequacies of the sixty-six-book Bible, it is necessary to search for an interpreter or supplement for it to find the full content of Christian moral law. The present book will consult all available ancient Christian literature up to a definite point in time, such point being determined by a major break in the continuity of extra-biblical tradition descended from the apostles. Scholars divide this literature into three main categories: "New Testament apocrypha", "histories of martyrs", and "the early church fathers". New Testament apocrypha consists of anonymous writings which purport to be scripture or first-hand accounts by Jesus' early disciples but which were not included in the present canon. Accounts of martyrdoms consist of government records of the questions of persecuting secular officials and the answers by Christians facing capital punishment for their faith and/or reports of eyewitnesses or contemporaries about the martyrs' trials and deaths. Like the authors of such accounts, the early church fathers did not purport to be composing scripture but were usually identifiable people who wrote in their own names. In the present volume, the three categories will be treated equally as witnesses to the original gospel. (In practice, there is almost no ethical guidance in New Testament apocrypha.) In addition, this book will also consider the few comments on Christian behaviour by ancient non-Christian authors.

There are at least fifty reasons for thus increasing the database of early Christian writings beyond the present Bible:

1. Paul the Apostle or his circle considered it necessary for Christians to be guided by tradition as well as by a written Bible:

    a) 1 Corinthians 11.2: "I commend you because you remember me in everything and maintain the traditions even as I have delivered them to you."

b) 2 Thessalonians 2.15: "stand firm and hold to the traditions which you were taught by us, either by word of mouth or by letter." Here the oral tradition is placed on a par with the epistles themselves.

c) 2 Thessalonians 3.6: "Now we command you...that you keep away from any brother who is living in idleness and not in accord with the tradition that you received from us."

2. The presence of four different gospels or biographies of Jesus in the commonly-accepted New Testament immeasurably increases our knowledge of the Lord by providing four different aspects of a single reality and thus gives us "a more sharply defined and a more realistic presentation of the person of Jesus".[299] In the same way, ancient Christian books not in the twenty-seven-book New Testament increase our knowledge and appreciation of those that are within this canon.

3. There is more information from which to draw conclusions, more dots to form a larger or clearer picture. The addition of this large volume of material enables the reader to learn more complete answers to ethical questions and to obtain clarification of points that are ambiguous in the commonly-accepted Scriptures. Tradition forms a larger context to Scripture.

4. The tradition as preserved by the early Christians helps to uncover the original meanings of New Testament texts and the original wording of New Testament passages now in doubt because of variations in manuscripts, just as the Dead Sea Scrolls do for our canonical Old Testament. Use of the early post-apostolic writings lessens the ambiguity of many unclear passages in the New Testament,[300] e.g. baptism for the dead in 1 Corinthians 15.29.[301]

5. Study of early non-canonical Christian literature in the original languages materially aids in determining the meanings of Biblical words and phrases as the first audiences of the New Testament would have understood them, or at least shed more light on them. As a case in point: the Greek language best known to secular studies, the language of the classics, is centuries older than that of the New Testament and was from a different cultural milieu while the extra-biblical Christian writings share the milieu and values of the New Testament authors, and the ones studied in the present book were more contemporaneous with them.[302]

6. Exegetes and scripture scholars of almost all denominations work on the basis that a Bible passage or book should be interpreted in context, drawing on one part of the context to better interpret another, so that the resultant interpretation will be that of a harmonious whole. Anglo-American courts do the same with statutes. But what is the context of any given New Testament book? It is not the other New Testament books alone, and perhaps the present canon does not constitute a single context. Except for writers like Paul who penned more than one epistle or book now in the New Testament, the writers of the several books worked largely in isolation from each other, separated by great geographical distances. This isolation is especially evident from the differences among

the four Gospels, whose contents, arrangement of events, and other details would have been harmonized or at least more in accord with each other had their authors been in physical proximity or communication. A collective effort, a single context, would have produced none of the variations that have taxed the brains and ingenuity of Bible scholars over the last nineteen centuries. Perhaps the four evangelists would have produced only one Gospel. The true context of an individual author was not another canonical writer working hundreds of kilometres away, but the living church of his local community, which consisted of Christians with their own memories and traditions of Jesus and His teachings. The Christian message was communicated largely temporally (from generation to generation) in local communities, only rarely geographically (from interchanges from one congregation to another) between distant regions. New Testament authors wrote to convert, preserve, strengthen and edify in their local communities. By far the majority of collaborative efforts was between generations of Christians in local towns and provinces rather than between individual writers of the same time period in distant provinces. Except for Luke and the late and spurious 2 Peter, there is no evidence that the various New Testament writers knew of each other's books, let alone had them in mind when writing their own. The exhortation of Paul to the Colossians (4.16) that they should read his letter to Laodicea does not prove that it was common practice to exchange and read New Testament other than the one he had sent to them. The fact that he had to tell them to share epistles suggests that they would not have otherwise done so.[303] Indeed, some of his letters (most noticeably 1-2 Corinthians and Galatians) are so addressed to local issues that it is doubtful if their contents would interest other congregations. Therefore, to find the context of any New Testament book or passage and interpret it through this context, we today must find and consult Christian material that was composed in the same community not long afterwards.

7. Consulting such early sources helps give us a better idea of the meaning or the most accurate meaning of New Testament parables and events. It does this because the early non-canonical sources reveal the presuppositions shared by the New Testament personages and their original hearers and thus disclose the interpretation and lesson that persons contemporaneous with the Biblical writers were intended to draw from them.[304] In this way, the ancient sources help inform us of Biblical concepts (which are sometimes quite different from ours) and help supply its conceptual framework so that we can better relate biblical paradigms to cases in which we must make moral decisions.

8. In any endeavour, knowledge of the thought and events of an era is most accurately obtained from contemporaries of it or—as second best—from material dating from neighbouring times and neighbouring geographical regions, i.e. with people who were well acquainted with the language, culture, thought-processes and actions of the personages whose thoughts and deeds are being studied. More reliable information can be obtained about the events in the New Testament and the thought of its writers by consulting ancient people who spoke the same language and shared the same culture and were familiar with—or shared—their way of looking at and perceiving the world than can be obtained

from persons who lived twelve to seventeen centuries later in different economic and social worlds in distant countries.

9. Christianity itself was born and passed its infancy in a world that was guided much more by tradition and custom than our own. Tradition as an overreaching source of guidance was the mind-set in which the New Testament and other early Christian literature were written.[305] The people of the Roman Empire in the early Christian period kept as much as possible to secular and religious traditions. The concern of Hellenistic secular education was not to develop students' reasoning faculty (as it is among us) so much as to hand on the great literature of the past.[306] Among the Romans the chief aim of education was to inculcate respect for old customs and mores in order to initiate the young in the traditional way of life so that they would unquestioningly keep to it.[307] This attitude was even more true of the common people. Among them, custom and tradition were a kind of ideology or oral dogma.[308] According to Professor Robert L. Wilken in describing the general Greco-Roman view[309]

> The ultimate legitimation of religious beliefs and practices did not rest on philosophical arguments about the nature of the gods but on ancient traditions that had been passed on from generation to generation. Age and custom were the final arbiters in religious matters.

To work with the Scriptures on their own terms we must take into consideration that they were written in a tradition-oriented mind-set. To fully understand the New Testament we must relate to it with the mentality of its authors and first readers.

10. Ancient Christians encountered many problems in the interpretation of the Bible and in other aspects of religion, and produced solutions for these problems. Such problems were often aberrant doctrines or practices originating outside the mainstream of Christianity, although some arose within the main body of the church. Some of these aberrant beliefs and practices have been raised anew in our era by fringe denominations which assert that they were part and parcel of the correct faith preached by the apostles. Instead of reinventing the wheel by producing new solutions, we today can search the early written tradition to find solutions formulated by Christians who were much closer to the milieu in which the New Testament was written and to the original faith preached and taught by Jesus and the apostles.

11. The ancient non-canonical writings indicate how people, who (like Paul) may have had the mind of Christ, followed Christ's example and teachings in situations neither he nor the new Testament writers had encountered.

12. Part of the non-canonical literature also gives answers to questions that were not asked until after the apostles and evangelists finished writing.

13. Early Christian literature teaches how some of the earliest recipients of grace through Christ responded to it under the supervision and example of the apostles and other early disciples who were appointed and inspired by God.

14. The ancient non-scriptural materials show what the near associates of the apostles and evangelists received in the way of criteria as to how Scripture is to be used, what authorizes variations on its themes, what parts of it are more important than others, and what is to be taken figuratively rather than literally.

15. Non-canonical authors provide reminders of moral principles and specific precepts found in the canonical writings.

16. Later authors help indicate what in the New Testament its writers and the rest of the ancient Christian communities regarded as local or temporary moral commands and directives (those meant to be confined to a particular time and place) as distinct from those meant to be valid for all times and places.

17. Later authors prove the timeless validity of the general principles and individual precepts laid down by Christ and His apostles, especially those recorded in New Testament books that were written earlier in time. According to seminary President McDonald, the canonical books written later in the New Testament period show how Christians of later generations recognized new applications of these principles and commandments in new contexts.[310] The same is true of post-biblical Christian writings, for their authors found newer applications in later generations to newer contexts, in a chain of teaching handed down as the generations passed.

18. Much early Christian literature recorded contemporary beliefs and practices during a period as to which most present-day Christians agree the Holy Spirit was still actively guiding the church.

19. In evaluating modern interpretations and methods of interpreting the Bible, Christians today can derive much assistance from what ancient Christians wrote on various issues before they became subjects of dispute.[311]

20. A consensus of early Christian authors on a point indicates what all wings of the ancient church agreed on, and what variations they considered to be matters of indifference and thus tolerable within the bosom of a single religion. The fact that they agreed on certain important things indicates that these things were handed down intact from the first century, for if each had departed from the genuine original faith, they would have evolved separately and randomly in matters of ethics and doctrine and thus contradicted each other on significant points.[312]

21. Use of early sources helps us to learn what are essentials and what are accidentals or nonessentials in the gospel and church life "for we may reasonably say that the essential elements of any movement or idea must have been at least inchoately present at their beginnings."[313]

22. Unanimity of ancient opinion on a point of ethics or other matter relating to the Christian faith raises a presumption that it is correct: "When the [church] Fathers agree among themselves as to what is central or essential, then it would seem that the Christian of today must either agree himself or have extremely cogent reasons for disagreeing."[314]

23. The non-canonical early literature helps us understand the role the canonical literature played in believing communities and the scope or varieties of hermeneutical methods that were allowed.[315]

24. The early non-canonical writings help us to reconstruct the world of thought in which authors of the present New Testament lived, taught and wrote.

25. Earlier non-canonical Christian writings (e.g. *1 Clement*) that predate later canonical ones (e.g. 2 Peter) may have been known to and entered into the consideration of canonical authors when producing their own works. In any event, at least some traditions the earlier non-canonical ones contain had an influence on the later canonical writers. The earlier works should therefore be consulted and studied for the same reason(s) that we now do when looking at the Old Testament for help in understanding the New.

26. It is more probable that the teaching of Jesus and His apostles was preserved among Christians who were contemporary with them or with the first few generations of Christians after them, instead of the true faith and practice disappearing around the death of the last apostle, then long afterwards being perfectly restored at the Reformation or by Mohammed in the seventh century or by Joseph Smith of the Latter-Day Saints in the nineteenth. Similarly, it is infinitely more credible that the correct interpretation of the Bible (whatever books it contains) was preserved by these early generations than suddenly lost and came to light over fifteen centuries later.

27. The probability is vanishingly remote that even the most dedicated and protracted study of the Scriptures in the sixteenth century or later would uncover a spiritual truth or moral precept unknown to early Christians. Christianity has never been a mere collection of writings that can be interpreted by one person as accurately as by another regardless of time or place. The Christian faith has always been a living community or group of communities in which the gospel is shared and transmitted. One Christian interacts with others; older members tell younger members; unwritten memories are recorded in writing by a later generation; and each person directly or indirectly interacts with other Christians from whom they are not isolated by geography. Everyone dies sometime and recollections grow dim, thus gradually weakening the recollections of earlier times and practices. The full meaning and milieu of the Christian message (including the New Testament) gradually fades over the generations. Thus, we need the witness of as many as possible of the early heirs of the gospel, i.e. believers who had been personally acquainted with the apostles or their early disciples who had inherited much fresher memories of Christ and His teaching than those of later years or centuries. For this reason I include New Testament apocrypha, accounts of martyrs, and the early fathers.

28. Unlike the authors of the New Testament (and perhaps of some "apocryphal" New Testament books), the early church fathers lived in a situation more like our own. In the four Gospels and other accounts of Jesus and His apostles, disciples were led and taught directly by God manifested in the flesh or by men He had personally selected and had filled with divine inspiration. Just as we do not enjoy these contacts today, neither did any Christians after the death of the last apostle. Indeed, almost all Christian life

has taken place in such "uninspired" circumstances. Early extra-Biblical Christian literature provides a more comparable model for today, a model in which modern spiritual conditions are paralleled but with the added benefit of fresher memories of the sources of the Faith.

29. For almost all of the second millennium, in which Luther, Calvin, the Wesleys and the founders of denominations in the nineteenth century lived, Christianity was by far the most influential—and sometimes the only—religion in Europe, colonies populated by its peoples and former such colonies (including the United States). Except for incidental and mostly inconsequential notice of Jews, these European and derived peoples lived, worked and thought with Christianity as the only faith of themselves and of their immediate neighbours and the only one they need consider. Any differences or disputes or negotiations were with other groups of Christians, nothing as distant or fundamentally different as Buddhism, Islam or Hinduism. In the relatively few cases when these religions were encountered, thought about them could be safely dismissed. Our twenty-first-century world finds Christian churches competing against totally different religions, not just other forms of Christianity that share their mind-set, fundamental conceptions of the world and the life after it and almost all of its doctrines and practices. Today Christians of European derivation must come to grips with totally alien conceptions of the divine, the world, and the life beyond it, and uncontemplated approaches to them. In this respect, Christians are now in a situation more like their brethren before the time of Constantine, when they were surrounded by non-Christian faiths and cultures and in competition with religions that put little or no stock in our Bible. We can thus learn more from the ancients in the Mediterranean world than from the sixteenth-century reformers and nineteenth-century religious leaders who lived in Europe or America.

30. The Christian Scriptures have no meaning or effect without the prior existence of people who already believe in the gospel. Unless there had been apostles and their successors to create such belief by testifying that Jesus had truly lived and died and risen again, there would be little or nothing to distinguish the accounts in the four written Gospels from similar ones about pagan deities which circulated in the eastern Mediterranean world in the same era. Without an oral handing-on of background information that the New Testament personages had been real and had actually spoken and acted as reported there, a person to whom this background has not been communicated might well regard the New Testament as just another historical novel or ancient myth. Nor could anybody in any age find or win converts to a new Christian denomination based on an allegedly superior interpretation of the Bible if there were no nearby people who already believed the Christian scriptures to be authoritative in religious belief and practice.

31. Consulting writings of early Christians furnishes an abundance of information about early believers: their concerns, their approaches to ethical problems, their ways of responding to God, and how they lived their commitment to Christ. These descriptions of the ways they acted in obedience to their Lord (and the rebukes they received when they did not) enable people in the twenty-first century to learn which moral teachings and commandments in

the New Testament were accepted as literally binding and those which were meant only figuratively, and which ones were considered more important than others.

32. The written word has no effect until read and understood by human beings, who vary in their ability to interpret and understand. The concept of rejecting guidance from outside the Scriptures is really guidance by an interpretation of Scripture, usually an interpretation which dates back no further than five hundred years at most. Bible passages do not select themselves nor do they arrange themselves of their own accord to produce the most correct exegesis.[316] In contrast, where the early Christian authors agree among themselves, it must be deduced that their interpretations were made within a structure received from the apostles not many years earlier. They too present only an interpretation but it is a better interpretation than those formulated since the sixteenth century because it was made closer in time, life and culture to the authors of the New Testament, with whom some of them were personally acquainted.

33. As originally instituted by Christ, the church had no scriptures except the Old Testament and even then for the full Christian interpretation of it had to rely on the oral teaching of the apostles and their first successors. The first writings in the present New Testament were not penned until the AD 50s and the last not until half a century or more later. Indeed, the New Testament itself is little more than a partial record of material that must have originally been handed on orally. In the first century, there were preaching, repentance, sacraments and other aspects of church life without the aid of distinctively Christian scriptures. For instance, Communion services were held for approximately thirty years before any writing mentioned them.[317] As Professor Hanson pointed out,[318]

> the life of the Christian Church was continuing uninterruptedly before the New Testament was written, while it was being written, and afterwards, when Clement and Origen were producing their works; indeed they must have implicitly assumed its existence and importance and did not maintain in their minds a clear separation between the evidence of Christian institutions and the evidence of the Bible such as the theology of a later day has tended to make.

Although advocating the supremacy of Scripture for our day, a professor of theology at Trinity Evangelical Divinity School similarly acknowledges the existence of the church and its activities to be prior to the New Testament by fifty to a hundred years.[319] Thus, God's first provision for Christianity was that its adherents be instructed by the apostolic tradition rather than by a book, or at least as the definitive interpreter of a book. Of course, as time passed, more and more of this oral tradition was committed to writing in the form of the twenty-seven-book New Testament and other early Christian works. Even when New Testament scriptures were introduced into these ancient congregations, they did not come all at once, in a complete collection of two dozen or more books. President McDonald holds the conviction that no "first century church had more than one gospel, and most likely only a few letters of Paul and perhaps only one or more Catholic Epistles."[320] As the Bible came piecemeal over the years to local congregations, Protestants in our own day who assert that there is no true

Christianity without a sixty-six book Bible (including a twenty-seven-book New Testament) face an insurmountable dilemma: at what point in the accumulation process over the decades or centuries did these early believers become genuinely at one with these self-proclaimed unsullied uncorrupted Bible-believers of our time?

34. The belief that the New Testament contains certain particular books and no others, no more and no fewer, is itself a product of a tradition, although a tradition dating, at the earliest, from half a century to a century after the death of the last apostle, and more likely two to two and one-half centuries. It is tortuously difficult to divide the Christian heritage in such a manner as to keep the twenty-seven-book canon while rejecting the parts of the tradition which interpret or expand upon it: "one cannot have scripture without also having tradition."[321]

35. Belief in the inspiration and inerrancy of the Scriptures does not include belief in the inspiration or inalterability of the twenty-seven-book canon. The earliest Christian literature was written by people who knew Jesus personally or by apostolic men who knew them or by people not many years afterwards, a time before His message could become corrupted. Due to its ancient origin, this letter faithfully records the whole gospel. On the other hand, the present canon—or any canon—was not decided upon until the fourth through sixth centuries, and even then with remarkable lack of unanimity. To assert that the boundaries of the present canon are as sacred as (some of) its contents necessarily entails the assumption that the church of the fourth through sixth centuries were as inspired and infallible as the apostles and other scripture-writers, and fails to account for the disagreements and contradictions among the canon-makers.

36. Rejecting the fathers and New Testament apocrypha in favour of using Scripture alone is itself accepting a tradition, although one which began over a thousand years after Jesus.[322] This later tradition is that of Calvin and other sixteenth-century reformers who rejected an existing tradition in their desire to purge the church of spurious and unedifying additions which they thought had originated in the Middle Ages.

37. As the Baptist scholar Stephen R. Holmes points out: "There is no escape from the mediation of our faith by the tradition".[323] Even if a twenty-first Christian seeks to be guided only by his or her reading of the Bible, Holmes shows, the all-encompassing effect of tradition is nevertheless present: if such a Christian reads a translation of the Bible, their perceptions are shaped by the traditions of Bible translating and translator(s). If she or he reads it in its original languages, the Christian is governed by lexicons and grammar books which hand on "a tradition of translating certain words and grammatical constructions in one way and not another".[324] If he or she accomplishes the monumental task of learning New Testament Greek without such aid and examines "every extant manuscript of the New Testament and developed her own canons for textual criticism"[325] there is still the effect of tradition from archaeology and bibliographic work and—the most influential tradition of all—her mother tongue and secondary languages she has studied.

38. The source of Christianity and the church is the gospel, the good news of Jesus Christ.[326] It cannot be confined to a book or even a collection of writings because the divine person

and the revelation existed before and independently of the writing, and would have existed even if writing had never been invented. The person and the revelation would not have been known to the world unless there were Christians who shared them with others. The apostolic tradition preserved in the New Testament and other ancient Christian literature was part of this sharing of the good news. Even among twenty-first century Baptists the absolute authority in religion belongs to Jesus Christ alone, final authority being in a person rather than in a book. To Baptists, as to the first Christians, the Bible is not the absolute and final authority but is merely a witness to Him.[327]

39. In our day-to-day conduct of important matters, we all prefer to obtain our information from first-hand sources or at least from people who are closer to them or whom we believe to be better versed than ourselves. For this reason, a police officer who is investigating a traffic accident questions the earliest witnesses, i.e. people present at the time of the collision or who were the first to arrive after it; the officer does not go to people who came along much later. In the same way, courts avoid relying on hearsay or on any evidence other than the best procurable as to the matter. Granted, courts sometime accept the testimony of accident reconstruction experts who did not personally witness the collision in question but have intensely studied a host of similar incidents; however, their testimony is dependent upon the observations of the first witnesses present, which is the raw data without which the experts cannot work. Similarly, ancient Christian writers are the best sources it is possible for us to have and are the earliest known witnesses to the matters on which we consult them. Accordingly, they are automatically preferable to people who came centuries later with pretensions to a knowledge superior to theirs.

40. In their writings, the New Testament authors assume knowledge and presuppositions which were in their own minds and in those of their first readers but are not contained in the Bible itself. For instance, many letters in the present New Testament present formal arguments that have special concerns or foci and do not set out the entire ethics of the authors or of the communities to which they were addressed.[328] Other early Christian literature, outside the New Testament, helps provide such background and thus contributes to ending the artificial divorce between the New Testament and the culture that surrounded it and its authors. This non-canonical literature reveals the meanings and concepts that a hearer of Christ or other person of the New Testament period would attach to phrases and allusions now in the twenty-seven-book New Testament and how such a hearer would understand, and was meant to understand, them.[329]

41. The early sources provide raw data, sometimes both pro and con, that faith communities today can use today when debating moral problems, applying them to new categories of situations and circumstances. This data helps set the structure for such debate.

42. The tradition can often break the tie between two equally probable mutually-incompatible interpretations of Scripture.

43. The church fathers, New Testament apocrypha and other ancient writings by Christians (i.e. early Christian tradition) show the response to life and solutions to life's problems formulated by believers who were closer than we to the ultimate source of Christian ethics.

44. Consulting material from all books of the New Testament and other relevant early sources should serve to minimize confusion attendant upon post-medieval differences in exegesis of the canonical ones stemming from different exegetes each selecting a different "canon within the canon".

45. Reflecting upon the contents of the books that have been admitted into the commonly-accepted canon and those that have not, especially those purporting to be scripture, help us determine what is the essence of the Christian faith, and what are peripherals, so that interpreters and systematic theologians are better informed when deciding upon a "canon within the canon".

46. As regards the actual wording of Jesus' teachings, non-canonical writings sometimes preserve less edited and less modified versions of Christ's words and teachings than those in the present New Testament. Being independently redacted and transmitted, Jesus' sayings in both their canonical and non-canonical expressions took on different forms to meet the needs of the early communities within which they were handed down; by studying and comparing them we can obtain a more complete insight into the process of transmission of His sayings within the present canon and also into the relation of such processes to the various groups within the ancient Christian movement.[330]

47. According to the Evangelical Robert E. Webber, a professor of theology at Wheaton College, "Evangelicals already have a commitment to historic Christianity and only need to be reminded of what that means."[331] Consulting the ancient authors reminds—or, more likely, informs—Evangelicals and other Christians of the content of original, historic Christianity.

48. Most reform and renewal movements in Christianity assert that their aim and teachings are a return to the original, pristine, Christian faith.[332] Study of the early sources is an indispensable guide to what this faith was like. It will at least gives such reformers possible scenarios of what might happen to their movement after they leave the scene when they see what happened after the deaths of the apostles.

49. To avoid reading into the Christian past, or any past, only what we want to see there, we must obtain knowledge of the real past, based on the best evidence procurable of what that past really was. Drawing from sources centuries after the events can yield all manner of errors and misconceptions. The best possible evidence comes from people who were personally acquainted with the characters, thought, and events of the era, or at least not many hands removed from them. Thus, consulting the earliest nonbiblical sources about New Testament and other pristine Christianity is superior to consulting sources that came much later in time—many over a millennium and a half in which there was plenty of opportunity for misconceptions, deceptions, and other errors to creep in and distort their perceptions and knowledge or render them wildly incorrect.

50. In a paragraph demonstrating that even denominations that claim to have no guide but the Bible nevertheless maintain strong traditions of their own, even a prominent Evangelical concedes that "although/84/the simple message of the gospel is sufficient for salvation, it is not sufficient for Christian worship, fellowship, community and life."[333]

51. An exegete that learns facts and interpretations assumed as common knowledge by the New Testament writers makes him/herself less ignorant and the contents of Paul's letters easier to understand. Broadening the New Testament exegete's knowledge base by including the near-biblical literature also provides a more stable ground for interpreting the undoubted Scriptures. In this way, a Christian will avoid or substantially reduce the risk of being among people that 2 Peter 3.16 characterizes as ignorant and unstable who twist the letters of Paul and other Scriptures to their own destruction.

Some Objections Considered

First, in some translations, 1 Corinthians 4.6 exhorts Christians "not to go beyond what is written", which Dr. Rosner considers "a remarkable statement about the sufficiency of the Scriptures for Christian conduct"[334] and which other people use as a proof-text that nothing outside the Bible is to be considered for this purpose.

Such a confining contention violently isolates 1 Corinthians 4.6 from the rest of the New Testament and its historical setting, because:

1) what was "written" in the way of scripture at the time 1 Corinthians was penned was the Old Testament. Excluding non-canonical Christian literature on the strength of 4.6 would also exclude all but those few New Testament books that were written before it.

2) such an argument clearly contradicts the exhortation of the author of 1 Corinthians 4.6 to follow both written and oral traditions (2 Thessalonians 2.15).

3) Rosner himself admits that these words constitute "a rather difficult phrase".[335] The Authorized (King James) Version reads "not to think *of men* above what is written" while, unless there is a misprint in the edition I use, the RSV has "live according to scripture", while the NSRV renders it "'Nothing beyond what is written'". This wording is too unclear to overthrow the plain wording of 2 Thessalonians and the universal practice of the Christians who were personally acquainted with the writer of 1 Corinthians 4.6 and had first-hand knowledge of the context in which he wrote and could ask him for clarification of it.

Second, certain advocates of *sola scriptura* may cite 2 Timothy 3.16f, laying stress on the latter verse:

> 16 All scripture is inspired by God, and profitable for teaching, for reproof, for correction, and for training in righteousness, 17 that the man of God may be complete, equipped for every good work.

The argument runs that the Bible is a *complete* and exhaustive textbook for *every* possible *good work* and that since it is *complete* for all ethical purposes, sources not in the present Bible are superfluous or perhaps harmful.

This position has five weaknesses:

1) although what was "written" in the way of scripture at the time 1 Timothy was penned was more than at the time of 1 Corinthians and included more parts of the present New Testament, yet 2 Peter, the Revelation of John and some other books now held to be canonical had not yet been composed.

2) such an indirect argument clearly contradicts the clearer exhortation of the author or circle of authors of 1 Timothy 3.16f to follow both written and oral traditions (2 Thessalonians 2.15).

3) The Greek original of the New Testament has no special word for "scripture" or "Bible". The Greek word used in 2 Timothy 3.16 is *graphē*, which is elsewhere translated "writing", indicating no special genre of "writing" but simply any recording of communication on a permanent surface. *Graphē* does not connote a special authority of one type of writing—religious or secular—over another, except that in the Biblical world (as in semi-literate cultures generally) writing of any sort is often regarded as somehow more authoritative than oral speech. *Graphē* in 2 Timothy 3.16 could thus refer to a wide host of writings. Certainly, Clement of Alexandria took it in a wide sense, for in addition to the Christian Bible he cited the writings of pagan poets and philosophers as authorities in his presentation.

4) Some public events in our time and culture include a reading that begins "Now let us praise famous men" (Sirach 44.1ff). The Greek text, which dates from the second century B.C., uses the word *graphē* in the phrase the Revised Standard Version renders as "those who composed musical tunes and set forth verses in writing" (v. 5). Hence, the word that 2 Timothy 3.16 translates as "scripture" included secular poetry and was not confined to canonical writings on religion.

5) In the New Testament itself, the word usually translated "scriptures" most often refers to the Old Testament:

(a) on the road to Emmaus, Jesus interpreted to His travelling companions "all the scriptures" that pertained to Himself (Luke 24.25). If "all the scriptures" included the New Testament, the travellers would have known these matters already.

(b) in John 5.39 Christ said to the Jerusalem Jews "You search the scriptures, because you think that in them you have eternal life". Certainly, these "scriptures" could not have included the New Testament books, because the Jews do not accept them as holy writ even to our own day and thus they would not be persuasive to them.

(c) Paul's Beroean audience "received the word with all eagerness, examining the scriptures daily to see if these things were so (Acts 17.11). There would have been no need for searching or examining very far if these "scriptures" contained the entire Pauline corpus or even just the four Gospels.

(d) Apollos of Alexandria had been instructed in the Christian Faith, accurately taught it to others, was "fervent in spirit" and—most importantly for our purposes—was "well versed in the scriptures" (Acts 18.24). Yet "he knew only the baptism of John" (18.25), which verses 1 through 5 of the next chapter indicate was inferior to Christian baptism and its recipients were required to be baptized again, this time in the name of Jesus. If the scriptures in which Apollos was "well versed" had included the New Testament, he would have received the latter baptism long before instead of only after Priscilla and Acquila "expounded to him the way of God more accurately (18.26). The "scriptures" in which Apollos was "well versed" were apparently insufficient because they lacked information on the rite of Christian initiation. This lack is to be expected of the Old Testament but not of the New.

(e) Apollos later "confuted the Jews in public, showing by the scriptures that the Christ was Jesus" (Acts 18.28). As with John 5.39 above, the Jews would not have accepted the New Testament as having any authority, so "the scriptures" must mean only the Old Testament in Acts 18.24 and 28 and 2 Timothy 3.16.

Third, many proponents of the sufficiency of Scripture might contend that 2 Timothy 3.15 proves their point in that it refers to the same genre and authority of writing as do verses 16 and 17:

> from childhood you have been acquainted with the sacred writings which are able to instruct you for salvation in Christ Jesus.

They can point out that what the Revised Standard Version translates as "sacred writings" in verse 15 the Authorized (King James) Version renders as "the holy scriptures".

However, verse 15 provides no support for the assertion that "scripture" includes all the New Testament and that the commonly-accepted Bible exhaustively and exclusively contains all possible material for the Christian life. There are four reasons why this argument is not sound:

1) The Greek words referring to writings in v. 15 (*hiera grammata*) are not the same as in verse 16 (*graphē*), which by making a distinction through changing his words the author did not intend the one to be equivalent to the other.

2) Verse 15 states that Timothy had been acquainted with "the sacred writings" since childhood. Acts 16.1-3 indicates that he was already a disciple and mature enough for missionary travel at the time of Paul's second missionary journey, which W. H. C. Frend dates from AD 49 to 52.[336] We are therefore looking at whatever "sacred writings" existed in the mid-40s at the latest. Scholars generally agree that the earliest book in the present New Testament was composed around AD 50, which excludes all but the Old Testament and some Old Testament apocrypha, which are neither the subject of the present book nor accepted by the sort of people who raise this sort of objection.

3) If the first argument under this Third heading is incorrect and "the sacred writings" in verse 15 are identical to "scripture" in verse 16, then the time constraints regarding

the man Timothy necessitate that these quoted words exclude the New Testament as being part of the writings that are "complete...for every good work."

4) If the meaning of the words "scriptures" and "sacred writings" are extended beyond the "Protestant" Old Testament, we fall into the same position as Tertullian when he used 2 Timothy 3.16 to argue *in favour of* the inspiration and canonicity of the Book of Enoch.[337]

Third, are Christians who claim "I go by the Bible, which is infinitely more reliable and unquestionable than whatever any human being might have said, no matter how close in time and place to its authors." Actually, what such people go by is not the Bible but their *interpretation* of it, and interpretation almost always from a translation and with little awareness of the milieu in which the Bible was written. The fact that a person can produce an interpretation of it does not mean that such translation is correct, unless we fall back on the old saw that the Bible can be infallibly interpreted by anyone at all, except the pope. The existence of hundreds of Christian denominations, debates in religious journals, and differing commentaries on the Bible indicate the opposite. When even a person who claims to accept only the New Testament without modifiers or intermediaries is in doubt as to whether their interpretation is complete or correct, s/he often consults a Christian brother or sister, usually their pastor, to compare thoughts and extract the fullest meaning from the sacred text. Should they not even more consult the interpretations of those ancient believers who were much closer to Jesus and the apostles in language, time, culture, assumptions, and locale? Such ancient believers—or those not many years or generations earlier—could have asked the New Testament writers for explanations or expansions upon what they had written and record them in their own writings. If a twenty-first-century cleric can contribute help or insight in interpreting holy writ, how much more an ancient one, even if only as a second opinion.

The fifth objection to the inadequacy of Scripture relies on an exegesis of the Revelation of John 22.18f, which through changes in the arrangement of New Testament books over the years now appears a few verses from the end of the present Bible:

> 18 I warn every one who hears the words of the prophecy of this book: if any one adds to them, God will add to him the plagues described in this book, 19 and if any one takes away from the words of the book of this prophecy, God will take away his share in the tree of life and in the holy city, which are described in this book.

The exegesis postulates that the Apostle John spoke in the name of God to prohibit the addition or deletion of any books, chapters, words or any other written material or teaching from the present sixty-six-book collection. Some Protestants apply this interpretation so thoroughly that they reject all creeds, catechisms or other written statements of faith, out of abundant caution that even such summaries, explanations or educational tools add to the definitive, unalterable, and changeless text of God's exhaustive and complete disclosure as to how He wants His people to behave and believe.

However, this objection is also without real substance, for six reasons:

1) Even though their argument requires God's instruction and revelation to end at 22.19, its proponents nevertheless accept verses 20 and 21, i. e. the last two verses of this book, which opens the question of where the line is to be drawn.

2) What verses 18 and 19 prohibit altering is only "the prophecy" of the Revelation of John, theoretically leaving human beings free to add to or subtract from the non-prophetic parts, e.g. those on ethics. If 2 Peter 1.20 be a part of it, the New Testament has a special solicitude for prophecy, e.g. prohibiting private interpretation of prophecy.

3) In the days when all books were copied by hand, one word at a time—a situation that existed until the invention of printing in the fifteenth century—copyists frequently left out or inserted words or lines. Often this was accidental due to the boredom attendant on such a mind-numbing task, but sometimes a copyist would deliberately make alterations in order to explain or "improve" the text from which he was copying, or would add into the text an explanation or gloss a previous copyist had penned in the margin. Some alterations were even more major, as when a copyist "corrected" a passage in an old text to make it conform to the orthodoxy of his own day, an orthodoxy different from that of an earlier copyist or the original author.[338] In reaction, it became fairly common practice for an author or even a copyist to include at the end of their work a curse such as that in Revelation of John 22.18f. This constituted a warning or prayer to discourage corruption of the original text by people who copied them. For instance, the famous *Letter of Aristeas* states that when the Septuagint translation of the Old Testament was first made public, the leaders of the people considered it so accurate and faithful a rendering of the word of God that they laid a curse on anyone who should add to, delete from or otherwise change any part of it. The *Letter* itself indicates that such a curse was customary.[339] Thus, 22.18f was just another much-used literary device in its day, and John was not trying to protect the integrity of the whole Bile but only of his own individual book, or the prophecies in it.

4) If the immediately preceding paragraph hereof is not accepted, with the result that Revelation of John 22.18f applies to the entire sixty-six-book collection, the *sola scriptura* position is still untenable because it fails to take into account the fact that certain Christian writings, some of them included in various early canons of Scripture, were written *before* the Revelation of John, e.g. *1 Clement* and quite likely *The Didache* and *The Gospel of Thomas*, yet are not in the current New Testament. Moreover, 2 Peter must be excluded because it was composed long *after* the Revelation of John, and John's own letters might face the same fate. In either case, applying 22.18f to the whole of the "Protestant" Bible would entail serious revamping of the canon because of the history of what was and what was not written at the time these two verses were penned.

5) The warning or curse in the Revelation of John 22.18f does not stand alone in any version of the Bible. In Deuteronomy 4.2 Moses admonishes: "You shall not add to the word which I command you, nor take from it; that you may keep the commandments of

the LORD your God which I command you", while in Deuteronomy 12.32 he instructs: "Everything that I command you you shall be careful to do; you shall not add to it or take from it." Unless this is a literary convention that applies to only one book or the books of one prophet instead of the whole written revelation of God, then the whole of our present Bible from Joshua to the Revelation of John must be excluded from the canon and we must confine our Scriptures to the Five Books of Moses, like the small Samaritan worshipping community that survives in Israel today.[340]

6) This objection also fails especially if early Christian writings outside the present New Testament be used only as interpreters of the Bible rather than as integral parts or supplements to it. If their use be thus limited, they would be in the same category as the creeds in their present form and confessions of faith and catechisms, most of which were formulated after the fifteenth century. Yet no Presbyterian believes that *The Westminster Confession* or its *Catechisms* add to the Bible or otherwise violate Revelation of John 22.18f; rather, s/he believes that they are merely summaries of it, bringing scattered points together into a more convenient arrangement for better comprehension, as a convenient or educational exposition of the main teachings of the sixty-six books.

Granted, there are denominations that eschew all confessions of faith, catechisms, statements of belief or practice, and even the creeds, and believe they possess no constitution or guide except the Scriptures, but even each such denomination possesses its own interpretation of the Bible, assumptions as to what is implied (although not explicit) in it, collective experiences, and unwritten convictions as to what is spiritually edifying, upbuilding or wise (which become their own latter-day oral "traditions"). As a result, there are a multitude of ecclesiastical organizations each claiming it follows only the plain word of the Bible yet differing from others that make the same claim. However high the aspirations, such a radical Bible-only position sometimes creates within a church an inner elite that "knows" the correct interpretation of holy writ on any given point, what is implied in it, and what is spiritually edifying, upbuilding or wise, while lay members outside the charmed circle must depend on the elite more heavily than do the rank and file of denominations that possess written statements or summaries of their denomination's teachings as to what the Bible says. In addition to other inequities, the non-elite often cannot ascertain the correct interpretation, etc., until after they have committed an act the elite speaking in the name of the whole body of believers condemns as a breach of good Christian conduct or belief.

Moreover, even churches that eschew all confessions, catechisms, statements of faith or practice, and all other written expositions of Biblical/church teaching nevertheless have sermons at every worship service in an attempt to explain the relevant portion of the Bible, such sermons being regarded as merely summaries of the Bible, bringing scattered points together into a more convenient arrangement for better comprehension, a convenient or pedagogical exposition of the main teachings of the sixty-six books.

Sixth, the reasonableness or inherent logic in supplementing or interpreting the Scriptures by using early Christian traditions do not in themselves prove that this was what Jesus had intended or that early believers did in fact use tradition in this manner. The desirability or wisdom of utilizing sources outside the present New Testament is not in itself conclusive evidence that this methodology was part of the original faith.

The rest of present chapter intends to adduce evidence from actual practice at the relevant time that the apostolic tradition was a factor in how early Christians thought, believed, acted and shared their faith.

Definition and Scope of "Tradition"

One definition of the word "tradition" as it pertains to Christianity is found in Rev. E. Flesseman-Van Leer *Tradition and Scripture in the Early Church*: "the proclamation of the message of Jesus in such a way that it becomes the heritage of the succeeding generation."[341] The brief introductory definition in the article "Tradition" in the *Encyclopedia of Early Christianity* is "Authoritative teaching transmitted in the church."[342] To Prof. R. P. C. Hanson, its primary meaning is "that which is handed down from the beginning of the Christian faith, the Christian teaching and gospel, the method by which it is handed over, and the sources from which it is derived."[343] According to Professor Richard B. Hays, "tradition" in a theological context does not refer to "general cultural customs but specifically to the church's time-honored practices of worship, service and critical reflection", including "the writings of individual theologians, particularly those who have been widely read and revered in the church over long periods of time".[344] The relevant part of the entry "tradition" in the *Concise Oxford English Dictionary* is that tradition is a doctrine etc. supposed to possess divine authority but not committed to writing, especially the oral teaching Christ gave to His immediate followers but which they did not record in writing. The Latin root and use of the word and its related forms all convey the meaning of a "handing over" or "handing down" or "passing along" of something that has value, from one generation or guardian or owner to another, often through a succession of persons in possession. In the present book, "tradition" means a religious teaching or practice or set of religious teachings or practices that have been handed down from an earlier Christian generation to the immediately succeeding generations. In this book, the term the "apostolic tradition", here more conveniently termed "the tradition", was the body of unwritten doctrines and practices accepted by Christians in the first centuries of the Common Era as the teaching and praxis of Jesus and His apostles, handed down orally to their first disciples and by them to succeeding generations. At first it was transmitted only by word of mouth, but as time passed more and more of it was written down. The rest of the present chapter will consider the evidence as to whether early Christians did in fact use the apostolic tradition as a supplement to Scripture or interpreter of it.

Tradition in the New Testament

The noun "tradition" appears in thirteen verses of the twenty-seven-book New Testament. At first sight, the New Testament appears to be inconsistent as to whether religious traditions should be a binding authority in addition to Scripture, e.g. as interpreters of Scripture. In the Gospels of Matthew and Mark,[345] Jesus rebukes the Pharisees for adhering to certain traditions that had been handed down to them:

1) Matthew 15.3: "you transgress the commandment of God for the sake of your tradition",

2) Matthew 15.6: "for the sake of your tradition you have made void the word of God",

3) Mark 7.8: "You leave the commandment of God and hold fast the tradition of men",

4) Mark 7.9 (sarcastically): "You have a fine way of rejecting the commandment of God, in order to keep your tradition!", and

5) Mark 7.13: "making void the word of God through your tradition which you hand on."

Two letters attributed to Paul also appear to deprecate adherence to religious tradition:

1) Galatians 1.14: "I advanced in Judaism beyond many of my own age among my people, so extremely zealous was I for the traditions of my fathers."

2) Colossians 2.8: "See to it that no one makes a prey of you by philosophy and empty deceit, according to human tradition, according to the elemental spirits of the universe and not according to Christ."

On the other hand, Paul or his circle elsewhere exhorts that tradition(s) be followed:

1) 1 Corinthians 11.2: "I commend you because you remember me in everything and maintain the traditions even as I have delivered them to you."

2) 2 Thessalonians 2.15: "So then, stand firm, and hold to the traditions which you were taught by us, either by word of mouth or by letter."

3) 2 Thessalonians 3.6: "Now we command you, brethren. in the name of our Lord Jesus Christ, that you keep away from any brother who is living in idleness and not in accord with the tradition that you received from us."

There are also references in Paul or his circle to what can only pertain to unwritten tradition because the recipients of the letters had accepted and implemented the gospel before it was put into writing:

1) Romans 6.17: "But thanks be to God that you...have become obedient to the standard of teaching to which you were committed",

2) 1 Corinthians 11.16: "we recognize no other practice, nor do the churches of God." This verse brings out an aspect stressed by later authors: for a practice to be considered part of the apostolic tradition it must be widespread throughout Christendom,

3) 1 Timothy 2.2 instructs a young cleric, who had been a travelling companion of Paul, to follow the tradition and to hand it on to later Christians so that they may transmit it to still later ones: "what you have heard from me before many witnesses entrust to faithful men who will be able to teach others also."

Close study of the foregoing verses resolves the seeming contradiction. In all cases where following tradition(s) is deprecated, the reference is to Pharisaic, Jewish or other human customs and practices. In all instances where acceptance of tradition is commanded, the references are to Christian traditions—the practices and teachings of Jesus and His apostles. What Jesus condemned was not tradition per se or its method of transmitting religious knowledge; what He condemned was the Pharisees' and scribes' abuse of it by (1) giving purely human teachings more value than ones which God had established and had commanded to be transmitted, and (2) attributing more value to their own customs and interpretations than to God's wishes.[346] Where the New Testament mandates that a tradition is to be observed, the people commanded to follow it were Christians who never enjoyed contact with Jesus in the flesh but were converted after His ascension.[347]

In the sense of transmitting or passing along a body of knowledge, the present New Testament has a verb with the same Greek root as the noun "tradition". The relationship between the original expressions is shown somewhat more clearly by the *New Revised Standard Version* than the *Revised Standard Version* in translating the verb as "handed on". Luke 1.2 uses the verbal form when stating that gospel-writers had recorded stories about Jesus "just as they were handed on to us by those who from the beginning were eyewitnesses." In 1 Corinthians 11.23 and 15.3 the Apostle Paul said that he had previously "handed on" to his readers important facts about Christ. Because of the use of the past tense and the early dates of these two works, the handing-on or tradition was almost certainly oral or at least not yet written in any of the twenty-seven books.

Neither translation shows the same clearness in bringing out the Greek verbal form in two other passages. The first is 2 Peter 2.21, which denounces believers who backslide from the divine commandment which had been handed down to them. The other is Jude 3 in mentioning that the Faith had been handed on to the saints. Although not as compelling as the verses cited in the immediately preceding paragraph hereof, it remains more likely than not that the Christians to whom these letters were first addressed had received their information, faith or knowledge from oral presentations which were reduced to writing only later.

The verb form is also used in this sense at Lukan Acts 16.4 in relating that emissaries from the summit meeting in Jerusalem handed on, down or over its decision to congregations in southern Turkey. According to Acts 15.23-32, this communication was partly *viva voce* and partly in writing, illustrating that, in its broader sense, tradition can be both oral and written. *First Clement* and some books of the New Testament and, and perhaps also the *Didache*, being the first parts of it to have been committed to writing.[348] The Letters of John (2 John 12 and 3 John 13f) indicate that this apostle also communicated the Faith partly orally and only partly in writing, and preferred the former.

Thus, even in the twenty-seven-book New Testament, there are endorsements of the concept of accepting traditions besides those in Scripture, the tradition being passed on to Paul, then Paul transmitting it to Timothy and others, and then Timothy teaching it to later believers. Even Paul, who had the privilege of at least one personal conversation with the Saviour, did not rely solely on this direct revelation or inward conviction but consulted the original apostles and other Christians to determine from the apostolic tradition whether his understanding of Christianity was accurate (Galatians 1.18f, 2.1f). This is not contradicted by his statement in Galatians 1.12 that the gospel did not come to him from man nor was it taught to him by man but came to him "through a revelation of Jesus Christ". The solution to this seeming contradiction is that although Paul in the last analysis owed his gospel to a direct revelation, it was delivered to him through the mediation of his predecessors in the Faith; although the momentous vision on the road to Damascus revealed Christ to him, the record that we have of it shows that it did not contain all that Paul knew of Christianity; rather, it was the unifying force of "all that he has heard about Jesus before and after his conversion"[349]—a unifying force, not the entire substance.

If Galatians 1.12 be interpreted to mean that the entire content of the gospel came to Saul/Paul by a vision or revelation directly from heaven without human input, then one verse of the New Testament is problematic or hopelessly contradicts it. In the operative part of such direct revelation in Acts 9.6, Jesus imparted almost nothing directly or mystically to him but commanded him: "rise and enter the city, and you will be told what you are to do." Verses 10 through 19 relate that some of the content of what "you are to do" was conveyed to him by human intermediaries who were already members of the church, by Ananias and "the disciples at Damascus". Even so rudimentary a precept as Christian baptism was communicated to Saul/Paul by the disciple Ananias, not in the vision from Jesus. It is a well-established principle of Anglo-American law and (I should hope) Christian exegesis that a document, such as the New Testament, is to be construed as a whole, with indistinctness in one part being resolved by reference to clearer statements in another/other part(s). This principle leads us to interpret Galatians 1.12 in conjunction with Galatians 1.18f, Galatians 2.1f and Acts 9.3-19 in such a way as to affirm that Saul/Paul's knowledge about the Christian faith came from a tradition mediated through earlier Christians.

Tradition in the Century after the Apostles

First Clement 42 and 44 refer to events involving the apostles not recorded in the twenty-seven-book New Testament. Writing on the basis that the recipients of the letter knew about these happenings, the author of *1 Clement* deals with them as being already accepted as fact both by himself and by his readers, thus appealing to a tradition or source of knowledge that is not recorded elsewhere. The two chapters state that the apostles appointed the first office-bearers in the Corinthian congregation "and afterwards gave instructions, that when these should fall asleep, other approved men should succeed in their ministry... with the consent of the whole Church".[350] Later, some Christians in Corinth deposed these officeholders and installed ones of their own choosing. *First Clement* seeks to restore the old order, the succession from the apostles. Although the letter draws comparisons with the Old Testament, the army, and natural phenomena as desirable models of the harmony and orderliness that should be practiced in the congregation, the letter relies on unwritten tradition as a major ground of argument. Indeed, at the beginning of his exhortation that his readers repent, the author called upon them to go "to the glorious and venerable rule of our tradition".[351]

In an exhortation to avoid heresy and false doctrine, Polycarp of Smyrna appealed not to "what is written" but to "the word which has been handed down to us from the beginning".[352]

Whenever opportunity arose, Bishop Papias of Hierapolis in the first third of the second century obtained and wrote down reminiscences of what had been said by the apostles and the first generation of disciples. He "asked minutely after their sayings".[353] Finally he compiled five books of these traditions, of which only fragments remain. Papias confined his research to oral traditions, regarding them as more profitable than written ones. This does not necessarily mean that he completely disregarded Scripture but more likely that he gave greater weight to oral accounts because written ones could not respond to his questions or clarify the precise meaning of a statement or elaborate or clarify and thus not enable him to assess their credibility. This is comparable to law courts in proceedings in which they will not consider written affidavits, although sworn, but insist on oral testimony. His practice of cross-examining his informants could not be put into effect with written statements because the authors were unknown or unavailable for the purposes of ascertaining the correctness or full content of the accounts or of learning of circumstances that might contribute to their interpretation. Not all the records compiled by Papias were of significant theological or moral import,[354] but his diligence in searching for Christian oral traditions down to trivial anecdotes indicates that they were accorded a high respect and that Scripture did not stand alone.

A few decades later, Justin Martyr in *1 Apology* 6 related that Christians taught inquirers about Christianity free of charge, in the same way that it had been handed on to them. Here again, information and belief came through personal oral relationships, not through reading. In *1 Apology* 66, he set forth the requirements for people to be admitted to Holy Communion. Using a verb with the same Greek root as "tradition", he included the requirement that they live according to the teaching that Christ had handed down. Because everyone agrees that Jesus never wrote a book and there is no evidence that He wrote more than a few words, this teaching could have been handed down only orally, at least at first.

A bishop of Hierapolis after Papias was Apolinarius (bishop-pastor from AD 161 to 180), who wrote a letter criticizing the Montanist denomination of Christians. In it, he referred to "the doctrines or precepts of the Gospel of the New Testament, which it is impossible for one who has chosen to live according to the Gospel, either to increase or to diminish"[355] and some lines later condemned the Montanists' prophesying because it was "in a manner contrary to the constant custom of the Church handed down by tradition from the beginning."[356] To Apolinarius, the gospel was unalterable, and one of the ways of ascertaining its content was by consulting tradition. Although the Montanists alleged that they were receiving revelations directly from God, Apolinarius tested the spirits and evaluated these allegations by what had been handed down by a source outside the Bible.

The Tradition in Irenaeus

Irenaeus of Lyons was a member of the denomination of Christians known as the "catholics" or "Great Church" and the first exponent of Christian tradition to write at length. His *Against Heresies* was a refutation of various denominations of Gnostic Christianity and their interpretations of the Scriptures. Much of the Gnostics' energies were applied to deciphering and explaining the Scriptures in ways that would promote their exotic religious and cosmological theories. In arguing against them, Irenaeus laboured under the impediments that any Bible passage can be interpreted more than one way and the Gnostics could argue that it was the catholic interpretation that was flawed by faulty hermeneutics rather than their own. To overcome this hurdle, he raised four arguments which were not available to them: (1) the orthodox/catholic church possessed a tradition of beliefs and practices or of hermeneutics which had been handed down unbroken and unimpaired from the apostles, (2) the guardians of this tradition, who were the successors of the apostles, accepted the catholic interpretation over the Gnostics', (3) orthodox Christian communities were found throughout the known world while heresies tended to be local in extent, and (4) adherents of the catholic interpretation were in unity with each other all over the known world. Irenaeus said that it was these four factors rather than any pretended superiority in the method of interpretation that ensured the correct exegesis of the Scripture. Tradition was the judge of hermeneutics, not vice versa.[357] The catholic church, he maintained, had received through tradition not only the Scriptures but also the correct interpretation of them, and that the latter was not shared by the Gnostics.

At the beginning of *Against Heresies*, Irenaeus stated that the orthodox (catholic) denomination "though dispersed throughout the whole world, even to ends of the earth, has received from the apostles and their disciples this faith".[358] This was the "rule of faith", which to us resembles a longer version of the Apostles' Creed.[359] Irenaeus thus appealed to a tradition alongside Scripture or to a system of hermeneutics descended from the apostles as a standard for judging the correctness of an interpretation of the Bible. In the present book, this "rule of faith" is regarded, quite properly, as a part of the apostolic tradition.

Irenaeus also contended that a diligent investigator can see the truth and "contemplate clearly the tradition of the apostles throughout the whole world" by consulting bishops who had been ordained by bishops who had themselves been ordained by bishops, etc., in lines stretching back to ordinations by apostles. He said that such lines of succession could be traced down to "our own times", i.e. the A.D. 180s.[360] Irenaeus asserted that all these bishops accepted the catholic faith (the faith that had been transmitted by tradition) and that these contemporary guardians of the apostolic tradition[361]

> neither taught nor knew of anything like what these [non-catholics] rave about. For if the apostles had known hidden mysteries, which they were in the habit of imparting to "the perfect" [the Gnostics' term for themselves] apart and privily from the rest, they would have delivered them especially to those to whom they were also committing the Churches themselves. For they were desirous that these men should be very perfect

and blameless in all things, whom also they were leaving behind as their successors, delivering up their own place of government to these men….

The rest of the chapter is occupied by succession-lists or pedigrees of ordinations to the clergy, down to the late second century. For Irenaeus, the Christian faith, including the tradition, was so important that God had instituted a special office of guardians to protect and impart it.

In defending a specific tenet of theology, Irenaeus contended that proof for it could be deduced from (1) the universality of human belief, even among pagans, (2) its acceptance from time immemorial, "from the tradition of the first-formed man", (3) the prophets reminding men of it, and (4) "The Universal Church, moreover, through the whole world, has received this tradition from the apostles."[362] Half of these arguments rely on tradition. Although people in the twenty-first-century West would be reluctant to accept a proposition in the physical sciences which relies on what was handed down from past ages, Irenaeus' statements illustrate that ancient Christians gave great weight to tradition in interpreting or supplementing the Scriptures and that it took priority over clever or seemingly-plausible exegeses.

On a more personal level than *Against Heresies*, Irenaeus wrote a letter to a Christian named Florinus to refute the belief that God is the author of evil. In criticizing Florinus' doctrines, Irenaeus stated that they were "not of sound judgment", "disagree with the Church", "not even the heretics outside of the Church have ever dared to publish" them, and "the presbyters who were before us, and who were companions of the apostles, did not deliver [them] to thee".[363] To reinforce the last mentioned, he reminisced about Polycarp, whom both Irenaeus and Florinus had known in their youth. Here Irenaeus uses extra-Biblical Christian tradition as an authority in a dispute with a dissident Christian who had first-hand knowledge of the extra-biblical sources Irenaeus cited and thus would have been able to refute Irenaeus' argument if the tradition supported Florinus' own position.

The Tradition in Clement of Alexandria

The whole of Clement's *Stromata* (A.D. 190s) is written as if the principle of the apostolic tradition as a guide and guarantor of accurate ethical and hermeneutical teaching were so well established that he did not need to promote or defend the concept. His preface states that his purposes in writing were to preserve the memory and teachings of those who had instructed him in the Faith and to pass them on to this readers. Part of his praise for his mentors was that[364]

> Well, they preserving the tradition of the blessed doctrine derived directly from the holy apostles, Peter, James, John, and Paul, the sons receiving it from the father (but few were like the fathers), came by God's will to us also to deposit those ancestral and apostolic seeds. And well I know that they will exult; I do not mean delighted with this tribute, but solely on account of the preservation of the truth, according as they delivered it. For such a sketch of

this, will, I think, be agreeable to a soul desirous of preserving from escape the blessed tradition.

Clement did not laud his fathers in the Faith for their creativity or originality in interpreting the Bible, although these qualities are prized in some religious circles in our day. Nor would his teachers have regarded such attributes as compliments. They sought only to preserve what had been handed over to them by their own teachers. (Irenaeus also deprecated creativity in matters of faith.[365]) In contrast to innovation and originality, Clement condemned the person who "has spurned the ecclesiastical tradition, and darted off to the opinions of heretical men"[366] and opposed "the divine tradition by human teachings".[367]

Elsewhere in the *Stromata* Clement used the word "tradition" to include Isaiah's prophecies and other books of the Bible[368] and to refer to Christian teaching in general,[369] including the beliefs of a model Christian about creation and theology.[370] To Clement, well-informed faith is inseparable from what was transmitted by God through tradition.[371] Clement believed that the full meaning of Isaiah's written prophecy had been handed on to him and his contemporaries by an unwritten rendering which Jesus had taught the apostles,[372] true religious knowledge having been imparted in unwritten form and descended by tradition to enlightened catholics of Clement's era.[373] Tradition is the "fullness of the blessing of Christ" in Romans 15.29.[374]

Christian tradition was Clement's catchphrase for the whole of ethical conduct and the correct interpretation of the Scriptures. He characterized the lifestyle of the model Christian as "nothing but deeds and words corresponding to the tradition of the Lord."[375] This sentiment is in a part of the *Stromata* in which Clement attacked his Christian theological opponents ("heretics") for their mishandling of Scripture. In this section he wanted to demonstrate scriptural truth using the Scriptures themselves. After pointing out the heretics' inconsistencies and other errors in hermeneutical methodology, he accused them of deliberately altering "the things delivered by the blessed apostles and teachers, which are wedded to inspired words; opposing divine tradition by human teachings, in order to establish the heresy."[376] The verb here translated "delivered" is from the same Greek root as "tradition".

In short, the teaching of Christ and the apostles was for Clement "the understanding and the practice of the godly tradition."[377] Not only did he himself have a supreme regard for it, but his alleging violations of it to attack "heretics" and appealing to an unaltered tradition to support his own arguments indicate that its high or even overriding value was accepted as a given by his opponents, or at least by his readers.

Clement indicated that the authority of apostolic tradition was so widely entrenched as a concept that the Gnostics asserted that they had received their distinctive teachings by means of a tradition.[378] Irenaeus also indicated that some heretics asserted this.[379] To these assertions, Irenaeus and Clement replied that for a tradition to be acceptable it must be traceable back to the apostles themselves and not be of later origin. In Clement's metaphor, the true (i.e. catholic) church is the possessor of the correct key to God's kingdom, which it received through the tradition, while heretics without the proper key try to use a counterfeit one or attempt to apply force to commit spiritual burglary.[380]

The Tradition in Tertullian

Tertullian is of double value in the study of the authority of tradition among early Christians. He wrote from inside of two different religious denominations, having transferred allegiance from the catholic/majority church to the Montanists partway through his life as a Christian author. In both denominations, his arguments relied upon the apostolic tradition, employing it both to support and to attack the catholic/Great Church. This is significant not so much as an indicator of what he himself believed but as what he as a skilled barrister thought was so well-accepted that it could be used as a means of persuasion.

Tertullian's appeals to the tradition increased after he became a Montanist even though the apostolic tradition was not integral to his later theology. The basis of Montanist belief contradicted the authority of tradition or subordinated it to the teachings of Montanus and the prophets with him. It was a cardinal tenet of Montanism that the Paraclete had bypassed the apostles and the catholic church and had descended instead on the Montanist prophets in the second century A.D. By placing the prophetic oracles over the teaching of the church, such a movement ran counter to the principle of receiving what had reputedly been handed down in the church from earlier generations through designated custodians. Yet the Montanist Tertullian resorted to the tradition when trying to convince his opponents.

This is not paradoxical. Tertullian's experience as a lawyer had taught him that in an argument the beliefs that are important are not those of the barrister himself but those of the judge or the opposing party. The method is to appeal to what the other person already believes and use it to lead him into accepting something you want him to. It was because the people whom Tertullian sought to convince were catholics and other non-Montanists who would be influenced by arguments from tradition that his later writings appeal to tradition more than do his earlier ones. This method of approach is similar to that of Valentinus and his followers in deliberately not citing characteristically Gnostic scriptures when writing for a Christian non-Gnostic audience: the Valentinians limited themselves to books which were already accepted by their prospective readers because the readers would be far more inclined to accept theses based on undisputed books than on obviously Gnostic ones.[381] Similarly, in his attempt to convert pagan Greeks to Christianity, Tatian sometime before AD 172 openly stated that he did not use Christian sources but ones already accepted by his pagan audience because "To do the former would be foolish, because it would not be allowed by you; but the other will surprise you, when, by contending against you with your own weapons, I adduce arguments of which you had no suspicion."[382] Like any skilled barrister, Tertullian and Tatian and the Valentinians appealed to what was already believed by their intended converts rather than argue on the basis of premises their audiences did not share and to which the writers were trying to lead them. Professor Cosgrove notes that some Christians engage in such a method of argumentation in our own day.[383]

Six of Tertullian's works significantly touch on Christian tradition. One is from his catholic period, the date and denominational leaning of one is disputed, and the other four are Montanist. The former will be discussed after the Montanist ones because the catholic one illustrates first-hand the Great Church's view of tradition as a guide in religious life, while the work of disputed date contains a seeming contradiction which illustrates the meaning and parameters of the apostolic tradition more precisely.

The Montanist Tertullian wrote *De corona* in support of the Christian prohibition against a particular practice. He began by admitting that there was no warrant in Scripture for the prohibition and he delved into the principles of authority in religion. He stated:[384]

> If no passage of Scripture has prescribed it, assuredly custom, which without doubt flowed from tradition, has confirmed it. For how can anything come into use, if it has not first been handed down?

and then gave examples of liturgical practices not attested in Scripture but nonetheless followed by Christians of his time. In reasoning from tradition, he said of these worship customs:[385]

> If, for these and other such rules, you insist upon having positive Scripture injunction, you will find none. Tradition will be held forth to you as the originator of them, custom as their strengthener, and faith as their observer. That reason will support tradition, and custom, and faith, you will either yourself perceive, or learn from some one who has. Meanwhile you will believe that there is some reason to which submission is due.

Next he gave a general rationale and description of tradition. These included authorization by an apostle and long-continued observance:[386]

> If I nowhere find a law, it follows that tradition has given the fashion in question to custom, to find subsequently (its authorization in) the apostle's sanction, from the true interpretation of reason. This instances, therefore, will make it sufficiently plain that you can vindicate the keeping of even unwritten tradition established by custom; the proper witness for tradition when demonstrated by long-continued observance.

In short, *De corona* says that where Scripture is silent, follow tradition.

Tertullian composed *Against Marcion* to refute the Marcionite denomination of Christians. Originating around A.D. 150, the Marcionites rejected the teaching which had been handed down by church tradition and instead based its faith and practice solely on the first known version of the New Testament. They rejected all the Old Testament and their scripture consisted solely of Luke's Gospel and ten Pauline epistles as edited by their first leader. The foundation of their belief was that the Creator God of the Old Testament was not the deity of Jesus and the New and that these two gods opposed each other. Marcion's position was that because the Old Testament was the word of the Creator, Christians should reject it and have scriptures of their own.

In his argument, Tertullian set out his requisites for a binding Christian tradition: (1) despite differences among Christians in apostolic times, nobody held Marcion's views on the godhead, (2) no matter what may have happened in the immediate post-apostolic era, belief in the unity or continuity of God between the two Testaments had not altered in the apostles' lifetimes, (3) "no other teaching will have the right of being received as apostolic than that which is at the present day proclaimed in the churches of apostolic foundation",[387] and (4) there is no church of such foundation that does not accept the Creator as the God of Jesus and of Christians. Tertullian then challenged the Marcionites to point to any congregation founded by an apostle which accepted their doctrines.[388] Later in the same work, Tertullian appealed to history in stating that "the earliest Christians are found on the side of the Creator, not of Marcion".[389]

Against Marcion not only sets forth criteria for tradition but also identifies its guardians in the early third century. Before writing this work, Tertullian had left the communion of the catholic bishops as guardians and condemned them for not yielding to the Montanist prophets, who had appeared comparatively recently in church history and came from outside the tradition. His invoking the apostolic tradition in *Against Marcion* indicates that his reliance it was due to either force of habit or a deeply entrenched regard for it among his readers.

The Montanist *On the Flesh of Christ* was directed against a number of Christian denominations including that of Marcion, but does not attack the Great/catholic church. Tertullian exhorted Marcion to "believe what has been handed down to us" and scolded him thus:[390]

> Now that which had been handed down was true, inasmuch as it had been transmitted by those whose duty it was to hand it down. Therefore, when rejecting that which had been handed down, you rejected that which was true. You had no authority for what you did.

In this work also he called upon Marcion to accept the binding force of tradition and to accept what was being handed down by its custodians, whom Tertullian and the other Montanists rejected.[391] This seeming contradiction is resolved by the principle that a barrister need not believe in the merits of the arguments he presents nor in the justness of the law he invokes. If there were no such principle, there would not be at least one lawyer on each side of every lawsuit. Lawyers' arguments are evidence not of what they themselves believe but what they think the judge or other decision-maker believes. A former barrister of some prominence, Tertullian's arguments show what his twenty years as a Christian had led him to think his readers would accept tradition as an authority.

In *De pudicitia* the Montanist Tertullian made the distinction between the Pharisaic and human traditions condemned by Jesus and the apostolic tradition commended by Paul. Tertullian praised Paul for "becoming an emulator not of ancestral but of Christian traditions".[392]

In *De praescriptione haereticorum* also, Tertullian made remarks on tradition relevant to our present study. This work dates from his catholic period and attempts to demonstrate that it was the catholic or Great Church, rather than its Christian opponents, that taught the uncorrupted message of Jesus Christ. Tertullian stated that the congregations founded by apostles had received their faith in two ways: oral preaching and written letters.[393] He attributed a number of important features of church life solely to the unimpaired continuation of such tradition: the apostolicity, unity, communion in peace, fraternal spirit and practice of mutual hospitality among catholic congregations.[394] In order to refute the proposition put forward by non-catholics that at one time or another in the first two centuries the Great Church had apostatized from the original gospel and remained apostate in Tertullian's day, he pointed to the accepted fact that its congregations throughout the known world all preached the same things and from this he argued that the sameness was proof that catholic churches were preaching and teaching the original and uncorrupted gospel. If, said Tertullian, distinctively catholic doctrine were the result of congregations straying from the original Christian message by creating something new, the various churches would necessarily have strayed haphazardly and randomly and have produced different beliefs and practices: "When, however, that which is deposited among many is found to be one and the same, it is not the result of error, but of tradition."[395] Here again we see tradition, then still largely oral, used as an argument that a denomination had continued in the true Faith, in contrast to allegations that a later interpretation of scripture is superior to the traditional one or that a religious truth was lost in the first one or two centuries AD, and was "discovered" or "restored" in more recent times. Tradition was a judge or safeguard of the correctness of hermeneutics, and not vice versa.

Tertullian's work most helpful to us at the present juncture is *De virginibus velandis*, or *On the Veiling of Virgins*. Present-day experts in early Christian literature are widely divided as to its date and whether its author was still in communion with the catholic denomination or already a Montanist.[396] This disagreement would tend to suggest that its contents are free enough of denominational bias to portray an even-handed and balanced representation of Tertulian's assessment of the general regard for tradition among Christians of his day, which scholars variously date between AD 204 and his death almost three decades later. At first sight its presentation of the tradition as an institution is the weakest of the six works and at points appears to undermine tradition's viability as an authority. The issue in *De virginibus velandis* was whether life-long celibate women, termed "virgins", were obliged to wear veils like married women in obedience to 1 Corinthians 11.5-16. In support of their contention, Tertullian's adversaries cited a local (Tunisian) custom that permitted virgins a choice as to veiling.

At the beginning of the treatise, Tertullian seemingly disputed the authority of tradition in order to argue that this local custom was illegitimate:[397]

> it behoves our virgins to be veiled from the time that they have passed the turning-point of their age:[398] that this observance is exacted by truth, on which no one can impose prescription---no space of times, no influence of persons, no privilege of regions. For these, for the most part, are the sources whence, from some ignorance or simplicity, custom finds its beginning; and then it is successively confirmed into an usage, and thus is maintained in opposition to truth. But our Lord Christ has surnamed Himself Truth, not Custom. If Christ is always, and prior to all, equally truth is sempiternal and ancient. Let those therefore look to themselves, to whom that is new which is intrinsically old. It is not so much novelty as truth which convicts heresies. Whatever savours of opposition to truth, this will be heresy, even (if it be an) ancient custom.

In confronting the contradiction between one custom and another or between custom and tradition, Tertullian joined Paul,[399] Irenaeus and Clement of Alexandria in applying the principle that for a custom to qualify as an apostolic tradition it must have been adhered to throughout the universal church, especially in congregations founded by apostles, and not in only one region:[400]

> Throughout Greece, and certain of its barbaric provinces, the majority of Churches keep their virgins covered. There are places, too, beneath this (African) sky, where this practice obtains; lest any ascribe the custom to Greek or barbaric Gentilehood.[401] But I have proposed (as models) those Churches which were founded by apostles or apostolic men; and antecedently, I think, to certain (founders, who shall be nameless).

This seeming contradiction is also dispelled by examining Tertullian's choice of Latin words in *De virginibus velandis*. For "tradition" in the sense of a firmly-binding inherited practice, Tertullian used the Latin word *traditio* while the word for "custom", to which his opponents appealed, was *consuetudo*. The meanings of *traditio* include "bequeath", "commit", "deliver", "entrust" and "hand down", while the English equivalents of *consuetudo* are the less solemn and less longstanding "custom" or "habit". By definition, a *traditio* is a practice which has been handed down from persons in authority in an earlier era in a line stretching back to the apostles, while a *consuetudo* is the usual (but not necessarily universal or long-term) way of acting and may spring up in a short time. Tertullian was pitting *consuetudo* against *traditio*. In *De corona* 3 and 4 Tertullian mentioned "custom" as only one of a number of elements that make a practice a "tradition" and is not in itself "tradition".

Tertullian's contentions are thus not self-contradictory. To have the force of law within the Christian community, a "tradition" must date back to the apostles, be shared by Christians everywhere and be handed down by the saints of previous generations. It is not something that emerged haphazardly from uncertain roots as a matter of convenience or unplanned repetition. Note also Tertullian's references to Greece, its non-Greek provinces and northern Africa: as with Irenaeus, a purely local practice does not qualify as "tradition". Take a contemporary example. The Ladies Auxiliary of Saint Arius' Church in Chicago has "always" used the Fellowship Room every Thursday afternoon. This is not an unbreakable "tradition" sanctified by God which inexorably prevents rescheduling to accommodate an African-American youth group. It is a mere "custom" because (1) it is not shared by congregations throughout the world and (2) the room scheduling of no United States church can possibly date back to apostolic times.

The Tradition in the *Letter to Diognetus*

An unknown Christian writer in the second or early third century indicated the high relative value his co-religionists accorded to "the tradition of the Apostles" by including it in the same category with "the fear of the law", "the grace of the prophets", "the faith of the gospels" and "the grace of the Church".[402]

The Tradition in Hippolytus

The early writings of Hippolytus were contemporary with those of Tertullian and his later ones with the earlier ones of Origen. Hippolytus' literary production continued until his martyrdom in or about A.D. 235. Origen had heard him preach.[403] Formerly a student of Irenaeus, Hippolytus was a bishop in central Italy from the early A.D. 200s until his death. In A.D. 217 he wrote *The Apostolic Tradition* "in order that those who have been rightly instructed may hold fast to that tradition which has continued until now".[404] He assured his readers that "The Holy Ghost bestows the fulness of grace on those who believe rightly that they may know how those who are at the head of the Church should teach the tradition and maintain it in all things".[405] As the second quotation indicates, the laity were to be educated in the tradition so that they could evaluate the correctness of their clergy's teaching, presumably to take measures against guardians who deviated from it.

In his *Little Labyrinth*, Hippolytus invoked tradition against the followers of Artemon. These were not Gnostics but originally members of the Great Church who believed that Jesus Christ was conceived and born an ordinary human being who was not divine from eternity but was adopted as the Son in adulthood. They maintained that this had been Christian doctrine from the beginning until Zephyrinus became bishop of Rome around the year 199. Hippolytus said that their beliefs were contradicted not only by the Scriptures but also by the writings of Justin Martyr, Justin's disciple Tatian, Miltiades, Clement of Alexandria, Irenaeus and Melito of Sardis, by Christian hymns, and by the actions of Zephyrinus' immediate predecessor.[406] The fact that Artemon and his followers themselves alleged that their doctrines had been handed down in a tradition which they said had only recently been corrupted shows the importance of the principle of tradition among early Christians. Note that both sides appealed to non-biblical Christian antiquity as a touchstone and criterion, with one citing Christian writings and official actions outside the canon of Scripture.

The Principle of Tradition among the Gnostics

Hippolytus recorded that the founders of a particular Gnostic denomination alleged that the Apostle Matthias had "communicated to them secret discourses, which, being specially instructed, he heard from the Saviour."[407] In addition, Ptolemy the Gnostic in the middle of the second century likewise asserted that his own denomination possessed a tradition descended from the apostles.[408] Still other Gnostic groups claimed to have received secret traditions from New Testament personages.[409] As noted above in the discussion of Clement of Alexandria, both Clement[410] and Irenaeus[411] recorded similar Gnostic allegations. It has been suggested that the idea of alleging that one's theology was transmitted by a tradition (as distinct from or in addition to the Scriptures) originated among the Gnostics rather than catholics.[412] Regardless of whether Gnostics or members of the catholic church fabricated a tradition solely to legitimize their existence, or whether there were parallel or competing traditions, both parties considered it necessary to possess an apostolic tradition in addition to criteria such as a correct interpretation of the Scriptures.

Tradition in Origen and his Circle

Nothing will be given here about Origen and tradition except an incident in his life. His writings on the topic of tradition as such will not be examined because there is a debate over the reliability of the texts that have come down to us. His most relevant work[413] has not survived in the original Greek but only in Latin translations, especially those of Jerome and Rufinus, both of whom flourished around AD 400. According to commentators in the nineteenth and part of the twentieth century, these translators and later copyists abridged, interpolated into, or otherwise altered Origen's writings to make them accord with the changed orthodoxy of their own day.[414] As a result, say these scholars, the texts we now have do not faithfully represent his thought, especially on the subject of tradition.[415] On the other hand, some twentieth-century scholars believed that the translations are faithful to the originals and that, despite the loss of his exact expression, they retain the essence of his thought.[416] Because the present book confines itself as much as possible to contemporary and uncontroverted texts and excludes doubtful sources, I will not present a study based on suspect evidence. This reservation or omission does not extend to my lists of specific moral precepts because the scholarly debate does not extend to Origen's teachings on ethics. No ancient or modern source I have consulted has alleged that his teachings on ethics were altered in the texts and translations available to us.[417]

Origen's preaching before being ordained did not make him a violator of tradition. In fact, the troubles it caused emphasize one of its aspects. While travelling in Palestine in A.D. 216 he was persuaded by the bishops of Jerusalem and Caesarea to expound the Scriptures to an assembly which included clergy. When his doing so was reported in Alexandria, his own bishop protested and recalled him to Egypt on the ground that it was contrary to tradition for a layman to preach to clergy. For his part, the bishop of Jerusalem asserted that there had never been a tradition against laymen preaching to clerics.[418] He even gave examples of the practice in Turkey, where he had been a bishop. This did not end the matter. Several years later, when Origen was again visiting Palestine, the same bishops ordained him to the presbyterate. The reaction of the bishop of Alexandria was to convoke synods in Egypt which defrocked and excommunicated him. This action was not recognized by the churches of Achaia (eastern Greece), Lebanon, Cappadocia (south-central Turkey), Arabia nor, naturally enough, Palestine.[419] The correct view of the tradition must be conceded to the Palestinian bishops for the reasons stated by Irenaeus, Tertullian and 1 Corinthians 11.16: for a practice or prohibition to be part of the apostolic tradition, it is not enough for it to have been of long standing; it must have been accepted by churches throughout the known world and not in only one locality.

The Tradition in Dionysius the Great

The bishop of Alexandria from the late 240s to the mid-260s was Dionysius, whose book *De natura* indirectly discloses a high regard for the apostolic tradition. He had been a student of Origen and later dean of the Alexandrian seminary and, later still, bishop. Before A.D. 250 he wrote the *De natura* to combat a movement which was a rival to Christianity. In doing so, he deemed it necessary to attempt to disprove the atomic theory of matter or the hypothesis that the universe is composed of a large number of tiny particles. He propounded arguments from logic, from commonplace observation, from analogy and from the Scriptures. Significantly, the one authority to which he did not appeal was Christian tradition. Because neither Jesus nor His apostles had said anything about the structure of matter, neither did the tradition, and thus Dionysius did not employ it in trying to disprove what science has since established to be correct. On the other hand, he felt free to use the Bible for his argument, much the same way as people use it today to advance other unscientific hypotheses. While it is possible for a determined exegete to argue that the atomic theory or other well-accepted scientific fact is contrary to the Bible, he or she can make such a pronouncement of faith only in the absence of the guidance of the apostolic tradition.

The Tradition in the Time of Cyprian

Although he tried to subvert the role of tradition in ways discussed in Chapter Five, Cyprian of Carthage appealed to it when writing to other Christians, probably in the same way Tertullian sometimes did: not necessarily because he himself believed in it but because an appeal to it would help win his readers to his view. The same may well be true of the members of his circle cited in the next two paragraphs hereof.

In a letter to laypeople, a presbyter and a deacon concerning the election of bishops favourable to his views, Cyprian and bishops of his party wrote: "you must diligently observe and keep the practice delivered from divine tradition and apostolic observance, which is also maintained among us, and almost throughout all the provinces".[420] Cyprian accepted the result of another episcopal election because it was "in conformity with the requirements alike of the sanctity and the truth of the divine tradition and ecclesiastical institution".[421] He added that bishops ought to work together to exclude opposition by maintaining the unity among the clergy that had been handed down (*traditum*) by the Lord through the apostles.[422]

For a few years beginning in AD 254, there was a controversy within the catholic or Great Church over the validity of baptisms administered by other Christian denominations. Firmilian of Caesarea in Cappadocia and northwest African bishops including Cyprian maintained that, in keeping with the apostolic tradition which had been transmitted to them over the generations, converts to catholicism from other denominations must be rebaptized. On the other side, Pope Stephen of Rome and Bishop Dionysius of Alexandria[423] held that the intending converts had been validly baptized into Christianity and should therefore be admitted into the Great Church through no more than the rite of reconciliation used for repentant catholics. Stephen insisted that his practice (the tradition that prevailed at Rome) must be followed everywhere, saying that the other approach was only recent and "nothing is to be innovated unless it has been handed down (by tradition)".[424] In reply, Cyprian questioned the source of Rome's longstanding practice,[425] while Firmilian denied that it had descended from the apostles[426] and dismissed it a mere "custom" (*consuetudo*)[427] or "human tradition".[428]

Cyprian also used the expression "human tradition"[429] to deprecate a liturgical practice with which he disagreed, and contrasted it with practices instituted by Christ, applying the condemnation in Mark 7.9 of Pharisaic tradition.[430] This is similar to his language on another subject when he characterized his ecclesiastical rivals as "those who reject the commandment of God and try to set up their own tradition",[431] again in conjunction with Mark 7.9.[432]

Also in relation to liturgical and sacramental matters, Cyprian advocated that a particular practice be abandoned on the ground that it was contrary to "the plan of evangelical truth, and of the tradition of the Lord",[433] and he admonished its practitioners "to keep the truth of the Lord's tradition",[434] i.e. to do what Cyprian wanted them to do. On another of such matters, he sought to win over his opponents by saying "we should return to our original and Lord, and to the evangelical and apostolical tradition".[435]

In trying to persuade persons then or formerly in danger of martyrdom for admitting to persecuting government officials that they were Christians, Cyprian invoked "ecclesiastical order", "evangelical law", "the unity of the Catholic institution", and "your confession and the divine tradition",[436] apparently as considerations of equal importance. To elicit compliance in another matter, Cyprian and his co-authors sought to bolster their paraenesis by stating "we do not depart from the traditions of the Gospel and of the apostles",[437] with the implication that the addressees would keep such traditions if they accepted the authors' directions.

For the purposes of the present chapter, what is significant in these controversies and the invocation of tradition in them is not who was right or wrong or whether particular longstanding practices really were of apostolic origin, but the fact that contending groups of Christians considered tradition as determinative for faith and practice, at least in order to persuade their correspondents, which indicates that their readers considered tradition to be authoritative. To be sure, Cyprian quoted Scripture verses to advance his contentions but, from the way they appear in the Bible, they favour his opponents' positions as much as his own and merely beg the question. These quotations would have been applicable only if he was in the right for some other reason, and from the face of his writings it appears that this reason was tradition——either as an independent source of authority or as a indication as to how Holy Writ is correctly interpreted.

The aforesaid controversies as to the content and teaching of tradition are also important for Chapter Five of the present book: where are we to draw the line between (1) genuine apostolic traditions and (2) beliefs and practices of later origin to which the term "tradition" was erroneously applied? As in the Easter Controversy of the late second century, both sides in the dispute over rebaptism alleged that their own positions had come to them through tradition from the apostles. This indicates that either (1) the apostles themselves had never established a tradition about that subject-matter and had left the point for individual congregations or geographical regions to decide for themselves, or (2) one or both parties had strayed from the original truth, each setting up a (non-apostolic) tradition or custom of its own, or (3) the allegations of at least one party were incorrect, with that party erroneously attributing to the apostles longstanding precepts or practices which were really of more recent origin. As observed by Professor Hanson:[438]

> We may even go so far as to say that by the end of the second century and certainly by the third century patristic writers have fallen into the habit of describing as 'apostolic' any custom whose immediate origin they could not trace and which they knew to be widely diffused throughout the Church.

For these reasons, it is imperative in a study such as the present book to seek the earliest available attestations rather than accept a statement not found until centuries or millennia later as to the antiquity (and therefore obligatory nature) of a practice or precept. For the same reasons, we must consult as many authors and geographical regions as possible in order to distinguish between (1) customs which were merely local and therefore probably originated after the apostles and their first disciples, and (2) the traditions they actually did hand down in the earliest times. For instance, in the matter of Origen as a layman preaching to clergy, the correct view of the tradition must be conceded to the Palestinian bishops for the reasons stated by Irenaeus, Tertullian and 1 Corinthians 11.16: to prove that a practice is part of the apostolic tradition it is not enough to show that it is of long standing; it must have been accepted by the Christians throughout the known world instead if in only one locality.

The Tradition in Callistratus the Martyr

Callistratus was a Christian layman who was martyred under the Emperor Diocletian (reigned AD 285 to 305). In a presentation to potential converts, Callistratus based his faith not only on written scripture but also on a family-based tradition that had begun with his great-grandfather, who had seen Jesus and Pilate, witnessed the crucifixion and burial of Jesus and seen the resurrected Christ, and was baptized on the day of Pentecost. He taught the Faith to his children and grandchildren and his teaching was passed on in the family where it was still relied on over two and a half centuries later.[439]

Conclusion

Chapter Two of the present book shows that instead of absorbing their moral guidance from the ad hoc application of generalized principles such as loving their neighbours or following the standards of secular society, early Christians were governed by a sizeable number of specific commandments and restrictions. Some of these were in the New Testament. As shown in Chapter Three and the present chapter, much of the teachings of Jesus are not included in the sixty-six-book Bible. Some were transmitted orally from Christ to the apostles, from the apostles to their disciples, and so on through the generations. In the present book this teaching is known as "the apostolic tradition". Rather than being a competitor to the Scriptures, the oral tradition was accepted by early Christians as a valuable or even necessary source of divine guidance, especially as a means of evaluating the correctness of an interpretation of the Bible. For instance, Tertullian wrote of the tradition as being found mainly in Scripture, with the New Testament being part of the tradition.[440] Never did he contrast tradition with written teaching.[441] We Christians must use the Bible and the oral tradition together.

Although he limits the scope of the oral tradition to the ancient liturgy and rule of faith, even the Evangelical Robert E. Webber, a professor of theology at Wheaton College, concedes that "Scripture was never separated from oral tradition as if the apostles had two mouths. Both the oral and the written tradition came from the same source and were not perceived as contradictory."[442]

Transition

The tradition was preserved and promoted by the New Testament writers, their friends in Christ and the first generations of believers. The question arises: how early must a source be to represent an accurate recollection of what the church taught decades or generations earlier. In addition to Prof. Hanson's observation, it is common experience that over time memories grow dim, comparative innovations are mistaken for longstanding practices, and self-interest often argues that something that is in fact spurious was authorized in antiquity. As compared to families and individuals, these weaknesses are not as great as when the memory is widespread and commonly known among Christians and thus subject to correction and reinforcement, but these weaknesses must nevertheless be taken into account. The time and circumstances at which reliability ended are considered in the next chapter.

Chapter Five

The Decian Discontinuity

Introduction

This book might be ten times longer if a combination of factors in the middle of the third century did not form a natural division in Christian history. A break at one point or another in the two thousand years was inevitable because lines of oral transmission weaken with the passage of time and become unreliable and distorted. In addition to tricks of memory over long periods that create misinformation, so also too great an attenuation of tradition through too long a succession of generations eventually renders it impossible to separate facts about the early period from intermediate inventions which are incorrectly attributed to the earlier period. New customs are introduced and, over time, are falsely attributed to the original tradition. Some genuine particles of truth may nevertheless be communicated from the time of the beginning into a later period, but there is no way of distinguishing them from more recent additions. In fact, after a long enough period of time, the teachings of office-bearers in the church may even contradict those of an earlier age. One example relates to Origen. Although he held the same convictions as other catholic Christians of the third century, at the end of the fourth it was possible to accuse him of heresy because in the interval catholic churchmen had deviated considerably from the original faith, which had been substantially modified through the passage of time.[443] Around A.D. 469 Pope Gelasius of Rome "forbade the use of all those works of Origen which Jerome had not sanctioned by turning them into Latin."[444] As mentioned in Chapter Four, it is widely believed that Jerome interpolated or modified Origen's text in the late fourth and early fifth centuries to accord with the orthodoxy of his own day. In the sixth century, Origen's thought—and that of Clement of Alexandria—was "crushed out by tyranny and the leaden ignorance of the age" by Christians.[445] The only method of ascertaining the content of the authentic tradition is by confining oneself to documents written during the period in which there is no doubt that it was pristine and unimpaired.

A culmination of trends and events marks the Decian Persecution of A.D. 249-251 as a distinct watershed in church history. That is why this study of traditional Christian moral law stops at that time. As illustrated below, the Decian Persecution signals an abrupt break in the apostolic tradition. This was caused by (1) egregious laxity among the clergy, (2) thinning of the numbers of dedicated Christians by widespread persecution, mass apostasy and natural disaster, (3) the rise of other, new, forms of misconduct in the church, especially threats and use of corporeal force, (4) introduction of replacements for the tradition, and (5) praising the example of churchmen apart from that of Jesus.

Corruption among the Clergy

"a long peace had corrupted the discipline that had been divinely delivered to us"[446]

In the decade before A.D. 249 Origen recorded that too many clergypersons were morally and intellectually unqualified. He deplored the phenomenon of "large numbers of Christians who do not sufficiently occupy themselves with the quest for the word, and who yet with this defect are promoted to high office".[447] He lamented that far too often[448]

> he who has a mean mind and cares for the things of this world occupies the exalted position of the priesthood or the chair of a teacher, whereas a truly spiritual man, and one who is altogether free from secular considerations,...either holds an inferior position in the ministry or even remains among the multitude of the laity.

Some Christians intrigued for positions of leadership in the church,[449] organizing banquets to influence electors for this purpose.[450] Origen complained that many clergypersons of his time were pedantic, "quite unfit, and often far more in need of such teaching as will improve their character and give order to their life".[451] Some men sought bishoprics only for the sake of earthly glory and praise or in order to take gifts from people who donated out of piety after hearing their sermons.[452] Origen characterized many a Christian shepherd (i.e. pastor) as the kind "who, being at the head of his flock, uses its milk and dresses in its wool, but does not visit the infirm, neither carries the lame, but overburdens the strong with labour."[453] Fraud and corruption were frequent among the clergy, who converted to their own use the offerings to the church and the fund for the relief of the poor.[454] Some clerics imitated secular government officials and terrorized the poor.[455]

Origen admitted that there were some good preachers among the clergy but added that for all practical purposes the mouths of others were sealed shut by their incompetence and sense of guilt over their own sins.[456] He protested that instead of preaching the Scriptures with meaning and freshness, many did no more than repeat old themes in old forms without reflection, imparting nothing; to these he said "Your lips move a lot but your minds are motionless."[457] Often the preaching was calculated to please the congregation by oratory rather than to teach it.[458] He also asserted that some clergy were too proud of their positions[459] and did not lead lives commensurate with their calling.[460] He found the latter accusation to be true during the Decian Persecution itself.[461]

By the eve of the Persecution, offices in the church had become regarded as personal property. Some presbyters and bishops used their power over appointments in the church in a way calculated to amass fortunes for themselves and their families instead of appointing on the basis of merit.[462] Many bishops and presbyters who presided over congregations sold many of them to "unsuitable persons" and ordained to the Christian ministry "undesirable men",[463] many or all of whom were "greedy, tyrannical, and wicked".[464] Origen noted that some clergy did not leave the selection of their successors to God but bequeathed their offices in their wills to their relatives and thus established dynasties within the church.[465] The natural conclusion is that the beneficiaries were of similar or lesser character and fitness as their immediate predecessors.

Some clerics feared men rather than God. The eminent (or at least much-published) Roman Catholic scholar Karl Rahner has noted the following about the catholic clergy of Origen's era in their dealings with wayward Christians:[466]

> the clergy were not infrequently afraid of being slandered by the accused. This applied even to bishops, few of whom were saints. The temptation was to appear not strict but lenient. Thus there was a continual risk of turning a blind eye even to offences which were clearly subject to excommunication.

This attitude could only encourage the laity to engage in new forms of misconduct (see below) as well as increase the practice of old ones, thus weakening the moral fibre of cleric and layperson alike.

More than two thousand kilometres to the west of Origen, Cyprian in Tunisia described a parallel situation:[467]

> Among the priests there was no devotedness of religion; among the ministers there was no sound faith: in their works there was no mercy; in their manners there was no discipline. .... Crafty frauds were used to deceive the hearts of the simple, subtle means for circumventing the brethren. .... They would swear not only rashly, but even more, would swear falsely; would despise those set over them with haughty swelling, would speak evil of one another with envenomed tongue, would quarrel with one another with obstinate hatred. Not a few bishops who ought to furnish both exhortation and example to others, despising their divine charge, became agents in secular business, forsook their [office], deserted their people, wandered about over foreign provinces, hunted the markets for gainful merchandise, while brethren were starving in the Church.

The clergy of the early third century also gained extra privileges which were bound to weaken their relations with the average Christian. In an age when the daily labour of the common people was directed mainly to obtaining enough to eat, the *Didascalia apostolorum* provided that presbyters and deacons were to receive twice as much as ordinary Christians at church meals and the bishop was to have four helpings.[468] In making requests for assistance, laity no longer enjoyed direct access to the bishop but had to go through the deacons,[469] which can only have reduced the bishop's contact with the day-to-day life of his flock. The *Didascalia* also provided that the bishop was to be the sole recipient and sole custodian of tithes and offerings to the church and the sole dispenser of the its gifts.[470] Besides teeming with opportunities for graft and favouritism, this system lacked elementary safeguards against corruption, for the *Didascalia* further provided:[471]

> And thou shall require no account of the bishop, nor observe him, how he dispenses and discharges his stewardship, or when he gives, or to whom, or where, or whether well or ill, or whether he gives fairly….

Of course, it can be alleged that in every age there is evidence that the conduct of the Christian clergy is open to criticism. Hans von Campenhausen writes of clerical misbehaviour of the middle and late second century as recorded in the *Shepherd of Hermas*[472] and Irenaeus' *Against Heresies*,[473] but this was quantitatively and qualitatively different from that of the mid-third century. Hermas' statements about the disinclination to be peaceful[474] and about strife and jealousy over precedence, honour,[475] and the prime seats in Christian assemblies[476] apply equally to clergy and laity and are of the same kind of paraenesis about minor offences as are found throughout pre-Decian Christian writings, including the New Testament. Campenhausen's citations that apply exclusively to Christian leaders are also exhortations to good stewardship, peace,[477] self-correction,[478] and other virtues[479] little different from those elsewhere in this literature. Hermas' denunciation of some prophets for asking for money[480] is paralleled in the *Didache* and Apollinarius' *Against Montanism*, but all these apply to Christian prophets—who never had a role in the administrative or economic aspects of church life. On another tack, Campenhausen's statement that *Hermas* is the first to note "the inner contradiction between the worth of the official and the spirit and authority of his office"[481] is not substantiated by the references in his footnotes. Similarly, Arnold Ehrhardt's statement that the *Epistle of the Apostles* revealed that in the second century the punishment of villainous bishops "was already a subject of popular discussion"[482] is not borne out in the translations of the *Epistle* by Montague Rhodes James[483] or C. Detlef G. Muller.[484]

Ehrhardt also draws parallels between Origen's criticisms and those of earlier times in the church.[485] Ehrhardt cites (1) *Hermas* Mandate 11.12,[486] but the earlier writer definitely referred only to prophets, and (2) Vision 2.2.6,[487] but this is a general exhortation to virtuous living, a statement of the kind that can be found in every era of Christian history.

Granted, Hermas complained that deacons or other clergy performed their duties improperly, plundering widows and orphans of their living and making a profit for themselves from their ministries,[488] and Irenaeus counselled catholics to avoid presbyters who were heretics or schismatics or who "serve their own lusts, and do not place the fear of God supreme in their hearts, but conduct themselves with contempt towards others, and are puffed up with the pride of holding the chief seat, and work evil deeds in secret";[489] however, both situations differ from those in the 240s and 250s in that the later ones were all regular catholic clerics whose actions the laity had no choice but to accept because church life had come more firmly under the control of the clergy in the intervening sixty to a hundred or more years.

It thus appears that the misconduct described by the second-century authors was hardly novel, less severe, and did not affect the church and its people as much as that in the third century.

Towards the middle of the third century, the clergy's opinion of themselves rose inversely to their spiritual decline. They magnified the importance of their offices, assumed high-sounding titles and became possessive of their authority. Origen noted that some of the higher clergy considered themselves "princes of the church".[490] In letters written while hiding from the Decian Persecution, Cyprian, bishop of Carthage, constantly invoked the "honour" and "dignity" of bishops, addressed other clergy as "my lord", and did not decline such honorifics when directed to himself.[491] He asserted "the Church is founded upon the bishops, and every act of the Church is controlled by these same rulers."[492] He criticized his presbyters for being insufficiently submissive to him, for acting too much on their own initiative in caring for the Carthaginian church in his absence of indefinite duration, and for not remembering "their own place".[493] This self-aggrandizement and spiritual arrogance were particularly out of place when all involved, including Cyprian himself, were in immanent danger of imprisonment, torture and death. These developments are not parallel to those in *1 Clement* or the letters of Ignatius of Antioch. The earlier authors sought to solidify the relationship between the laity of other congregations and their clergy. Here Cyprian is lecturing his own clergy in order to increase his own power over them.

Two of these developments in the first half of the third century, at least in Tunisia, are noted by an eminent Fellow of the British Academy:[494]

> Cyprian's letters show that in the generation that separated him from Tertullian many changes had taken place in the African Church:
>
> . . .
>
> (b) It was now entirely episcopal. Power lay in the hands of councils of bishops.
> (c) Much of the evangelical fire of Tertullian's time had evaporated. It was not unusual for clergy, even bishops, to hold secular appointments (cf. Cyprian, *De Lapsis* 6.)

(Actually, *De Lapsis* [*On the Lapsed*] 6 does not say that clergy received appointments in secular government but only, as to suggest that this was unprecedented, that some had become merchants and moneylenders and accepted appointments as agents in profit-making enterprises.)

The Persecution and the Apostasy

In December A.D. 249 the Roman Emperor Decius launched the first thoroughgoing and Empire-wide persecution against Christians generally. There had been previous persecutions but none had been as efficient or as complete. The most recent crackdown had been in A.D. 235-238 but it was directed only against clergy. The last persecution comparable to A.D. 249-251, against all Christians, had ended in A.D. 206, and was thus beyond the memory of most people of Decius' time. Christians were not prepared for a persecution of any sort, let alone the worst to date. Indeed, Origen had noted shortly before A.D. 249 that Christians were "not being persecuted by the authorities as in old times."[495]

Under Decius, a new Imperial law required all subjects of the Empire to sacrifice to the gods of Rome, an act Christians had always considered idolatry and a disavowal of the divine lordship of Christ. Refusal to perform the pagan rite was the main reason for government execution of the faithful. Under Decius, the only ways of avoiding torture and death were sacrifice, long-term hiding, or producing a certificate from a corrupt government official falsely stating that the bearer had performed the rite.

The Emperor's program was highly successful. "Decius was able to weaken the churches by throwing them into internal chaos".[496] Cyprian's *On the Lapsed* describes how the majority of Christians traded their religious convictions for earthly considerations:[497]

> Immediately at the first words of the threatening foe, the greatest number of the brethren betrayed their faith, and were cast down, not by the onset of persecution, but cast themselves down by voluntary lapse. .... Nor did they even leave it to be said for them, that they seemed to sacrifice to idols unwillingly. They ran to the market-place of their own accord; freely they hastened to [spiritual] death, as if they had formerly wished it, as if they would embrace an opportunity now given which they had always desired.

There were so many intending apostates that in some places the government officials had to ask them to come back another day.[498] Not satisfied with denying their own faith, some Christians urged others to sacrifice.[499]

The Persecution in Egypt was described by Dionysius of Alexandria, who had become bishop of the city in A.D. 246. Dionysius related the categories of reactions to the Emperor's decree that all must sacrifice or be put to death:[500]

> "a large number...speedily accommodated themselves to the decree in fear"

> "others, who were engaged in public service, were drawn into compliance"

> "others were dragged on to it by their friends"

> "others yielded pale and trembling"

> "others...hurried up to the altars with greater alacrity, stoutly asserting that they had never been Christians at all"

Whatever the individual motivation or enthusiasm of compliance, the moral fibre of a great many members of the church was not up to the Christian tradition of martyrdom for Christ or observing the important precept of Christian law against worshipping or doing homage to more than one God.

It strains credibility to assert that by A.D. 249 one hundred percent of Christians or even one hundred percent of clergy were thoroughly self-seeking at the expense of Christ. However, common experience of human character in every age teaches us that when confronted by a choice between punishment and denial of principles, it is the lax who tend to survive by compromising their consciences while the more dedicated opt for punishment. In the Decian Persecution the punishment was death, which means that it was the less dedicated who survived and carried their traits and practices into the following generations.

The Epidemic of A.D. 251

Continuity within Christianity was also impaired by a widespread natural disaster in the year 251. A devastating epidemic swept the Roman Empire, killing five thousand people a day in the City of Rome, depopulating Alexandria by two-thirds, and hitting rural areas just as hard or harder.[501] Thus, the memories of many Christians who could remember and pass on the apostolic tradition were cut prematurely short by a demographic catastrophe unprecedented since the smallpox epidemic of seventy to eighty-five years earlier.[502]

The Rise of New Forms of Misconduct in the Church

Despite the threat of impending torture and death, Christians in Origen's parishes continued to devote Sundays to secular pleasures and money-making activities. Many attended public worship only on high holydays and even then spent the time in private conversations instead of paying attention to the service.[503] Even in this dark hour Cyprian found that a letter to him purporting to come from the church at Rome had probably been forged by a Christian third party, and fraudulently altered by a fourth.[504] Nor was Cyprian himself above writing a poison-pen letter in A.D. 254 as a reply in kind to a Christian who had defamed him.[505]

More portentous for the future of Christianity was the behaviour of those who had sacrificed to idols and later sought readmission to the Great Church. Government violence was followed by violence within the church. Sacrificers airily asked for reinstatement, and then demanded it. When some clergy insisted on a waiting period with signs of repentance, they threatened them with violence.[506] Cyprian recorded that apostates who sought readmission did so "not with prayers but with threats,...not with lamentation and atonements, but with terrors".[507] He found it necessary to help a bishop who had been subjected to verbal and physical assaults by a deacon.[508] Excommunicated persons assailed the bishop of Rome with threats and terror and tried to intimidate the absent Cyprian with "clubs and stones and swords".[509] He also considered it necessary to alert his Roman confrere to Christians who were spreading detractions about him.[510]

The church at Rome had additional problems arising from the mass apostasy. This church divided over the policy for readmitting repentant sacrificers. Breaking into two denominations, one faction elected Cornelius bishop while the other chose Novatian, who had been acting head of the Roman Church during the Persecution and now opposed any earthly forgiveness for the apostates. When the Carthaginian church appeared inclined to recognize Cornelius, the Novatianists sent representatives to win support in Tunisia. They were not peaceful and gentlemanly but adopted the violence around them. They burst into a solemn assembly of Carthage's clergy and broadcasted accusations, abuse and disruptive clamour.[511] When these tactics failed, they stumped the country, alleging serious sins and crimes against their opponents,[512] as did Cyprian against them.[513]

Resort to violence may also have been prompted by knowledge that petitioners would not receive a fair hearing from a local church. Ecclesiastical decision-makers had forgotten the basic principle of natural justice that they must hear both sides before deciding; even the pagans observed this principle.[514] The Carthaginian clergy refused to allow Novatian's party to make an oral presentation or file documents concerning the disputed Roman election. The decision was manipulated and one-sided, without regard for the merits.[515] In such an atmosphere, the first casualty is truth and there arise abuses in the church, such as disregarding or materially distorting the apostolic tradition.

Violence as an instrument of church procedure was unprecedented. Although there had been disagreements and schisms among Christians in the previous two centuries, at least they had been free from physical force. Neither Paul nor his opponents resorted to terror-tactics. The apostles confined themselves to nothing stronger than straightforward epithets. *First Clement* mentions a revolt in the Corinthian congregation but with no physical violence and with a conspicuous lack of verbal abuse. The adversaries of the Montanists uttered uncomplimentary remarks but never advocated corporeal action. Hippolytus' criticisms of his opponents were unflattering but he did not suggest physical interference. Church fathers prior to A.D. 249 employed reasoning, persuasion and negative comparisons with Jesus and Old Testament worthies. It was not until the reign of Decius that we find Christians accusing each other of sins and crimes irrelevant to the topic in issue, using force against each other, or threatening violence. Where force and violence become factors in decision-making, there is little or no room for reason, truth or respect for traditions.

The Persecution did not cure the spiritual maladies of the clergy. After toleration had been restored, Cyprian still stressed "the priestly authority"[516] and he referred to the bishop's seat as "a throne".[517] Within three years after the Persecution Cyprian repeated views like his earlier "the Church is founded upon the bishops" when he opined that "the bishop is in the Church, and the Church in the bishop; and if anyone be not with the bishop, that he is not in the Church".[518] To Cyprian, being outside such a church was a sin worse than idolatry and murder such that even the martyrdoms of non-catholics were without value.[519] In the same vein, he stated that "neither have heresies arisen, nor have schisms originated, from any other source than from this, that God's priest is not obeyed."[520] He wrote that all heresies and schisms arise when clergy do not receive enough respect and deference.[521] Cyprian taught that whoever rejected him or rejected other bishops rejected God; and equated himself with the High Priest of Israel in a letter in which he tirelessly boasted of his own humility.[522]

Among Cyprian's favourite proof-texts, both before and after the Persecution, were (1) 1 Samuel 8.7: "And the Lord said to Samuel 'Hearken to the voice of the people in all that they say to you; for they have not rejected you, but they have rejected me'",[523] (2) Acts 23.5: "And Paul said, 'I did not know, brethren, that he was the high priest; for it is written, "You shall not speak evil of a ruler of your people"'"[524] and (3) Deuteronomy 17.12f: "The man who acts presumptuously, by not obeying the priest who stands to minister there before the Lord your God, or the judge, that man shall die; so you shall purge the evil from Israel. And all the people shall hear, and fear, and not act presumptuously again."[525] Cyprian applied to himself and bishops of his party these and other scriptures that magnify the authority and supremacy of clergy over laypeople and that discountenance any lay criticism or disobedience to Jewish or Christian priests.

Nevertheless, Cyprian continued the culpable leniency toward sin that Rahner in the above quotation noted was born of clerical fear of malefactors. Cyprian himself admitted: "I remit everything. I shut my eyes to many things, with the desire and the wish to gather together the brotherhood. Even those things which are committed against God I do not investigate with the full judgment of religion. I almost sin myself in remitting sins more than I ought.[526] By being negligent in his ministry in order to gather together a brotherhood including recent apostates, Cyprian apparently valued the number of Christians who would subject themselves to him over holiness of life and steadfastness in persecution. After all, laypersons of higher quality might be more inclined to think for themselves and question Cyprian's yoke on them.

We thus see the nominal guardians of the tradition magnifying the importance of themselves and their office to exclude such considerations as the brotherhood of Christians, fair play in the church, and openness to correction. The elitism of the ostensible protectors of the apostolic morality eclipsed its content, thereby creating a substantial doubt as to the continued reliability in the process of transmission.

History soon provided two examples of the privileged positions of the official guardians displacing the ethical teachings of the tradition. Paul of Samosata bore a striking resemblance to some twentieth-century televangelists. Penniless when consecrated bishop of Antioch around A.D. 260, he soon amassed a fortune through blackmail, misuse of church funds, bribes and other corrupt practices. He turned his flock into a personality cult and adopted the pomp, lifestyle and bearing of a high secular official. He cultivated connections with the local government for his own secular advantage. His clergy and the neighbouring bishops did not oppose him because he shared his ill-gotten gains and mistresses with them. In A.D. 268 a large synod with emissaries from an unusually large geographic area convicted him of heresy and excommunicated him but he retained enough accomplices to keep control of the church's property. Only the intervention of the Roman emperor was sufficient to dislodge him.[527] What was significant was not that one cleric strayed so far but that he was able to succeed for the better part of a decade and had no lack of collaborators. Tolerating and abetting his activity revealed a lack of idealism which persisted despite attempted intervention by outside clergy.

The necessity of bringing in the secular authorities, which had been putting Christians to death only one or two decades earlier, is forceful testimony to breakdown of moral law and authority within the Christian community.

On behalf of himself and three other Egyptian bishops, Bishop Phileas of Thmuis sent a complaint to Meletius, a bishop from Upper Egypt, concerning his conduct in a later persecution. After Bishop Peter of Alexandria had fled during the persecution of A.D. 303-311 without making provision for public worship or pastoral care, Meletius in good faith ordained two men to provide for the spiritual needs of the flock. Phileas and his co-authors assailed Meletius for breaking church law, undermining "the honour of our great bishop", "doing violence to ecclesiastical order" and disrespect for the office of bishop in general.[528] What mattered were jurisdiction, the dignity of the clerical office, and solidarity of the priestly class over the salvation and welfare of the laity. Peter's own letter on the subject reveals him as a prelate possessive of his clergy, jealous of the territory of his bishopric, and vindictive toward anyone who provided for his flock when he did not.[529] Peter's letter presumes Meletius' guilt and bad faith, before hearing Meletius' account of the matter.

Replacing Parts of the Tradition

Despite continued lip-service to the apostolic tradition, some survivors of the Decian Persecution undermined it or tried to redefine the substance out of it. This is most clearly indicated during the rebaptism controversy of A.D. 254-258, where alternatives to the tradition were enunciated. In another difference of opinion, a personal letter on the contents of the eucharistic chalice manifests some of the thinking of the new era.

In a less ecumenical age than our own, the question arose whether converts to the catholic church from other denominations (e.g. Marcionites, Montanists, and even Novatianists) should be baptized a second time in the belief that non-catholic baptism was invalid. This was the Rebaptism Controversy mentioned in Chapter Four of the present work, in which Bishop Stephen of Rome and his party held for its validity while Cyprian, Firmilian and their party insisted on rebaptism. That chapter tries to show that in this controversy each side argued that its own practice had been handed down as part of tradition, with the clear implication that tradition was determinative. The present chapter illustrates how and what one party argued when tradition was not clearly in favour of its practice, with the result that it asserted new alternatives to tradition or began to modify its authority.

Cyprian vaguely asserted that his position was not a new one but had been decreed by his predecessors long before.[530] However, he cited no authority older than a local synod of less than forty years earlier. Although his practice may have descended from those in authority, it was neither traceable to apostolic times nor accepted throughout Christendom. Such a reference is a confession that he could find no better authorization; in law, reliance on a weak argument in the absence of other arguments is an indication that there is no better argument. It is nevertheless significant that he felt obliged to tie his position to a tradition of some sort.

In advancing his choice of procedure, Cyprian argued "Neither must we prescribe this from custom, but overcome opposite custom by reason":[531] Cyprian relied not so much on his own interpretation of tradition but on reason as the supreme arbiter of Christian praxis. Yet when his opponents argued from reason, he dismissed them as being "overcome by reason"[532] in asserting "it is in vain that some who are overcome by reason oppose to us custom, as if custom were greater than truth."[533] Cyprian apparently derived his "truth" from a source other than tradition or reason.

In their own minds, the rebaptizers sought to replace custom with truth or overcome a tradition with what they believed was truth. For Cyprian, custom must not prevent "the truth" from being accepted and required evidence of truth independently of tradition.[534] Firmilian, Bishop of Caesarea in Cappadocia, and friend of the recently-deceased Origen, boasted on behalf of the rebaptizers in Turkey that "we join custom to truth, and to the Romans' custom we oppose custom, but the custom of truth; holding from the beginning that which was delivered by Christ and the apostles."[535] In keeping with the bitter spirit of the dispute, he accused the Roman church of setting up custom against truth and of perversely preferring the former to the latter.[536] The existence of different customs for different regions was not the issue for the bishop of Rome, and perhaps not for Firmilian: his truth must prevail over the contrary practice everywhere. Sentiments similar to Cyprian's and Firmilian's were expressed in a synod of eighty-seven clergy in September A.D. 256 which drew representation from what are now Morocco, Algeria, Tunisia and western Libya. With the concurrence of the whole assembly, speakers urged following "the truth" instead of traditional practices of which they disapproved, and preferring "reason and truth" over them. Bishop Libosus asserted that although there had been inter-Christian conversions without rebaptism in the past, now that "the truth" had been manifested all contrary practices must be discontinued.[537] Astoundingly, Bishop Felix of Bussacene proclaimed that "reason and truth always exclude custom."[538] Shortly after the synod, Cyprian considered the objection that converted heretics in past ages had been accepted into the Great Church without rebaptism. He admitted that this had been the practice, at least in some congregations, but added that error should never be perpetuated and that error is to be abandoned after the truth becomes known.[539]

To Cyprian's party, religious truth could be lost even though it had once been widespread in Christendom. It could disappear despite the vigilance of its guardians, a group to which Cyprian and the bishops in his party belonged. To them, truth could be newly discovered generations after the early disciples, having been unknown to the intervening generations. This approach is strikingly similar to those of denominations that originated in the nineteenth and twentieth centuries that base their claims on new religious truths they have "found" or "restored". Such an approach is tenable in the physical sciences, which are concerned with a universe full of data to be discovered and analysed. However, the scientific method does not apply to religion.[540] The essence of Christianity is that a single person appeared for a definite period in human history and taught all the "data" to His disciples. There is no religious truth apart from this source; there are no reliable discoveries outside the tradition and teachings He began.

It is significant that both sides in the rebaptism controversy relied on long-established practices which they asserted were of universal validity; the bishop of Rome at least was not inclined to tolerate the use of a different practice, even at the local level. This difference and the fact that neither party to the dispute could provide evidence from before the third century in support of its position indicate that neither the apostles nor their early followers held a unified tradition—and therefore probably no tradition—in the matter. As noted elsewhere in the present book, the ancients believed that for a practice to be considered part of the apostolic tradition, it must be found throughout Christendom. To use Tertullian's language, the parties were contending for custom (*consuetudo*) not for *traditio*. They also illustrate the propensity to incorrectly attribute customs of more recent origin to the remoter past of the original tradition after memories have become attenuated by the passage of time.

For all their emphasis on "truth", the rebaptizers only begged the question. They believed that they had the truth about reception of converted heretics but provided scant information on how they knew it to be the truth or on the means of deriving truths about other matters of Christian praxis apart from a disputed custom of no great antiquity. On the few occasions when this information was given, it was rooted in Scripture apart from the tradition.

As part of his exposition against the Roman practice, Cyprian advocated a "return to the head and source of divine tradition" in order to bring an end to "human error".[541] He said that to justify their practice Stephen and his adherents must produce an authority for it from the Gospels or the Acts of the Apostles or the epistles of the New Testament.[542] In proposing the "return to our original and Lord, and to the evangelical and apostolical tradition",[543] Cyprian liberally cited Scripture as an authority which overruled tradition.[544] He had forgotten that the New Testament is part of the tradition and that earlier Christians had never contrasted tradition with the written teaching of the holy books.[545]

Cyprian's concept of the paramountcy of the Bible was more fully developed in his dissertation in letter form that the eucharistic cup must contain both water and wine, never water alone. While agreeing that "the tradition of the Lord must be observed"[546] he confined this "tradition" to the contents of the Bible.[547] To him, following the tradition of Christ meant relying on only what was recorded there and discarding customs with which Cyprian disagreed. In support of his position he cited thirty-four Scripture passages, most of them of no obvious relevance and which opposed only Pharisaic and other human traditions, not Christian traditions as mentioned in the New Testament epistles. About half of his proof-texts were drawn from the Old Testament even though the eucharist did not begin until the New Testament.

In developing arguments against traditions they disliked, Cyprian and his party shifted from reason to "the truth" and then to exclusive reliance on Scripture, or rather on one interpretation of Scripture. We today would find this method of interpretation to be specious because the Bible passages quoted have only tangential or, more often, no bearing on the point Cyprian or his party was trying to prove. Unlike the previous two hundred years, the period after the Decian Persecution witnessed a Christian hostility to the authority of tradition[548] and reliance on the interpretation of the Bible independently of tradition.

Beginning of Praising Churchmen Apart from Christ

The death of Cyprian in A.D. 258 marks another change in Christian devotion and practice. According to Robert Louis Wilken,[549] prior to this time the stories of heroes in the Scriptures, the marvels of apostles in New Testament apocrypha, and the accounts of martyrs were told and read only to the extent that these saints imitated Jesus Christ. Jesus Himself said in John 13.15 that it was He who was an example of how His disciples should act. Although the events in the life of Paul the Apostle, with its travels, preaching, whippings, stoning and shipwrecks, would have been excellent material for praise of the Apostle himself, Paul himself said only "Be imitators of me, as I am of Christ."[550] Ignatius exhorted the Philadelphians to imitate Christ even as He imitated His Father.[551]

According to Professor Wilken, the martyrdom of Cyprian marked the beginning of writing of lives of virtuous later Christians as examples in themselves to be imitated. Cyprian's deacon Pontius wrote the first story of a Christian saint praising the saint himself independently of Christ. Rather than tell the story in the manner of earlier acts of martyrs, Pontius consciously broke with tradition by describing Cyprian's teachings and accomplishments as noble and meritorious independent of the martyrdom. Pontius consciously sought to preserve in writing the accomplishments and great deeds of Cyprian's entire life. This was a marked departure from traditional reliance on Jesus or God as the ultimate examples to be imitated, and the earlier rule that the human saint is to be regarded as an example, not in themself but only to the degree that he or she imitated the Lord. Later writers followed Pontius' innovation.

It is my own observation that we thus have another development in the middle of the third century that sought to deflect Christians' attention away from the centrality of the Lord and His tradition and towards glorification of individual men and their novel ideas and methods.

Conclusion

Corruption among the clergy, persecution on an unprecedented scale, unparalleled mass apostasy, a devastating epidemic, the introduction of force and defamation into church disputes, a desperate grasping for arguments to support a party's position, and decline in piety combined to weaken Christians' continued acceptance of unimpaired apostolic tradition and make its reliability after the Decian Persecution a matter of debate and uncertainty.

The present book submits that Christian tradition is a dependable source of information on Christian moral law only until A.D. 249-251. It does not allege that the apostolic tradition ceased all at once, forever and completely—like the fall of the Romanovs—but only that forces and events which coalesced in the mid-third century make suspect all attributions to apostolic tradition not recorded until after the Decian Persecution. The martyrdoms of numerous clergy and laity (especially the more dedicated), the predominance of self-seeking ones, the attenuation of the lines of oral transmission, the steamroller effect of violence within the church, the instituting of alternatives to tradition and the low level of dedication do not necessarily invalidate all post-Decian claims to the traditional nature of a practice but only render them too doubtful and unreliable for use in ascertaining the moral law of Christ and the original believers.

Chapter Six

Determining the Specifics of Early Christian Law

As described in earlier chapters, the apostolic tradition ("the tradition") was the body of teaching accepted by Christians in the first centuries as the doctrine and practice favoured by Jesus and His apostles. For at least members of the catholic/orthodox/Great Church, the apostolic tradition (including the New Testament) was a binding source of authority. The tradition was handed down from one generation of early believers to another. Transmitted orally at first, elements of it were gradually reduced to writing. Because of factors that came to a head around A.D. 249 to 251, the tradition as attested by Christian writings after the middle of the third century is suspect and without the degree or kind of reliability as works written before that time.

<u>Contents of the Lists</u>

The apostolic tradition contained many commandments or rules of morals to which a believer's attitudes and actions were required to conform in order for him or her to live according to God's will. Conversely, there were many specific prohibitions or negative rules of morals from which a believer was required to refrain or avoid. In the present book, this part of the tradition is called "Christian moral law". These rules are set forth and consolidated in the following two lists. One of these lists is a compilation of references from the applicable literature to affirmative or positive duties or commandments. The other list is a compilation of similar references to acts and attitudes forbidden in the pre-Decian records.

The far left-hand side of a line (before the first dash) indicates in succinct form a behaviour, state, or attitude mentioned or commented on by a pre-Decian author or anonymous work. The words after the first dash on the left-hand side cite the author (or the work if it is anonymous or better known by title), then the work itself, and lastly the verse and chapter where each is found in the work. In the first list—that of affirmatives, commandments and duties—the words before the first dash indicates contains the substance or essence of the moral duties or commandments, etc.; the reader is to preface each of them with "Be a ...", "Do a ...", "God wants a Christian to do/be...", etc. The second list—the list of negatives and prohibitions— similarly states the behaviour, etc., giving the substance or essence and without the negative qualifiers. This brevity obliges the reader to mentally add "Do not ...", "Do not be a ...", "... is forbidden to Christians", as the case may be.

The behaviours, states of mind or attitudes included in the lists are:

1) those which the author himself or work itself commands or states that something is part of God's commandments or expectations from a Christian.

2) precepts contained in an excerpt that the author quotes from the Old Testament or the words of Jesus recorded in the four canonical gospels.

3) those which an author describes as a general Christian practice.

The behaviours, states of mind, or attitudes omitted from the lists are:

1) references to moral duties or prohibitions that the author cites or quotes from another Christian author in the list (usually the New Testament) without explicitly and unequivocally adopting or approbating that precept as one which he himself believes is part of Christian moral law,

2) those that the author mentions as possible moral precepts but does not explicitly and unequivocally command or approbate as his own e.g. Romans 1.24-32, and Tertullian's comments on adultery and concupiscence at *On Repentance* 3; in the case of Romans 1.24 to 32, I do not include homosexuality and the other behaviours mentioned there because Paul speaks of them as penalties for moral misdeeds rather than as moral misdeeds in themselves.[552] In instances where there is reasonable doubt as to whether a writer adopts a deed or attitude in his own statement of Christian moral law, I have excluded it on the ground that mere allusions or casual mention of an activity are insufficient when the author does not explicitly indicate whether God and Christians considered it desirable or undesirable. As stated above in "The Early Third Century: Tertullian" of Chapter Two, I use only indisputable evidence that an author regarded a particular attitude or activity as binding on Christians, instead of my relying on statements which are open to more than one conclusion as to whether they were part of Christian moral law. This exclusion eliminates ambiguous and debatable statements which an author might not have intended as a firm rule,

3) attributions to Christians or a denomination to which the writer is hostile. This exclusion also saves a user of the lists from being misled when a writer attributes a particular rule or practice to a denomination to which s/he is hostile. The statements of such a writer may well lack balance or even include intentional or inadvertent distortions. One does not consult *The Watchtower* magazine for the most accurate or definitive treatment of Roman Catholic faith or morals. However, I have included

commandments and prohibitions which an author attributes as binding Christians as a whole, because (a) Christian authors included themselves and their denomination as part of the larger Christian movement and (b) pagan authors who describe general Christian traits can be weeded out by a user of the lists because the fact that they were not Christians is stated in the thumbnail sketches in "Guide to Authors and Works Cited in the Lists",

4) those pertaining to master-slave relations because they are (I hope) irrelevant in the milieux in which I anticipate this book will be used, and may give twenty-first-century employers totally misleading ideas for norms of labour relations in the modern world. In addition, there are already specialist works addressing the subject of slavery in antiquity,

5) liturgy,

6) doctrine, including decisions as to what doctrines constitute a heresy, and exhortations to avoid heresy. Like liturgy, doctrine lacks the necessarily interpersonal elements to qualify it as part of ethics and is not usually regarded as part of its subject matter. However, the lists includes statements about how to treat or act toward heretics, because this necessarily entails the personal interaction which is the substance of ethics,

7) words used in metaphors and similes, e.g. "darkness" and the various components of armour in Ephesians 6.13-17,

8) instructions or exhortations of a purely personal nature that are not obvious from the context to be of general application, e.g. the "love one another" spoken to the two Christians in *Passion of Perpetua and Felicitas* 6.3, "use a little wine for the sake of your...frequent ailments" (1 Timothy 5.27), and Christ's injunctions in the Gospels that the person cured by His miracle should not tell other people. Thus, the exhortation to be watchful and pray that a person not enter into temptation is treated differently according to context: it appears on the list for its occurrence in Origen's *Homilies on Genesis* 10.1 because there it is a general statement intended for all Christians, while I omit its occurrence in Matthew 26.41 and Mark 14.38 because there it appears to be directed to only a few apostles for the specific circumstances of Christ's praying before his arrest,

9) general terms which in themselves require elucidation and a value judgment and are not self-explanatory, such as "righteousness", "sin", "immoral", "justice", and "good", because the purpose of two detailed lists is to enable the reader to construct the meaning of these general terms from the lists of specific behaviours, attitudes, etc. However, I include such words in the lists when they are indispensable elements of another duty or prohibition,

10) the method, requirements and procedure for obtaining remission of sins, whether before or after baptism, because of the volume of the subject matter, the need for in-depth discussion of individual authors, and the orientation of the lists toward maintaining a state of grace/holiness rather than toward remedies for losing it.

Advanced scholars of early Christianity may take issue with my omission of a particular ancient writing when there is doubt that it dates from before Decius. I have included only those works on which there is no reasonable argument as to dating before A.D. 250. I do so on the ground that the possible inclusion of writings that may be of a later date is more harmful than the exclusion of a work that dates from before that emperor. The distortion caused by including later works is more serious than omitting pre-Decian ones from a list that already contains a very broad spectrum of the relevant literature.

The Contrary View

I am not unaware of the opinion of Susanne Heine that[553]

> There are contradictory strands of tradition, contradictions within a tradition or even a person, contradictions in receptions and analysis. Anyone who cuts swathes determined by his or her own interest will always find enough points of contact to endorse that interest.

Actually, the situation is not as nebulous or questionable as Professor Heine's oversimplification would indicate. For example, looking at the lists under such precepts as "Adultery", "Fornication", "Patience" and "Love your enemies" reveals total agreement on particular ethical points among the widest range of Christian authors. It is true that for some precepts there is disagreement or merely no mention by some writers but on a broad range of issues there is a uniformity surprising for such a large number of people (some of them belonging to different denominations) in a large number of geographic areas over a period of two centuries. As present readers will find for themselves, disagreements and contradictions in the lists are amazingly few. One might say that the early writers agree on essentials and disagree only on non-essentials, if one applies the reasonable albeit circular criterion that "essentials" were what all ancient Christian writers agreed on while "non-essentials" were those thoughts and behaviours on which liberty was tolerated and hence a lack of uniformity.

Although the instances of contradictions are more negligible than Professor Heine would have us believe, the reader in making his or her analysis should nevertheless proceed with the procedures, considerations and safeguards recommended in the following heading hereof.

Associate Professor Allen Verhey denies the validity of the entire concept of consolidating and interfiling early Christian moral precepts into lists such as those found in the present book: "To fashion the great variety of New Testament ethics into one massive, undifferentiated whole is impossible and impoverishing."[554] I naturally take issue with this statement, on four grounds:

1) Although comprehensively itemizing and interfiling the various points of ethics might have been impossible or at least unwieldy when he wrote in 1984, developments in computer technology—especially much larger database storage capacity—make such a project feasible today.

2) Eighteen pages later, Dr. Verhey appears to indicate that such a project is desirable, at least to Christian Fundamentalists for the canonical books: "In this view, the tasks for Christian ethics are to harmonize and systematize the biblical rules and commands and moral teachings and to apply them to cases as a contemporary code."[555] One of the uses to which my lists can be put is by such Fundamentalists ignoring all the non-biblical tradition and using as a code only those books in the present New Testament.

3) Despite his great labour and erudition, Dr. Verhey in his book really poses little alternative to such a fashioning into an entire compendium of New Testament ethics. His book does not answer the question "How am I as a Christian to act in these particular circumstances?" but consists of pure theory without solid guidance or clear, quick, practical methodology. Rather, his lack of specific, affirmative criteria for making ethical decisions and his belabouring the point that perhaps not all New Testament precepts are binding today—again without a methodology for deciding which ones—render his volume a possible textbook of excuses for not following many clear biblical directives.

4) Verhey's reasoning against compiling a code of New Testament precepts includes "These writings—in all their variety and relativity to particular situations—not only were a part of a developing moral tradition but also are a part, the normative part, of a continuing moral tradition."[556] Much of the thrust and rationale of the present book and the *raison d'être* of its lists are that the New Testament is inadequate unless set in such tradition, at least for the period that such tradition is reliable. Thus, a massive and undifferentiated compendium is not impoverishing when it includes relevant similar elements of the apostolic tradition as a normative tradition as it continued until the Decian disruption.

5) The greatest failing of Verhey's approach (as with Hauerwas and Birch and Rasmussen)[557] is its advocacy that moral decisions be made by the church, which to me seems too time-consuming and cumbersome when an individual Christian must make a quick moral decision within a limited time. The sort of contemporary code produced from a massive compendium such as the lists in the present book would allow early and quick decisions by an otherwise-unaided individual.

Considerations as to the Authorities

The following preferences and advice are largely hypothetical and mentioned here only out of abundant caution. The incidences of disparities and variations in patterns are almost nonexistent, but a good lawyer makes provision even for what is unlikely to happen.

I submit that the most feasible way for people in the twenty-first century to reconstruct the content of early Christian moral law is to find the particular precept in the appropriate list, look at all the other works cited for the same precept, form a tentative conclusion, and then examine the other list for references to the contrary, and (if there is nothing to the contrary) to form a final conclusion on the relevant topic. In every case, the reader should look for a consensus of the ancient authors to reveal a common source in Jesus or the apostles. In the rare instances where there is a contradiction between the lists, the reader is to apply Paul's injunction to "test everything" (1 Thessalonians 5.21). Some readers may wish to work within the three procedural guidelines Professor Hays has recommended for finding coherence in the moral teachings of the various New Testament writers.[558] In the very few instances where one author contradicts others, the sources must be weighed. Such weighing involves more than simply using the lists alone or applying no more than the considerations contained in the subheadings of the present chapter; on the contrary, readers—especially those who wish to write an in-depth sermon or article on a point of ethics—must look up the full texts of the references cited in the lists in order to learn and consider the original authors' surrounding statements, manner of expression, and expanded discussions, which the lists by the essential nature of their brevity cannot include. Such weighing would also include looking at the denominations or schools of the authors: it is quite likely that one or both authors were expressing the teaching of only their own group. If they belonged to the same denomination or school but it was not shared by writers outside it, the natural conclusion is that the issue on which there was liberty of belief or of opinion other than within the group, with no Christianity-wide "official" position on the matter.

As for types of sources, the lists are as inclusive as possible, for they include references to the church fathers, works by "heretics", the few comments by secular authors, and anonymous works. This breadth and inclusiveness is to accommodate the various approaches different readers may wish to apply to the ancient writings:

- whether to accept all genres of literature or to confine oneself to the church fathers and omit the New Testament apocrypha, on the grounds that little or nothing is known about the authors of the latter: they may well have been sectarian, heretical or otherwise deviant,
- conversely, whether to confine oneself to works which purport to be inspired scripture, and thus omit the church fathers and accounts of martyrdoms,
- whether to accept only authors who adhered to the orthodox/catholic church, and thereby exclude the works of pagan authors and minority Christian denominations,
- whether to cut off research at a date earlier than A.D. 250, and
- whether to accept only the evidence of the authorized guardians of the tradition as the sole legitimate informants on the tradition.

The last two considerations are given extended treatment below under "Whether to Choose a Cut-off Date Other than A.D. 249-251" and "Transmission by the Authorized Guardians: Which Church Officers?"

Ancient voices may assist some readers who wish to select among authorities. Writing from the perspective of the catholic/orthodox church, Irenaeus, Tertullian and Clement of Alexandria were agreed that in order to qualify as part of the apostolic tradition, a practice or teaching must meet four tests: (1) it must have been widespread through the known world rather than found in only one or a few localities, (2) it must have been transmitted by the authorized guardians of the tradition, rather than by the self-appointed, (3) it must have been open and ascertainable rather than handed down secretly within a small inner circle, and (4) it must not have been a recent innovation but be traceable back to the apostles or at least date back to a time when no memory knew of the contrary. Tests 1 and 2 are given extended treatment below. Of course, non-catholics might have applied other criteria; for an overview of the approach of some Gnostic denominations, see Elaine Pagels' *The Gnostic Gospels*.[559]

Idiosyncrasies must be guarded against. In using the lists, we must take the precaution of remembering that any given author may have written something that was not part of the apostolic tradition. He or she may have put down purely personal ideas and interpretations, local (in distinction from universal) Christian customs, or the beliefs and practices of a small group who shared merely local or personal ideas. Put another way, a statement in one or two early authors does not necessarily prove that it was the teaching of all ancient Christianity. By including all references, the lists allow a reader to determine how widespread was the particular teaching and thus whether to include it in his or her consideration of the contents of the traditional moral law.[560]

The lists contain as many authors and works as possible also to provide an abundant range of views and authorities to present readers and enable them to make comparisons and draw parallels to determine what was included in the general tradition.

Whether to Choose a Cut-off Date Other than A.D. 249-251

In addition to that proposed in Chapter Five of the present work, there are a number of opinions as to what should be the cut-off date for the reliability of contemporaneous writings relating to the apostolic tradition. For example, Hegesippus, the first church chronicler, took the view that the church maintained pristine orthodoxy until the death of the first generation after the apostles, after which heresy and schism became widespread.[561] In effect, Hegesippus would place the dividing line around A.D. 100 instead of 250, although regarding himself and his denomination as correct and true in the second or third quarter of the second century.

Although the factors in the second third of the second century did not involve number or severity of circumstances enumerated in Chapter Five, it might be argued that a break had been effected at the time of the smallpox epidemic of A.D. 165 to 180.

According to R. P. C. Hanson of the University of Nottingham, the continuity of an oral tradition independent of the Scriptures, in the sense I have used it, was broken between the time of Clement of Alexandria and that of Origen.[562] His statement quoted in Chapter Four of the present book bears repeating:[563]

> by the end of the second century and certainly by the third century patristic writers have fallen into the habit of describing as 'apostolic' any custom whose immediate origin they could not trace and which they knew to be widely diffused throughout the Church.

In one of his books on the canon, Lee M. McDonald arrives at a similar or later date for the ending of Christians' reliance on tradition as an authority. The lack of concern in earliest Christian times about a closed collection of Scriptures was due, he says, to the fact that oral tradition was still current and fresh among believers in the early second century.[564] The attempts to draft an exclusive and fixed canon began in the fourth century because by that time oral tradition was no longer as fresh or regarded as reliable as it had been in the earliest period. The authority of oral tradition passed into the authority of the written tradition. Citing Dr. Sundberg, McDonald says that this transition began with Irenaeus and was completed in Origen's time.[565] McDonald applies to all the New Testament what Sundberg said only about the four gospels as a canon. In Sundberg's own words:[566]

> Thus we find in Irenaeus the transition in authority from oral to written gospel. In Origen this transition has been accomplished. For him it is the 4-fold [sic] gospel that is authoritative and no question of oral tradition appears as an alternative authority.

Thus we have a date slightly earlier, but not much earlier, than the concatenation of events at the time of the Decian Persecution.

Although for purposes different from those of the present book, another twentieth-century author finds a natural cut-off point in Christian history to be the decade after that in Chapter Five:[567]

> The martyr-death of Cyprian in 258 during the Valerian persecution marked the end of one of the most formative and productive eras of the Church's history. No really outstanding theologians or ecclesiastical personalities come upon the scene in the East or the West for the next 100 years.

(The end of this hundred years was after the catholic denomination had become officially approved and favoured by the government of the Roman Empire.)

It is also worth noting that the Decian Persecution marked the end of Origen's literary endeavours while those of Cyprian were just beginning.

Of course, Mormons and most Protestants would draw the line at the penning of the last book of the commonly-accepted New Testament, ignoring the fact that *1 Clement* and probably some other books not in the present canon were composed before this last book.

Widespread Distribution of A Precept or Teaching

As mentioned above, according to Irenaeus, Clement of Alexandria and Tertullian, to qualify as a part of the tradition, a matter must *inter alia* have been found throughout Christendom, not in only one geographical area. If a precept in the lists is found in only one or two localities or in only one or two authors, there is a good probability that it was a merely local or idiosyncratic view. There is no inherent authority for requiring two or three or any set number of authors or geographical areas in order to consider a particular precept to be within the apostolic law. However, ancient patterns of routine travel and interaction indicate that writers in pre-Decian Christianity generally coalesced in nine localities: Tunisia, Egypt, mainland Greece, western Turkey, France, Italy, Iraq-east Syria, Lebanon-west Syria, and Palestine. Indeed, President McDonald of Acadia Divinity College groups the writings of the eastern church fathers by geographical area when discussing the use of pre-New Testament literature because, he notes, "their tendencies are linked to their locale."[568] On the other hand, these were not totally exclusive, e.g. Origen wrote in both Egypt and Palestine and he and some other eastern Christian writers had visited the City of Rome. He also visited Christians throughout the eastern Mediterranean basin. It is only reasonable that an author who flourished in more than one of these areas should not be regarded as an independent witness to the acceptance of a point of ethics in more than one of these areas. In all events, the reader must look for the unity of teaching in order to determine what specifics were part of the original faith and practice. This is more clearly established when there is a wider distribution of authors and regions.

On the other hand, more weight might be given to those Christians who travelled much from one Christian community to another, e.g. Irenaeus, Justin Martyr and—par excellence—Origen. In addition to the Christian teachings handed down to them in their main area of activity, such travellers would have been acquainted with those in distant congregations and thus have been better enabled to perceive on what points there was a consensus among the different communities and to distinguish universal beliefs and practices from the merely local, to separate "custom" from "tradition" as differentiated in Chapter Four above.

Transmission by the Authorized Guardians: Which Church Officers?

According to Irenaeus, Clement of Alexandria and Tertullian, another qualification for a doctrine, practice or teaching to be considered part of the tradition is that it had been transmitted by authorized guardians instead of by people without apparent accreditation. However, the early sources are not clear as to who were the divinely sanctioned custodians. Not everyone identified the bishops as the sole guardians. *First Clement* 42 states that the apostles appointed both bishops and deacons as their successors, and uses "presbyter" and "bishop" interchangeably throughout the letter. According to Irenaeus, the guardians of the tradition were also the clergy, in some cases presbyters,[569] in others bishops,[570] and in still others presbyters and bishops together.[571] The greatest significance of this to the present study and the lists is that Tertullian, Clement of Alexandria and Origen were presbyters and not bishops.

In Clement of Alexandria it appears that the tradition of truth was transmitted through scholars and experts in the interpretation of Scriptures.[572] These worked as individuals within the church, teaching select students rather than members of the church as a whole. He opined that religious truth was transmitted not through those in what we today term holy orders but through talented Christians who were advanced in Bible study working separately from a clergy composed of bishops and presbyters.

In the Preface to *De Principiis*[573] Origen laid great and repeated emphasis on the proposition that the true teaching was imparted to "the church" but the Preface does not identify any officer or body within it as the authorized custodian of this teaching. At Preface 2f and 4.14 he agreed with Clement that there is sufficient scope within the tradition for a gifted individual to find scriptural truths that are concealed from less scholarly or less perceptive Christians.[574] At 4.9 Origen wrote that the apostles handed down the standards they had received in a succession from Christ to the "teachers" of the church. In his *Commentary* on Luke 10.30-36, Origen regarded both bishops and teachers (*didaskaloi*) to be the successors of the apostles as ministers of the church and therefore as guardians of the tradition.[575] In keeping with reliance on scholars who might not be clergy, Origen proposed in his *Commentary on the Gospel of Matthew* that whenever a question arises on a point of the Christian religion, the disputants should "go to any of those who have been appointed by God as teachers in the church".[576] To Origen, the guardians of the faith were "the teachers", not "the bishops", although he does not deny that through study a bishop may be also a scholar and therefore a teacher. Indeed, Origen had no specific word for "preacher" but called himself simply a *didaskalos* or teacher, a kind of educator.[577]

Such teachers held an ancient office in Christianity, older than that of presbyters (including bishops) and deacons. The usual title of Christ in the four Gospels is "teacher", especially in the synoptics.[578] In the twenty-seven-book New Testament He is referred to as "bishop" only in 1 Peter 2.25 and nowhere as "presbyter" or "elder". In 1 Corinthians 12.28 Paul places teachers below only apostles and prophets as God's appointees in the function of the church while governors/administrators, who were bishops and presbyters or the predecessors of bishops and presbyters, rank seventh or next to last. Second Peter 2.1 to 22 is a lengthy warning against false teachers in the church, which could well indicate that Christians of the time were acquainted with the office of an orthodox teacher. Second Timothy 4.3 is to the same effect. Hermas spoke of apostles, bishops, deacons and teachers as distinct ministries.[579] When Christianity was first introduced to a locality it was by apostles, prophets or teachers preaching the word, winning converts and nurturing them in the faith; bishops/presbyters and deacons did not make an appearance until after the labours of an apostle, prophet or teacher resulted in the establishment of a Christian congregation there.[580] It is prophets and teachers that Hermas mentioned as preaching Jesus.[581]

For over two centuries of early Christianity, the offices in 1 Corinthians 12.28 were not mutually exclusive: it was not as if a person were unable to hold only one of the eight offices at a time. Both Paul and Barnabas were teachers as well as prophets and apostles.[582] According to the Pastoral Epistles, most or all bishops/presbyters were also teachers.[583] Ephesians 4.11 links teachers with pastors as a function in the church distinct from those of apostles, prophets and preachers. *Didache* 15.1 speaks of bishops and deacons as performing the ministry of teachers and prophets, although the following verse appears to indicate that the latter two held a distinct ministry. It was not until the era described in Chapter Five of the present book as a time of departure from the original patterns of Christianity that the teaching office became exclusively monopolized by bishops and presbyters.[584] The offices of apostle, teacher and prophet disappeared by this point.[585] Another reason that Irenaeus of Lyons did not make a distinction between the teacher as distinct from the clergy of bishops, presbyters and deacons was that he combined the offices of teacher and cleric in his own person.[586]

In his earlier period, Tertullian's view was similar to that of Irenaeus that the apostolic tradition was transmitted through bishops and/or presbyters,[587] but for Tertullian it was the congregations as corporate bodies that were the guardians, with the bishops imparting traditional teaching only as agents of the congregations, and the succession-lists of bishops being merely the indicators that particular churches were of apostolic origin or at least in comity with churches that had been founded personally by apostles or apostolic men.[588] According to Tertullian, the later congregations received the fullness of the tradition from those of apostolic foundation by being in communion with the earlier ones.[589] However, in this earlier period Tertullian began to identify the church and the Holy Spirit as a single entity.[590] This was significant in his later views. Under the influence of Montanism, Tertullian engaged in an elitism comparable to that of the Alexandrians: the Spirit, the true church, was represented on earth by people of advanced spirituality and "not the Church which consists of a number of bishops."[591]

Thus it appears that there is legitimate latitude as to which categories of ancient Christians can be regarded as reliable sources of the tradition. Because of this, I have incorporated into the lists all available pre-Decian sources and allow the reader to draw his or her own conclusion based on reliable and objective considerations.

To my way of thinking, it is only common sense to prefer the evidence of church office-bearers over that of laypersons. We can safely assume that the former were more familiar with church matters, if only through their day-to-day experience (although they had probably received some formal training). Such experience would have extended over many years because at least elders/presbyters and bishops at this time held office for life. Such experience would also acquaint them with those troublesome borderline cases in which precise lines needed to be drawn and distinctions made and much study of the sources made in order to determine exactly what the traditional law provided and how it would apply to a specific case. Even a bishop who was no scholar but only an administrator would nevertheless have gained such experience if only as a judge in church courts.

By the same reasoning, the writings of Christians should be preferred to those of non-Christians because the latter's sources were second-hand or more remote and their knowledge not in the same depth as for Christian authors, except perhaps for Celsus.

If two contradictory statements by two different authors—or by the same author—cannot be harmonized and their qualifications and office within the church are the same, we must conclude that there was no single apostolic tradition on the point and that their statements reflect a purely personal or local—and most probably post-apostolic—view. However, the diligent reader will discover that these are rare indeed.

Conclusion

Again, the above considerations and advice have been added only to cover every possible contingency, whether probable or not, in order to treat the subject with exhaustive thoroughness and provide for the miniscule number of contradictions or inconsistencies among ancient Christian authors. (Pagan authors do contradict Christian ones on some points, but non-Christian attestations tend to be unreliable for the reasons given in the last preceding paragraph hereof.) Having in mind the opinions of Lohse, Marxsen and Heine, I anticipate that these lists will be intently scrutinized in order to seize upon the least discrepancy that their schools of thought might construe as support for their theses, even though such theses are founded on premises not based on empirical evidence. My considerations as to choosing among writers, classes of writers, books, dates and other factors are designed to minimize or provide other solution for what some people may strain to construe as disparate, varying, contradictory or able to "be brought into agreement only with difficulty."[592]

Notes on Terms Used

AEDILE. An elected Roman official who superintended public buildings and public works, such as (pagan) temples, communal baths, sewers, aqueducts, circuses (in the Roman sense), roads and streets. An aedile also regulated the market place, taverns, weights and measures, the costs of funerals, and (to prevent their dilapidation) private buildings. There was always more than one aedile at a time.

BATH-HOUSES; BATHING. Most inhabitants of the Roman Empire did not have bathtubs or shower stalls in their homes, but used communal pools shared by everyone in the geographical community. All bathers were stark naked when using the facility. Outside the largest cities, men and women used the same pool or bath. Although not all mixed bathhouses had different hours for males and females, by custom the proportions of bathers by sex were more common at some hours than others.

BAILMENT. A bailment is money or other tangible property that has been transferred to a person by the owner or another person in lawful possession, for a fee or gratuitously, for the benefit of one or both parties, with the expectation that it will be returned.

BIGAMY. Digamy was the state of having married more than once, but only to one spouse at a time. By contrast, bigamy was the state of having more than one spouse at the same time. Remarriage by a widow or widower is digamy but not bigamy.

BISHOP. In the pre-Decian period, a bishop had charge of only one congregation. The modern equivalent is a congregational pastor. Presbyters and deacons were associated with him in leading, governing and serving the congregation.

CATECHUMENS were persons desirous of joining the Christian church. In ancient times they were first obliged to be taught its beliefs and ethics. This was like our "church membership class" or "convert class" but was much more intensive, rigorous, and longer in duration.

In some places, this student status went on for years, and the catechumens had their lives monitored by their teachers.

CIRCUS (IN THE ROMAN SENSE). The Roman "circus" was a collection of games or combats which were often harmful or fatal to the participants, e.g. gladiatorial contests, combats between people and large carnivores, dangerous chariot-races. Because such sports are not encompassed by any modern English term, the phrase "(in the Roman sense)" is always added in the lists and is used to translate the Latin word "spectacula". For details of the games and other activities in the Roman circus, see pages 169 to 174 of Gregory J. Riley *One Jesus: Many Christs* (Minneapolis: Fortress Press, 2000 © 1997).

CLEANLINESS; IMPURE; IMPURITY; PURE; PURITY; UNCLEAN; UNCLEANESS. For extended, in-depth, treatments of these terms, see L. William Countryman *Dirt Greed and Sex: Sexual Ethics in the New Testament and Their Implications for Today* (Philadelphia: Fortress Press, 1988).

CONFESSOR. A "confessor" was a Christian who was imprisoned or otherwise suffered persecution for his faith but was not yet put to death. The term "confessor" applied both to an imprisoned Christian awaiting execution and to one who was later released without being executed. Confessors were different from martyrs in that martyrs had already been put to death for their faith.

CORONA. "Corona" is variously translated into English as "crown", "garland" or "wreath". It consisted of a circle of interwoven flowers and was worn around the head. This produced a surprisingly large Christian literature for a practice that Christians of the twenty-first century would be hard-pressed to find objectionable. Some pre-Decian believers so closely linked the corona with paganism that they regarded it as a confession of pagan faith on the part of the wearer.

DIGAMY. Digamy was the state of having married more than once, but only to one spouse at a time. By contrast, bigamy was the state of having more than one spouse at the same time. The most common situation of digamy comes about when a widow or widower takes a new spouse after the death of a previous spouse.

DEPOSIT. A form of bailment.

DIVINATION. Augury was the Roman practice of predicting the future by means of interpreting omens. Auruspices was soothsaying by means of examining the entrails of sacrificed animals. Ornithomancy was divination by interpreting the flight of birds.

GOLDEN RULE. The entries followed by "(positive form)" indicate that there is to be positive action: do to others what you wish them to do to you. The entries followed by "(negative form)" indicate merely refraining from action: do not do to others what you do not wish them to do to you.

FLAMEN. A priest who lit the sacrificial fires for a particular pagan deity. At first, each god had three flamens; later there were fifteen. A flamen held office for life or until the death of his wife because it was essential that she help him in the ceremonies.

LAST POST. This is the modern term for the ancient practice of playing a trumpet over a soldier's grave. (Tertulllan *De Corona* 11).

LECTIONARY. This term may not be completely accurate in that nothing to my knowledge, and certainly not in the texts of the homilies, indicates whether the Scripture readings which preceded them in public worship were in the form of (1) a complete unedited collection of biblical books, (2) separate monographs each containing a biblical book, or (3) a lectionary properly so called: a collection of selected portions of the Scriptures under one cover. In the lists, the word "lectionary" is used to indicate the Scripture readings in Christian public worship regardless of the form or completeness of the volume containing them.

LOFTY EYE (Didache 3.4). In a learned discussion at pages 149f of his monumental *The Didache: Faith, Hope & Life of the Earliest Christian Communities, 50-70 CE* (New York; Mahwah, NJ: Newman Press, 2003), Professor Aaron Milavec interprets "lofty eye" as a male looking at the eyes or top of the face and/or the feet of another man's wife or other respectable freewoman. In a culture that insisted on female modesty much more than our own, these body parts and the hands were the only part of a respectable woman not covered by clothing.

PALLIUM. A simple garment worn by both sexes and children among Greeks and Romans, especially philosophers and the poor. It consisted of a square piece of cloth taken directly from the loom, without tailoring or other processing. Versatile, it doubled as a curtain, carpet, or blanket, and could cover its owner's sleeping body, using the same pallium by night as by day. Unless intricately woven or decorated after weaving, it possessed no grace of appearance. Only the wealthy wore a different one in summer than in winter. In Tertullian's time, Roman citizens who were proud of their status or pretentious in dress wore the toga instead of the pallium whenever feasible.

By contrast, the TOGA was a formal garment, worn only by (male) Roman citizens and boys of wealthy families in public or on ceremonial occasions. It was so uncomfortable and difficult to keep on that it was not worn outside public view. It made body movements awkward, and the wearer usually needed to maintain his left arm bent to keep it in place. It was so difficult to put on that specially trained slaves were required to help dress the wearer.

PASCHA. The original languages do not make as clear a distinction as English between the Jewish Passover, the Feast of Unleavened Bread, Easter Sunday and the whole of the Easter season. In the lists, the untranslated word "Pascha" is used in reference to all of these.

PURPLE. In ancient times, purple was a very expensive dye. Its use was correspondingly confined to the wealthy and to high government officials.

VIRGINS were a distinct category of Christians who consecrated themselves so much to God and Christ that they became or remained lifelong celibates. Although most references to virgins in early Christian literature are to females, there were also male ones. Early virgins were unlike their successors, the monks and nuns, in a number of respects: virgins did not belong to formal separate organizations ("orders") nor were they governed through centralized or even local authorities, (2) they did not include poverty or obedience to a superior as a compulsory part of their ministry, (3) they owned property privately, and (4) they did not necessarily live in groups, under one roof, although writers like that of *Two Letters to Virgins* advocated prohibitions on certain types of shared accommodation. In short, unlike medieval and modern monks and nuns, being a virgin was largely an individual rather than a collective endeavour.

VOLUNTEER. This term is used in the lists in its legal sense, i.e. a person who voluntarily performs a service without a prior agreement that s/he be paid and as such has no legal right to payment. An early twenty-first-century example is a "squeegee kid".

WIDOW. The term "widow" has two meanings in early Christian literature. One is the ordinary sense of a woman whose husband has died; this is the only meaning in the four canonical Gospels. The other is a technical term which refers to a member of "the order of widows", a class of widows in the first sense who were supported or assisted by the church in return for prayer and other services, like the present-day nuns; this is the usual meaning in the *Didascalia*.

XEROPHAGY. Food cooked and served without oil, e.g. no fried food, nor oil-and-vinegar dressing on salad.

Guide to Authors and Works Cited in the Lists

in addition to books of the present New Testament

Abercius. Composed his own epitaph in the late second century AD. Bishop of Hierapolis in western Turkey.

Abercius Marcellus, Three Books to, Against the Cataphrygians. Turkey. AD 192.

Abraham, Testament of. First or second century AD.

Against All Heresies (pseudo-Tertullian). First half of third century AD. Rome.

De Aleatoribus = On Dice-Players. Late second century AD. A sermon of Latin (western Mediterranean) origin by a bishop.

Apollonius. Wrote against Montanism. AD 211.

Apostles, Epistle of. Anonymous (New Testament apocrypha). Written in Asia Minor or Egypt sometime between AD 140 and 160.

Appelles. Marcionite. Second century AD.

Aristides. Athenian philosopher. Wrote his *Apology* ca AD 125.

Athenagoras. Athenian philosopher. Wrote *Presbeia* (= *Embassy* = *Plea* = *Apology*) ca AD 177 and *Treatise on the Resurrection of the Dead* shortly afterwards.

Authentikos Logos = Authoritative Teaching. Alexandria, Egypt. Last few decades of second century AD, before Clement of Alexandria.

Babylonian Talmud. Rabbinic Judaism. Combines *Mishna* and *Tosephta* with *Gemara.* Among other matters, it contains descriptions of the practices and beliefs of Christians of the day, as seen from the viewpoint of Rabbinic Judaism, in order to condemn them. Completed ca AD 500-550. The material in the lists extracted from the tractate *Sanhedrin* dates from ca. AD 95. That from *Shabbath,* which is *Gemara,* from the late first or early second century AD, and most likely originates in Palestine. That from *Pesah* dates to the first half of the third century. The source of the excerpt from *Taanith* (on fasting) is from the middle of the third century.

Bardesan. Lived AD 154 to 222/223. Eastern Syria. His work is called *De Fato* (= *On Fate*) or *Liber legem regionum* (= *Book on the Laws of Countries*).

Barnabas, Letter of. Written in an Egyptian milieu sometime between AD 70 and 132. In widespread use during the early Christian centuries. Regarded as scripture by Clement of Alexandria, Origen, and the compilers of the Codex Sinaiticus (an early Christian Bible).

Baruch, Greek Apocalypse of, also known as *3 Baruch.* First or second century AD. Either an originally Jewish work with extensive Christian reworking, or a Christian book that made extensive use of Jewish traditions. Survives in Greek and Slavonic versions. Except where otherwise stated in the Chapter/Verse column, the precepts are identical in both versions.

Basilides. Gnostic. Flourished between AD 120 and 145.

Bruce Codex *Untitled Text.* Sethian Gnostic. First or second century AD.

Celsus. Pagan philosopher. Last third of second century AD. Well versed in Christian literature and practice, he wrote the earliest known systematic attack on Christianity. His book is reconstructed from Origen's *Against Celsus,* which preserves about seventy percent of the text. The numbers at the far right-hand side of the lists are the page numbers in R. Joseph Hoffman's translation, titled *On the True Doctrine* (New York: Oxford University Press, 1987). The Greek title can also mean true discourse, true teaching and true treatise.

Churches of Vienne and Lyons. *Letter to the Churches of Asia and Phrygia.* Gaul. AD 177.

1 Clement. Letter from the church at Rome to the church at Corinth. Between AD 70 and 97. Widely regarded as scripture in the early Christian centuries.

2 Clement. Anonymous. Rome, Alexandria or Corinth, most likely the last-mentioned. Mid-second century AD. The oldest surviving Christian sermon outside the New Testament.

Clement of Alexandria. Wrote in Alexandria, Egypt, between AD 192 and 202. Presbyter and dean/principal of the foremost Christian theological school of his time.

Cyprian. Bishop of Carthage, Tunisia, ca AD 248 to 258. Only his pre-Decian works containing ethical teaching are considered in the lists.

Dialogue of the Savior. Gnostic. Second century. The number to the left of the dot indicates the page number in *Nag Hammadi Codex III*; the number to the right indicates the line.

Diatessaron. A harmonized interweaving of the four Gospels, and perhaps of a fifth, by Tatian in the mid-second century AD. The standard text of the gospel in Syria until the fifth century.

Didache (= Teaching of the Twelve Apostles). Anonymous church manual written in Egypt or Syria in the late first century or early second century AD.

Didascalia Apostolorum. Church manual and code of church law compiled in the first three decades of the third century, probably in Syria, perhaps in Palestine.

Diognetus, Letter to. An anonymous apology for Christianity, possibly by a tutor of the Roman Emperor Marcus Aurelius (lived AD 121 to 180). Late second century or early third.

Doctrina (apostolorum). An early and independent witness of part of the text of the *Didache*, or of a still older common source for both the *Didache* and the *Letter of Barnabas*. The number subdivisions in the lists are those in Willy Rordorf and André Tuilier *La Doctrine des douze apôtres (Didachè)* (Paris: Cerf, 1978) pp. [207]-210.

Dionysius of Alexandria, called "Dionysius the Great". Student of Origen. Became head of the Alexandrian theological school circa AD 231. Bishop of Alexandria, AD 247/8 to 264/5. Only his pre-Decian work containing ethical teaching is considered in the lists.

Egerton 2 = British Museum Gospel = Unknown Gospel with Johannine Elements. First half of second century AD; probably older than the present Gospel of John. With one exception, all the extant manuscripts of the common-accepted New Testament are younger than this fragment.

Egyptians, Gospel of (Greek). Gnostic with Encratite tendencies. Second century. Not the same as the (Coptic) *Gospel of the Egyptians = Holy Book of the Great Invisible Spirit*. Number references are to Clement of Alexandria's *Stromata*, wherein it is quoted.

Elchasai, Book of. Gnostic. Of Semitic origin. Written in the first fifteen years of the second century AD. Number references are to the *Panarion* of Epiphanius of Salamis.

3/5 Esdras (= first two chapters of 2/4 Esdras). Anonymous. Of Latin (western Mediterranean) origin. Mid-second century to early third century AD. The first two chapters of 2 Esdras in the Revised Standard Version Apocrypha.

Exegesis on the Soul = Expository Treatise on the Soul. Anonymous. Third century AD. Number references are to Nag Hammadi Codex 2.

Galen. Pagan philosopher and physician. Lived ca. AD 129 to ca. 199. Resided in Rome and western Turkey. The material for the lists comes through brief quotations preserved in Arabic of otherwise lost works.

Gregory Thaumaturgus. Bishop of Neocaesarea in Pontus, AD 240s to 260. Only his pre-Decian works containing ethical teaching are considered in the lists. These are his *Metaphrase of Ecclesiastes*, written while a student of Origen's, and his *Oration and Panegyric to Origen*, written upon his graduation in AD 238.

Gnostic Apocalypse of Peter. Gnostic. Late second century or early third century AD. Also called *Coptic Gnostic Apocalypse of Peter*. Number references are to the page and line number(s) in Nag Hammadi Codex 7. Not the same as the (Ethiopic) *Revelation of Peter*, which in this book is referred to simply as the *Revelation of Peter*.

Hebrews, Gospel of. Jewish-Christian. Alexandria (Egypt). Second century AD.

Hermas, Shepherd of. Also known as the *Pastor of Hermas* and the *Pastor*. A series of revelations at Rome dating from the first half of the second century AD. Accepted as scripture by many early Christians.

Hippolytus. Studied under Irenaeus. Presbyter in central Italy in early third century. Rival bishop of Rome, AD 217 to 235. The books in the lists of known date are *Apostolic Tradition* AD 217, *Commentary on Daniel* AD 203, and *Philosophumena* between AD 222 and 235.

Hippolytus. See also: *Against All Heresies* (pseudo-Tertullian)

Ignatius. Bishop of Antioch. Just before AD 107 he wrote letters to the church at Rome; to bishop Polycarp of Smyrna, and to five churches in the Aegean basin: Ephesus, Magnesia, Philadelphia, Smyrna and Tralles.

Irenaeus. Bishop of Lyons in last quarter of the second century. Grew up a Christian in Smyrna (western Turkey), where he studied under Polycarp. His *Demonstratio* is also known as *Epideixis*, *Demonstration of the Apostolic Preaching* and *Proof of the Apostolic Preaching*.

Isaiah, Ascension of. Anonynous (New Testament apocrypha). Late first century or early second century AD.

Isidore. Disciple of Basilides. Second century AD.

James, 1 (First) Apocalypse of. Valentinian Gnostic. East Syria. End of second century to first half of third century AD. The number reference before the dot in the Chapter/Verse column is the page number in *Nag Hammadi Codex 5*; the number(s) after the dot indicate the line(s).

James, Ascents of. Greek-speaking Jewish-Christian. Second half of second century AD. Probably composed in what is today the country of Jordan. As reconstructed by Robert E. Van Voorst in *The Ascents of James: History and Theology of a Jewish-Christian Community* (Atlanta, Ga: Scholars Press, 1989). The original Greek being lost, it survives in two versions: the Latin translation of Rufinus, and Syriac. Except where otherwise stated in the Chapter/Verse column, the precepts are identical in both versions. Also called *The Steps of James.*

Jeou, Second Book of. Gnostic. First or second century AD.

Jerusalem Talmud. Rabbinic Judaism. Among other matters, it contains descriptions of the practices and beliefs of Christians of the day, as seen from the viewpoint of Rabbinic Judaism, in order to condemn them. Completed AD 400 to 425. The material cited in the lists originated from one or two generations after the Revolt of AD 135.

Job, Testament of. First century BC or first century AD.

John, Acts of. Anonynous (New Testament apocrypha). Mid-second century AD. East Syria, Turkey or Egypt.

John, Apocryphon of. Sethian Gnostic. Circa AD 185.

Judas, Gospel of. Sethian Gnostic. Between AD 100 and 180. Number references are to the pages in the Codex Tchacos.

Justin Martyr. Philosopher. Widely travelled. Flourished at Rome in the mid-second century AD.

(pseudo-Justin) See *Oratio ad Graecos.*

Justinus *Baruch.* Second century AD. Gnostic. The only extant quotations of this work are in 5.21 and 5.22 of Hippolytus' *Philosophumena.*

Kerygmata Petrou Anonymous. Jewish-Christian. Syria. Circa AD 200. As reconstructed by Georg Strecker in E. Hennecke: *New Testament Apocrypha* ed. Wm. Schneemelcher 1964; English trans. ed. by R. McL. Wilson (London: Lutterworth, 1965). Not the same as *Kerygma Petrou = The Preaching of Peter.*

De Laude Martyrii. Anonymous layman. Of Latin (western Mediterranean) origin. Between second century and AD 250.

Lucian of Samosata. Pagan satirist who had travelled widely in Syria, western Turkey, Italy and Gaul before settling at Athens. Written in the late AD 160s, soon after the events it describes, his *Passing of Peregrinus* is the story of an actual Cynic philosopher who had briefly converted to Christianity and been active in a Christian community in Syria-Palestine

Marcus Aurelius. (Pagan) Roman Emperor, lived AD 121 to 180, reigned AD 161 to 180.

Mary, Gospel of. Anonymous (New Testament apocrypha). Early third century AD. Gnostic. Number references are to the Berlin Gnostic Codex 8502.

Matthias, Traditions of. Egypt. First half of second century. May be the same as the *Gospel of Matthias*. Number references are to Clement of Alexandria's *Stromata*, wherein it is quoted.

Melito. Bishop of Sardis in western Turkey in the third quarter of the second century. Number references in his unidentified homily are to Stuart George Hall's *Melito of Sardis: On Pascha and Fragments* (Oxford; Clarendon, 1979) Fragment 2.

Midrash. Rabbinic Judaism. Among other matters, it contains descriptions of the practices and beliefs of Christians of the day, as seen from the viewpoint of Rabbinic Judaism, in order to condemn them. Completed around AD 1100. The material extracted in the affirmatives list dates from about AD 230.

Minucius Felix. *Octavius.* Rome or Tunisia. Written sometime between AD 166 and 249. Minucius Felix was a lawyer.

Mishna. Rabbinic Judaism. Among other matters, it contains descriptions of the practices and beliefs of Christians of the day, as seen from the viewpoint of Rabbinic Judaism, in order to condemn them. Compiled and edited in the first decade of the third century AD. The material cited in the affirmatives list come from the end of the first century.

Nazaraeans, Gospel of. Originated among Aramaic-speaking Jewish Christians in the first half of the second century AD.

Novatian. A leading presbyter a Rome in the mid-third century. Of all his works, only *On the Trinity* is indexed in the lists because it is the only one that all modern authorities agree was written before the Decian Persecution. Later a controversial figure, he founded an important schism. Martyred.

Oratio ad Graecos = Discourse to the Greeks. Anonymous; once mistakenly attributed to Justin Martyr. First half of third century AD. There are two recensions: a shorter one in Greek and a longer one in Syriac.

Origen (AD 185 to 254/255). Foremost Christian theologian and teacher of the third century. The most prolific Christian writer prior to Martin Luther. Presbyter after AD 230. From AD 202 to 230 or 233 he was the dean/principal of the same institution of higher learning as Clement of Alexandria. In AD 231 or 233 Origen established his own at Caesarea in Palestine. Travelled much in the eastern Roman Empire as a theological consultant to local churches. Most probable dates of individual works:

Against Celsus: between AD 245 and 249

Commentary on Canticles: between AD 244 and AD 247

Commentary on 1 Corinthians: between AD 232 and 242

Commentary on Ephesians between AD 232 and 244

Commentary on Genesis: between AD 224 and 234

Commentary on Hebrews: between AD 231 and 249

Commentary on Isaiah between AD 232 and 249

Commentary on John's Gospel: second quarter of third century

Commentary on Matthew's Gospel: between AD 246 and 248

Commentary on Philemon: circa AD 243

Commentary on Proverbs: AD 246/247

Commentary on Psalms: between AD 222 and 247

Commentary / Except on Psalm 1: AD 246/247

Commentary on Psalms 1 to 25: between AD 222 and 229

Commentary on Psalms 26 to 150: between AD 230 and 251

Commentary on Romans: between AD 239 and 245

Commentary on 1 Thessalonians: between AD 239 and 242

Commentary on Titus: circa AD 243

De Principiis: between AD 220 and 230

Dialogue with Heraclides: between AD 244 and 249

Exhortation to Martyrdom: between AD 234 and 238

Homilies on Canticles: between AD 244 and AD 247

Homilies on Exodus: between AD 238 and 244

Homilies on Ezekiel: between AD 239 and 242

Homilies on Genesis: between AD 238 and 244

Homilies on Isaiah: between AD 239 and 242

Homilies on Jeremiah: between AD 241 and 244

Homilies on Joshua: between AD 249 and 250

Homilies on Judges: between AD 239 and 242

Homilies on Leviticus: between AD 239 and 242

Homilies on Luke: between AD 233 and 234

Homilies on Numbers: between AD 244 and 249

Homilies on Psalms 36, 37 and 38: between AD 246 and 248

Other *Homilies on Psalms*: between AD 239 and 249

Homilies on Samuel: between AD 239 and 241

Letter to Friends in Alexandria: circa AD 231

On Prayer: between AD 233 and 235

On the Pasch: circa AD 245

Treatise on the Resurrection: between AD 222 and 225

Stromata: between AD 222 and 229

Due to the preservation of different parts of Origen's *Commentary on Romans* in different forms and manuscripts, some extracts from it in the lists bear notations beginning "3.5-5.7 at" in the chapter and verse column. The numbers to the right-hand side of the "at" indicate the subdivisions in "Commentaire sur l'Epître aux Romains" Tomes 5 and 6 of Jean Scherer's 1957 Cairo edition. Those not preceded by this designation are from Rufinus, condensation and translation into Latin.

De Pascha Computus. AD 243. Of Latin (western Mediterranean) origin.

Paul, Acts of. Western Turkey. Written by an orthodox presbyter ca AD 160-170, who was later removed from office for this attempt to forge new scripture. Parts of these *Acts* were very popular and widely circulated. The part known as *3 Corinthians* was in Syriac and Armenian Bibles for centuries.

Periodoi Petrou. Mid-third century AD. Number references are to *Philocalia* 23.

Perpetua and Felicitas, Passion of. Tunisia. Written shortly after the event in AD 202. Montanist.

Peter, Acts of. Eastern Mediterranean. Between AD 180 and 200.

Peter, Revelation of. First half of second century AD. Regarded as scripture by Clement of Alexandria and some other early Christians. Not the same as the *Coptic Gnostic Apocalypse of Peter*, which in this book is referred to as the *Gnostic Apocalypse of Peter*.

Philip, Gospel of. Syria. Between AD 150 and 250.

Pionius, Martyrdom of. Western Turkey. Circa AD 250.

Pliny the Younger. *Letter 10.96.* Circa AD 112. Letter to the Emperor Trajan by a pagan provincial governor of Bithynia (in northwestern Turkey). Friend of Tacitus.

Poimandres. Second century AD. Gnostic.

Polycarp. *Letter to the Philippians.* Western Turkey. First third of the second century. Polycarp was a disciple of the Apostle John and may have been the "angel of Smyrna" mentioned in Revelation 2.8.

Polycarp, Martyrdom of. Western Turkey. Circa AD 156.

Potamiaena and Basilides, Martyrdom of. These martyrdoms took place under Subatianus Aquila, who was prefect of Egypt from AD 205/6 to 210. Basilides, and perhaps Potamiaena, was a follower of Origen.

Ptolemy the Gnostic. Valentinian. Italy. Mid-second century AD. Number references in his *Letter to Flora* are to Epiphanius of Salamis *Panarion* 33.

Savior, Gospel of. Greek. Second century. The number subdivisions in the lists are those in Stephen Emmel "The Recently Published *Gospel of the Savior* ('Unbekanntes Berliner Evangelium'): Righting the Order of Pages and Events" (2002) 95 *Harvard Theological Review* 45-72 as reproduced at pp. 53-56 of Bart D. Ehrman *Lost Scriptures: Books That Did Not Make It into the New Testament* (Oxford: Oxford University Press, 2003)

Scillitan Martyrs. Tunisia. Late second century AD. Government/judicial account of a martyrdom that took place on 17 July AD 180.

Sentences of Sextus. Of Graeco-Roman origin. First half of second century.

Sibylline Oracles. Ascribed to ancient Roman pagan prophetess(es), this collection of books has mixed origins: some books are of Jewish origin but interpolated into by eastern Christians, others are of completely Christian composition, while some may have pagan roots but also subjected to Christian interpolation and expansion. Only material that is definitely Christian and written within the relevant time period is used for the two lists.

Silvanus, Teaching of. Late second century or early third century. Number references in the lists are to Nag Hammadi Codex VII.

Solomon, Odes of. Syria or Palestine. Late first to early third century AD. A collection of baptismal hymns.

Sophia of Jesus Christ. First two centuries AD. Gnostic. The number to the left of the dot on the lists is the page number in Nag Hammadi Codex III; the number to the right indicates the page number(s).

Tacitus. Pagan Roman noble and historian. The material which appears in the lists was written after AD 100. Friend of Pliny the Younger.

Tatian the Syrian. Mid-second century AD. Student of Justin Martyr and a confessor, later an Encratite. His *On Perfection According to the Saviour* is extant only in fragments in Clement of Alexandria's *Stromata* 3.12. See also *Diatessaron*.

Tertullian. A lawyer in Rome who upon conversion to Christianity gave up secular law and became a presbyter in Tunisia. Later a Montanist. The most prolific ante-Nicene Christian author writing in Latin. Approximate dates of individual works:

Against Hermogenes: AD 203/203

Against Marcion: between AD 207 and 212

Against Praxeas: ca. AD 213

Against the Valentinians: between AD 208 and 212

Answer to the Jews: between AD 197 and 202

Apology = Apologeticum: AD 197

Exhortation to Chastity: between AD 204 and 212

On Baptism: between AD 198 and 202

De Corona = On Garlands: AD 211/212

On Fasting: sometime in his Montanist period

On the Flesh of Christ: between AD 208 and 212

On Flight in Persecution: AD 211/212

On Idolatry: between AD 208 and 212

On Modesty = De Pudicitia: sometime in his Montanist period

On Monogamy: sometime in his Montanist period

Ad Nationes = To the Heathen: circa AD 197

On the Pallium: between AD 208 and 212

On Patience: between AD 198 and 203

On Penitence = De Poenitentia = On Repentance: between AD 198 and 203

On Prayer: between AD 198 and 202

On the Resurrection of the Flesh: between AD 208 and 212

On the Soul = De Anima: between AD 208 and 212

On the Veiling of Virgins = De Virginibus Velandis: or sometime in his Montanist period

Praescriptio = De Praescriptione Haereticorum: between AD 198 and 207

To Scapula: AD 212/213

Scorpiace: between AD 208 and 212

De Spectaculis = On Shows: between AD 198 and 204

Testimony of the Soul = De Testimonio Animae AD 197

To His Wife = Ad Uxorem: between AD 198 and 206

On Women's Apparel = De Cultu Feminarum: between AD 198 and 204

(pseudo-Tertullian) See: *Against All Heresies*.

Testimonies Against the Jews = To Quirinus (pseudo-Cyprian). Shortly before AD 249. Probably written in Tunisia. Some modern authors attribute it to Cyprian, bishop of Carthage.

Testimony of Truth. Gnostic with Encratite views. Alexandria, Egypt. Late second century AD or early third.

Theophilus. *To Autolycus*. Third quarter of second century. Theophilus was bishop of Antioch.

Thomas, Acts of. Eastern Syria. Early third century AD.

Thomas, (Gnostic) Gospel of. New Testament apocrypha. Between AD 150 and 200. Gnostic. Syria. Also know as the *Coptic Gospel of Thomas*. Not the same as the *(Infancy) Gospel of Thomas*.

Thomas the Contender. Syria. First half of third century AD.

Tosepta or *Tosephta*. Rabbinic Judaism. Among other matters, it contains descriptions of the practices and beliefs of Christians of the day, as seen from the viewpoint of Rabbinic Judaism, in order to condemn them. Published a generation after the *Mishna*, about AD 220 to 230. The material in the affirmatives list is from Rabbi Tarphon, who lived in the early second century AD.

Valentinus. Gnostic teacher and author. Flourished in the middle of the second century in Rome and Cyprus. Almost elected bishop of Rome.

Vienne and Lyons, Churches at. *Letter to the Churches of Asia and Phrygia*. Southern France. Shortly after AD 177.

Virgins, Two Letters to. Probably Syria. First half of third century AD. Anonymous, at one time incorrectly attributed to Clement of Rome.

Zephaniah, Apocalypse of. Between 100 BC and AD 175.

Zephyrinus, bishop of Rome. See: *Against All Heresies* (pseudo-Tertullian).

Sources Consulted for the Lists

The terms "fragment" and "fragments" do not necessarily mean that only a few lines survive or were consulted. They indicate only that the text available to me was not 100% complete. In many cases, the fragment or fragments run to several pages.

Abercius of Hierapolis [epitaph]

Abricius Marcellus, Three Books to = *Against the Cataphrygians* [fragments]

Abraham, Testament of [fragments]

Adam, Revelation of

Against All Heresies (pseudo-Tertullian)

Aleatoribus, De

Alexander of Cappadocia and Jerusalem *Letter to Demetrius, Bishop of Alexandria*

Alexander of Cappadocia and Jerusalem *Letter to Antioch*

Alexander of Cappadocia and Jerusalem *Letter to Antinoé* [fragment]

Alexander of Cappadocia and Jerusalem *Letter to Origen* [fragment]

Apelles *On Genesis 3* [fragment]

Apelles *Syllogisms* fragment 3

Apollinaris of Hierapolis *Apology for the Christians to Marcus Aurelius Antonium* [fragment]

Apollinaris of Hierapolis *On the Pasch* [fragments]

Apollonius [*Against the Montanists*] [fragments]

Apostles, Letter of

Aristides *Apology*

Aristo of Pella *Disputation between Jason and Papiscus* [fragments]

Ascension of Isaiah

Ascents of James [fragments]

Athenagoras *A Presbeia for the Christians*

Athenagoras *Treatise on the Resurrection of the Dead*

Attis, Hymn to

Attis, Exegesis of Hymn to

Aurelia Ammeia, Zotikos, Allexandreia, and Telesphoros [epitaph] for Allexandros

Aurelios Satorneinos [epitaph]

Authoritative Teaching = Authenikos logos

Bardesan *De Fato* = *Book of the Laws of Regions*

Barnabas, Letter of

Barsabas of Jerusalem *On Christ and the Churches*

2 Baruch = *Apocalypse of Baruch* = *Syriac Apocalypse of Baruch*

3 Baruch = *Greek Apocalypse of Baruch*

4 Baruch see *Jeremiah, Paraleipomena of*

Basilides *Exegetics* = *Commentary* Book 23 [fragment]

British Museum Gospel = *Unknown Gospel with Johannine Elements* = *Egerton 2* [fragment]

Bruce Codex *Untitled Text*

Carpus, Papylus and Agothonicé, Martyrdom of

Celsus *True Discourse* [fragments]

1 Clement

2 Clement

Clement of Alexandria *Against Judaizers* = *Ecclesiastical Canon*

Clement of Alexandria *Eclogae propheticae*

Clement of Alexandria *Excerpts on Theodotus*

Clement of Alexandria *Exhortation to Endurance* = *To the Newly Baptized*

Clement of Alexandria *Hypotyposes = Outlines* [fragments]

Clement of Alexandria *Letters* [fragments]

Clement of Alexandria *On Marriage* [fragment]

Clement of Alexandria *On Providence* [framents]

Clement of Alexandria *On Slander* [fragments]

Clement of Alexandria *On the Soul* [fragments]

Clement of Alexandria *Paedagogus*

Clement of Alexandria *Protrepticus*

Clement of Alexandria *Quis dives salvetur* Title variously translated as *The Rich Man's Salvation, What Rich Man Can Be Saved?, Who is the Rich Man that is Saved?,* and *Who is the Rich Man that Shall Be Saved?*

Clement of Alexandria *Stromata*

Clement of Alexandria [unidentified fragments]

3 Corinthians see *Paul, Acts of*

Cyprian *Letters* 1 to 5 and 7 to 43

Cyprian *On the Dress of Virgins*

Dialogue of the Saviour [fragments]

Diatessaron

Didache

Didascalia apostolorum

Diognetus, Letter to [fragments]

Dionysius of Alexandria *Luke: an Interpretation* [fragments]

Dionysius of Alexandria *On Nature* [fragments]

Dionysius of Alexandria *On Promises* [fragments]

Dionysius of Corinth *Letter to the Roman Church* [fragments]

Discourse on the Eighth and Ninth

Doctrina Apostolorum

Ebionities, Gospel of [fragments]

Egyptian Gospel Commentary (Skeat and Idris Bell)

Egyptians, Gospel of (Coptic) = *Holy Book of the Great Invisible Spirit*

Egyptians, Gospel of (Greek) [fragments in Clement of Alexandria *Stromata* 3]

Elchasai, Book of [fragments]

Epictetus, in Arrian *Discourses of Epictetus* 4.7.6

Epiphanes *Justice* [fragments in Hippolytus *Philosophumena* 6]

3/5 Esdras

5 Esdras

6 Esdras

Eugnostus Letter of

Eve, Gospel of [fragment]

Exegesis on the Soul = *Expository Treatise on the Soul* [fragment]

Ezekiel, Apocryphon of

Gaius of Rome *Dialogue with Proclus* [fragments]

Galus of Rome *Disputation* [fragments]

Gaius of Rome *On the Alogoi* [fragments]

Galen in Walzer, Richard *Galen on Jews and Christians* (Oxford: University Press, 1949)

Gibson, Elsa (trans. and ed.) *The "Christians for Christians" Inscriptions of Phrygia: Greek Texts, Translation and Commentary* (Missoula, Montana: Scholars Press, 1978) Inscriptions 22 and 42

Gnostic Apocalypse of Peter

Gospel of the Savior [fragments]

Gospel of Truth

Gregory Thaumaturgus *Metaphrase of Ecclesiastes*

Gregory Thaumaturgus *Oration and Panegyric to Origen* = *Prosphoneticus*

Hadrian, Roman Emperor *Rescript to Municius Fundamus*

Hebrews, Gospel of [fragments]

Hegesippus *Hypomnemata* [fragments]

Heracleon the Gnostic *Commentary on the Gospel of John* [fragments]

Herford, R. Travers *Christianity in Talmud and Midrash* (London: Williams & Norgate, 1903)

Hermas, Shepherd of

Hippolytus *Against Plato = On the Cause of the Universe* [fragment]

Hippolytus *Apostolic Tradition*

Hippolytus *Citation de Hippolyte sous le nom d'Irénée*

Hippolytus *Commentary on Canticles*

Hippolytus *Commentary on Daniel*

Hippolytus *Commentary on Ezekiel* [fragment]

Hippolytus *Commentary on Genesis 1.5* [fragment]

Hippolytus *Commentary on Genesis 2.7* [fragment]

Hippolytus *Commentary on Genesis 27.1 to 28.5* [fragment]

Hippolytus *Commentary on Genesis 49.3 to 49.27* [fragment]

Hippolytus *Commentary on Proverbs* [fragments]

Hippolytus *Homily on the Psalms* [fragments]

Hippolytus *Letter to the Empress Mammaea on the Resurrection* [fragments]

Hippolytus *Little Labyrinth = Against the Heresy of Artemon* [fragments]

Hippolytus *On a Maiden of Corinth and Magistrianus* [fragments]

Hippolytus *On Christ and Antichrist*

Hippolytus *On David and Goliath*

Hippolytus *On Elkanah and Hannah* [fragments]

Hippolytus *On Judges 6.11*

Hippolytus *On Judges 6.27*

Hippolytus *On Judges 15.19*

Hippolytus *On Psalm 23* [fragments]

Hippolytus *On the Apocalypse = On the Resurrection* [fragments]

Hippolytus *On the Beginning of Isaiah* [fragment]

Hippolytus *On the Blessings of Balaam* [fragment]

Hippolytus *On the Blessings of Isaac and Jacob*

Hippolytus *On the Blessings of Moses*

Hippolytus *On the Distribution of Talents* [fragment]

Hippolytus *On the Great Song* [fragment]

Hippolytus *On the Pasch* [fragment]

Hippolytus *On the Psalms* [fragments]

Hippolytus *On the Quails and Manna* [fragment]

Hippolytus *On the Resurrection and Incorruptibility* [fragment]

Hippolytus *On the Two Thieves* [fragments]

Hippolytus *On the Witch of Endor* [fragment]

Hippolytus *Oration on Daniel, Second* [fragments]

Hippolytus *Philosophumena = Refutation of All Heresies* 1-2

Hippolytus *Philosophumena = Refutation of All Heresies* 4-10

Hippolytus *Scholia on Daniel*

Hippolytus *Syntagma = Against Thirty-two Heresies = Against All Heresies = Against Noetus* [fragments]

Hypomnemata see *Oratio ad Graecos*

Hypostasis of the Archons

Ignatius of Antioch *Letters*

Ignorance of God

Irenaeus of Lyons *The Blessings of Balaam* see Hippolytus

Irenaeus of Lyons *Against Heresies*

Irenaeus of Lyons *Demonstration of the Apostolic Preaching*

Irenaeus of Lyons *On Judges 6.27* see Hippolytus

Irenaeus of Lyons *Letter to a certain Alexandrian* [fragment]

Irenaeus of Lyons *Letter to Florinus on the Sole Sovereignty of God* [fragment]

Irenaeus of Lyons *Letter to Victor on Easter* [fragments]

Irenaeus of Lyons *Letter to Victor on Florinus* [fragment]

Irenaeus of Lyons *The Ogdoad* [fragment]

Isidore *The Adhering Soul* [fragment]

Isidore *Ethics* [fragment]

Isidore *Expositions of the Prophet Parchor* [= *Barcoph*] [fragment]

Jacob, Testament of

James, Apocryphon of

James, 1 Apocalypse of [fragments]

James, Ascents of [fragments]

James, Protoevangelium of

1 Jeou

2 Jeou

Jesus's Wife, Gospel of [fragment]

Job, Testament of

Jeremiah, Paraleipomena of = *4 Baruch*

John, Acts of [fragments]

John, Apocryphon of

Judas, Gospel of [fragments]

Julius Africanus *Chronography* = *Chronicles* [fragments]

Julius Africanus *Kestoi* [fragments]

Julius Africanus *Letter to Aristides*

Julius Africanus *Letter to Origen*

Julius Cassianus *On Eunuchry* = *De contientia* [fragment]

Julius Cassianus *Exegetica* [fragment]

Justin Martyr *Against Marcion* [fragment]

Justin Martyr *1 Apology*

Justin Martyr *2 Apology*

Justin Martyr *Dialogue with Trypho*

Justin and Companions, Martyrdom of = *Acts of Justin and Companions*

Justinus *Baruch* [fragments]

Kerygma Petrou = Preaching of Peter [fragments]

Kerygmata Petrou = Preachings of Peter

Krator = Monad

De laude martyrii

Lucian of Samosata *Alexander the False Prophet*

Lucian of Samosata *The Passing of Perigrinus*

Lyons, confessors of *Letter to Eleutherus of Rome* [fragment]

Marcionite Prologues to the Letters of Paul

Marcus Aurelius, Roman Emperor *Meditations* 11.3

Marsanes [fragments]

Mary, Gospel of

Matthias, Traditions of [fragments in Clement of Alexandria *Stromata*]

Melito of Sardis *Apology = Petition Addressed to Marcus Aurelius Antoninus* [fragments]

Melito of Sardis *Book of Extracts = Prooemium Eklogôn* [fragment]

Melito of Sardis *Discourse in the Presence of Antoninus Caesar = Oratio ad Antoninum Caesarem*

Melito of Sardis *Discourse on the Body and Soul* Book 3 [fragment]

Melito of Sardis *fragment de Méliton, évêque d'Attique ville*

Melito of Sardis *Hymn to the Father*

Melito of Sardis *Letter to Onesimus*

Melito of Sardis *On Baptism* [fragment]

Melito of Sardis *On Genesis 22* [fragments]

Melito of Sardis *On our Lord's Passion* [fragment]

Melito of Sardis *On the Cross* [fragment]

Melito of Sardis *On the Devil and the Revelation of John* [fragment]

Melito of Sardis *On the Faith* [fragment]

Melito of Sardis *On the Body and Soul* [fragment]

Melito of Sardis *On the Incarnation of Christ* [fragment]

Melito of Sardis *On the Lord's Day* [fragment]

Melito of Sardis *On the Pasch*

Melito of Sardis [unidentified fragment]

Melito of Sardis [unidentified homily]

Midrash see Herford, R. Travers

Miltiades [fragments]

Minucius Felix *Octavius*

Mishna see Herford, R. Travers

Monoimus [fragments in Hippolytus *Philosophumena* 8]

De montibus Sina et Sion

Moses, Testament of [fragment]

Muratorian Canon [fragment]

Naassene Hymn

Naassene Sermon [fragment in Hippolytus *Philosophumena* 5]

Narcissus of Jerusalem *Encyclical Letter on the Date of Easter* [fragment]

Nazareans, Gospel of [fragments]

Novatian [two] *Letters to Cyprian*

Novatian *On the Trinity*

Oratio ad Graecos (pseudo-Justin)

Origen *Against Celsus*

Origen *Commentary on Canticles* [fragments]

Origen *Commentary on Colossians* [fragment in Pamphilus *Apology*]

Origen *Commentary on 1 Corinthians* 14.34-35 [catena fragment]

Origen *Commentary on 1 Corinthians* 15.23 [fragment]

Origen *Commentary on Ephesians* [fragments]

Origen *Commentary on Ezekiel* [fragment in *Philocalia*]

Origen *Commentary on Galatians* [fragments in Pamphilus *Apology*]

Origen *Commentary on Genesis* [fragments]

Origen *Commentary on Genesis 1.16-18*

Origen *Commentary on Genesis 1.-5.1* [fragments]

Origen *Commentary on Genesis 3* [fragments in *Philocalia*]

Origen *Commentary on Hebrews* [fragments in Pamphilus *Apology*]

Origen *Commentary on Hosea* [fragment]

Origen *Commentary on Isaiah* [fragments in Pamphilus *Apology*]

Origen *Commentary on John* [fragments]

Origen *Commentary on Luke* [fragments]

Origen *Commentary on Matthew* Books 2 [fragment] and 10-14

Origen *Commentary on Matthew Commentariorum Series* [selected fragments]

Origen *Commentary on Philemon* [fragment in Pamphilus *Apology*]

Origen *Commentary on Psalm 1* [fragment]

Origen *Commentary on Psalm 4.6*

Origen *Commentary on Psalms 26 to 150*

Origen *Commentary on Psalm 50*

Origen *Commentary on Psalms* [fragments]

Origen *Commentary on Romans* [only translation of Rufinus, *Philocalia*, Cairo Museum Papyrus 88748, and Vaticanus gr. 762]

Origen *Commentary on Romans 3.5 to 5.7*

Origen *Commentary on 1 Thessalonians* [fragment in Jerome]

Origen *Commentary on Titus* [fragments in Pamphilus *Apology*]

Origen *De Principiis*

Origen *Dialogue with Candidus*

Origen *Dialogue with Heraclides and the Bishops with Him*

Origen *Exhortation to Martyrdom*

Origen *Homilies on Acts* [fragment]

Origen *Homilies on Canticles*

Origen *Homilies on Exodus*

Origen *Homilies on Ezekiel*

Origen *Homilies on Genesis*

Origen *Homilies on Hebrews* [fragments]

Origen *Homilies on Isaiah* [fragments]

Origen *Homilies on Jeremiah* [fragments]

Origen *Homilies on Joshua*

Origen *Homilies on Judges*

Origen *Homilies on Leviticus*

Origen *Homilies on Luke* [fragments]

Origen *Homilies on Numbers*

Origen *Homilies on Psalms* [fragments]

Origen *Homilies on Samuel* [fragments]

Origen *Letter to Alexander of Cappadocia and Jerusalem* [fragment]

Origen *Letter to Ambrose* [fragment]

Origen *Letter to Fabian of Rome* see *Letter to Ambrose*

Origen *Letter to Firmilian of Cappadocia* [fragment]

Origen *Letter to friends in Alexandria*

Origen *Letter to Gobar* [fragments]

Origen *Letter to Gregory*

Origen *Letter to Julius Africanus*

Origen *On First Principles = De principiis*

Origen *On Nature* [fragment]

Origen *On Prayer*

Origen *On the Pasch*

Origen *Scholia on Exodus* [fragments]

Origen *Scholia on the Apocalypse*

Origen *Scholia on the Whole Psalter* [fragments]

Origen *Scholia on Psalms 1 to 25 = Alexandrian Commentary on Psalms 1 to 25* [fragments]

Origen *Selecta on Psalms* (Lommatzsch 11.384 to 391) [fragment]

Origen *Selecta on Psalms* (Lommatzsch 12.129) [fragment]

Origen *Selecta on Psalms* (Lommatzsch 12.160 to 162) [fragment]

Origen *Selecta on Psalms* (Lommatzsch 13.82f)

Origen *Stromateis* Book 6 [fragment]

Origen *Stromateis* [unidentified quotation]

Origen *Treatise on the Resurrection* [fragments in Pamphilus *Apology*]

Pantaenus [fragments]

Papias *Expositions of the Oracles of the Lord* [fragments]

De pascha computus

Paul, Acts of [fragments]

Periodoi Petrou [fragment]

Perpetua and Felicitas, Passion of

Peter, Acts of

Peter and the Twelve Apostles, Acts of [fragments]

Peter, Coptic Gnostic Apocalypse of

Peter, Gospel of [fragment]

Peter *Letter to Philip* [fragments]

Peter, Revelation of (Ethiopic Text I and Akhmim Fragment)

Peter and the Twelve Apostles, Acts of [fragments]

Philip, Gospel of

Pionius, Martyrdom of

Pliny the Younger *Letter* 10.96

Poimandres

Polycarp *Letter to the Philippians*

Polycarp, Martyrdom of

Polycrates of Ephesus *Letter to Victor and the Roman Church* [fragments]

Tertullian *Against the Valentinians*

Tertullian *Answer to the Jews*

Tertullian *Apologeticum*

Tertullian *De censu animae* [fragment]

Tertullian *De exstasi* [fragment]

Tertullian *De paradiso = De spe fidelium* [fragment]

Tertullian *Exhortation to Chastity*

Tertullian *On Baptism*

Tertullian *On the Flesh of Christ*

Tertullian *On Fasting*

Tertullian *On Flight in Persecution*

Tertullian *On Garlands = On Crowns = De corona*

Tertullian *On Idolatry*

Tertullian *On Modesty*

Tertullian *On Monogamy*

Tertullian *On Patience*

Tertullian *On Penitence*

Tertullian *On Prayer*

Tertullian *On the Pallium*

Tertullian *On the Resurrection of the Flesh*

Tertullian *On the Soul*

Tertullian *On the Veiling of Virgins*

Tertullian *On Women's Apparel*

Tertullian *De praescriptione haereticorum*

Tertullian *Scorpiace*

Tertullian *De spectaculis*

Tertullian *Testimony of the Soul*

Tertullian *To his Wife*

Tertullian *To Scapula*

Tertullian *To the Martyrs*

Tertullian *To the Nations = Ad Nationes*

Testimonies against the Jews (pseudo-Cyprian)

Testimony of Truth [fragments]

Theophilus of Antioch *To Autolycus*

Thomas, Acts of

Thomas, Gospel of (Gnostic)

Thomas, Gospel of (Infancy)

Thomas the Contender

Tosephta see Herford, R. Travers

Trajan, Roman Emperor *Letter to Pliny Secundus*

Trimorphic Protennoia [fragments]

Valentinus [fragments]

Vanity of Idols (pseudo-Cyprian)

Vienne and Lyons, Churches at *Letter to the Churches of Asia and Phrygia* [fragments]

Virginity, Two Letters on = Two Letters to Virgins (pseudo-Clement)

Wessely, Charles (ed.) *Les plus anciens monuments du Christianisme écrit sur papyrus* (1907) 4 *Patriologia orientalis*, reprinted 1946

Xanthippe and Polyxena, Acts of

Zephaniah, Apocryphon of

The twenty-seven books of the New Testament as commonly received

Bibliography of Secondary Sources

Avis, Paul "The Churches of the Anglican Communion" in his *The Christian Church: An Introduction to the Major Traditions* (London: SPCK, 2002) pp. [132]-156

Barclay, William *The Men, The Making, The Message of the New Testament* (Philadelphia: Westminster, 1976)

Barkley, Gary Wayne introduction to *Origen: Homilies on Leviticus 1-16* (Washington, D.C.: Catholic University of America Press, 1990)

Barr, James *Holy Scripture; Canon, Authority, Criticism* (Oxford: Clarendon, 1983)

Barthel, Manfred *What the Bible Really Says* (New York; Avenel. N. J.: Wings, 1992) Translation and adaptation by Mark Howson of *Was Wirklich in der Bibel Steht* (Econ; 1980)

Beach, Waldo, and H. Richard Niebuhr *Christian Ethics: Sources of the Living Tradition* (New York: Ronald Press, 1955)

Beagle, Dewey M. *Scripture, Tradition and Infallibility* (Grand Rapids, MI: Eerdmans, 1973)

Bebis, George "The Concept of Tradition in the Fathers of the Church" (1970) 15 *Greek Orthodox Theological Review* pp. 22-55

Benko, Stephen *Pagan Rome and the Early Christians* (Bloomington, Indiana University Press, 1984)

Bigg, Charles *The Christian Platonists of Alexandria* (Oxford: Clarendon, 1886; reissued with revisions by F. E. Brightman, Oxford: Clarendon: 1913; reprinted 1968)

Birch, Bruce C., and Larry L. Rasmussen *Bible & Ethics in the Christian Life* Rev. ed. (Minneapolis: Augsburg. 1989)

Bochmuehl, Markus "Jewish and Christian Public Ethics in the Early Roman Empire" in Graham N. Stanton and Guy G. Stousma (ed.) *Tolerance and Intolerance in Early Judaism and Christianity* (Cambridge: Cambridge University Press, 1998) pp. 342-355

Bochmuehl, Markus *Jewish Law in Gentile Churches: Halakhah and the Beginning of Christian Public Ethics* (Edinburgh: T & T Clark, 2000)

Bourgeault, Guy *Décalogue et morale chrétienne: enquête patristique sur l'utilisation et l'interprétation du Décalogue de c. 60 à c.220* (Paris: Desclée; Montreal: Bellarmin, 1971)

Brooks, R. J. *Ask the Bible* (New York: Gramercy, 1989)

Brown, Harold O. J. "Proclamation & Preservation: The Necessity & Temptations of Church Tradition" in James S. Cutsinger (ed.) *Reclaiming the Great Tradition: Evangelicals, Catholics & Orthodox in Dialogue* (Downers Grove, Illinois: InterVarsity, 1997) pp. [69]-87

Bruce, Frederick F. *The Canon of Scripture* (Downer's Grove, Ill.: InterVarsity, 1988)

Bruce, Frederick F. *Peter, Stephen, James and John: Studies in Early Non-Pauline Christianity* (Grand Rapids, MI: Eerdmans, 1980)

Bruce, Frederick F. *The Spreading Flame: The Rise and Progress of Christianity from its First Beginnings to the Conversion of the English* (Greenwood, S.C.: Attic Press, 1978 c. 1958)

Bruce, Frederick F., and E. G. Ruff (ed.) *Holy Book and Holy Tradition: International Colloquium Held in the Faculty of Theology, University of Manchester* (Grand Rapids, MI: Eerdmans, 1968)

Burns, J. Patout "On Rebaptism: Social Organization in the Third Century Church" (1993) 1 *Journal of Early Christian Studies* pp. 367 to 403

Cahill, Lisa Sowle "Christian Character, Biblical Community and Human Values" in William P. Brown (ed.) *Character and Scripture: Moral Formation, Community and Biblical Interpretation* (Grand Rapids, MI: William B. Eerdmans, 2002) pp. 3-17

Campenhausen, Hans von *Ecclesiastical Authority and Spiritual Power in the Church of the First Three Centuries* translated by A. Baker (London: Adam and Charles Black 1969). Translation of *Kirchliches Amt und Geistliche Vollmacht* (Tübingen: J.C. Mohr (Paul Siebeck), 1953)

Campenhausen, Hans von *Tradition and Life in the Church: Essays and Lectures in Church History* translated by A. V. Littledale (Philadelphia; Fortress, 1968). Translation of *Tradition und Leben: Krafte der der Kirchgeschichte* (Tübingen: Mohr, 1960)

Carmody, Denise Lardner, and John Tully Carmody *Christian Ethics: An Introduction through History and Current Issues* (Englewood Cliffs, NJ: Prentice-Hall, 1993)

Chester, Andrew "Messianism, Torah and Early Christian Tradition" in Graham N. Stanton and Guy G. Stousma (ed.) *Tolerance and Intolerance in Early Judaism and Christianity* (Cambridge: Cambridge University Press, 1998) pp. 318-341

Chilton, Bruce D., and James I. H. MacDonald *Jesus and the Ethics of the Kingdom* (London. SPCK, 1987)

Clark, Elizabeth A. *Reading Renunciation: Asceticism and Scripture in Early Christianity* (Princeton, NJ: Princeton University Press, 1999)

Cole, Graham "Sola Scriptura: Some Historical and Contemporary Perspectives" (1990), 104 *The Churchman: A Journal of Anglican Theology* pp. 20-34

Congar, Yves M.-J. *Tradition and Traditions; An Historical and a Theological Essay* Translated Michael Naseby and Thomas Rainborough (New York: Macmillan, 1967 c. 1966). Translation of *La tradition et les traditions* (Paris: Athème Fayard, 1960 and 1961)

Conybeare, F. C. *The Armenian Apology and Acts of Apollonius and Other Monuments of Early Christianity* 2d ed. (London: Swan Sonnenschein; New York: Macmillan, 1896)

Countryman, L. William *Dirt Greed and Sex: Sexual Ethics in the New Testament and Their Implications for Today* (Philadelphia: Fortress Press, 1988)

Cosgrove, Charles H. *Appealing to Scripture in Moral Debate: Five Hermeneutical Rules* (Grand Rapids, MI: Eerdmans, 2002)

Cross, Frank L. *The Early Christian Fathers* (London: Duckworth, 1960)

Crouzel, Henri *Origen* Translated by A. S. Worrall (Edinburgh: T. & T. Clark, 1989) trans. of *Origène* (1985)

Cullman, Oscar *The Early Church* ed. A. J. B. Higgins (London: S.C.M., 1956)

Curran, Charles E. "Method in Moral Theology: An Overview from an American Perspective" (1980) 18 *Studia Moralia* pp. 107- 128

Davies, W. D. "The Moral Teaching of the Early Church" in James M. Efird (ed.) *The Use of the Old Testament in the New and Other Essays: Studies in Honor of William Franklin Stinespring* (Durham, NC: Duke University Press, 1972) pp. 310-332

Davies, W. D. "The Relevance of the Moral Teaching of the Early Church" in E. Earle Ellis and Max Wilcox (ed.) *Neotestamentica et Semitica: Studies in Honour of Matthew Black* (Edinburgh: T. & T. Clark, 1969) pp. 30-49

Dodd, C. H. "Ennomous Khristou" in his *More New Testament Studies* (Grand Rapids, MI: Eerdmans, 1968) pp. 134-148

Dodd, C. H. *Gospel and Law: The Relation of Faith and Ethics in Early Christianity* (New York: Columbia University Press, 1950)

Dodds, Eric R. *Pagan and Christian in an Age of Anxiety* (Cambridge: Cambridge University Press, 1965)

Edwards, Otis Carl, Jr. *How Holy Writ was Written* (Nashville, Tenn.: Abingdon, 1989)

Ehrhardt, Arnold *The Apostolic Succession in the First Two Centuries of the Church* (London; Lutterworth, 1953)

Ehrman, Bart D. *The Orthodox Corruption of Scripture: The Effect of Early Christological Controversies on the Text of the New Testament* (New York; Oxford: Oxford University Press, 1993)

Elliott, James K. (ed. and trans.) *Apocryphal New Testament* rev. ed. (Oxford: Oxford University Press, 1993)

Eusebius *The Church History of Eusebius* Translated by Arthur Cushman McGiffert (New York; Christian Literature Co.; Oxford and London: Parker, 1890 reprinted Grand Rapids, MI: Eerdmans; Edinburgh: T & T Clark, 1997). Translation of *Historia ecclesiastica*

Eusebius *History of the Church from Christ to Constantine* Translated by G. A. Williamson (Minneapolis: Augsburg, 1965). Translation of *Historia ecclesiastica*

Eusebius *Preparation évangélique* Translated by Edouard des Places (Paris: Cerf, 1987). Translation of Praeparatio evangelica

Evans, Craig A. *Ancient Texts for New Testament Studies: A Guide to the Background Literature* (Peabody, MA: Hendrickson, 2005)

Evans, Craig A. *Noncanonical Writings and New Testament Interpretation* (Peabody, MA: Hendrickson, 1992)

Fairweather, Ian C. M., and James I. H. MacDonald *The Quest for Christian Ethics: An Inquiry into Ethics and Christian Ethics* (Edinburgh: Hansel Press, 1984)

Faruqi, Ismail R. A. al- *Christian Ethics: A Historical and Systematic Analysis of its Dominant Ideas* (Montreal: McGill, 1967)

Ferguson, Everett (ed.) *Christian Life: Ethics, Morality, and Discipline in the Early Church* (New York and London: Garland, 1993)

Ferguson, Everett "Dionysius of Alexandria" in *Encyclopedia of Early Christianity* (New York: Garland, 1990) pp. 266f

Fischer, Bonifatius "Limitations of Latin in Representing Greek" as reprinted in Metzger, Bruce M. *The Early Versions of the New Testament: Their Origins Transmission and Limitations* (Oxford: Clarendon, 1977) pp. 362-374. Originally published as "Das neue Testament in lateinischer Sprache" in K. Aland (ed.) *Die altern Übersetzungen des Neuen Testaments, die Kirchenvätersitate und lektionare* (Berlin; New York, 1972) pp. 1-92

Flesseman-Van Leer, E. *Tradition and Scripture in the Early Church* (Assen, Netherlands: van Gorckum, 1954)

Florovsky, Georges "The Function of Tradition in the Ancient Church" (1964) 9 *Greek Orthodox Theological Review* pp. 181-200

Foerster, Werner (ed.) *Gnosis: A Selection of Gnostic Texts* trans R. McL. Wilson (Oxford: Clarendon, 1972-74)

Forell, George W. *History of Christian Ethics vol. 1: From the New Testament to Augustine* (Minneapolis; Augsburg, 1979)

Frend, William H. C. *Saints and Sinners in the Early Church: Differing and Conflicting Traditions in the First Six Centuries* (Wilmington: Glazier, 1985)

Freyne, Séan "The Bible and Christian Morality" in *Introduction to Christian Ethics: A Reader* ed. Ronald P. Hamel and Kenneth R, Hynes (New York: Paulist, 1989) pp. 9-32

Froehlich, Karlfried (ed. and trans.) *Biblical Interpretation in the Early Church* (Philadelphia: Fortress, 1984)

Fuch, Josef *Christian Morality: The Word becomes Flesh* (Dublin: Gill and Macmillan; Washington, DC: Georgetown University Press, 1987) Trans. Brian McNeil

Gager, John G. *Kingdom and Community: The Social World of Early Christianity* (Englewood Cliffs: Prentice-Hall, 1975)

Gamble, Harry Y. *The New Testament Canon: Its Making and Meaning* (Philadelphia: Fortress, 1985)

Gibson, Elsa *The "Christians for Christians" Inscriptions of Phrygia: Greek Texts, Translation and Commentary* (Missoula, Montana: Scholars Press, 1978)

Goodspeed, Edgar J. *A History of Early Christian Literature* rev. Robert M. Grant (Chicago: University of Chicago Press. 1966; Midway reprint 1983)

Grant, Michael *Greeks and Romans: A Social History* (London: Weidenfeld and Nicolson, 1992)

Grant, Robert M. *After the New Testament* (Philadelphia: Fortress, 1967)

Grant, Robert M. *Augustus to Constantine: The Rise and Triumph of Christianity in the Roman World* new preface, foreword and bibliography by Margaret M. Mitchell (Louisville, Ky: Westminster John Knox, 2004)

Grenz, Stanley J. *The Moral Quest: Foundations of Christian Ethics* (Downer's Grove, Ill.: InterVarsity, 1997)

Gustafson, James M. *Can Ethics be Christian?* (Chicago: University of Chicago Press, 1975)

Gustafson, James M. *Christ and the Moral Life* (New York: Harper & Row, 1968)

Gustafson, James M. *Protestant and Roman Catholic Ethics: Prospects for Rapprochement* (Chicago and London: University of Chicago Press, 1978)

Hanson, Richard P. C. *Origen's Doctrine of Tradition* (London: SPCK, 1954)

Hanson, Richard P. C. *Tradition in the Early Church* (London: S.C.M., 1962)

Harden, J. M. *An Introduction to Ethiopic Christian Literature* (London: SPCK; New York: Macmillan, 1926)

Harnack, Adolf von *The Constitution & Law of the Church in the First Two Centuries* Translated by F. L. Pogson (London; Williams & Norgate; New York: Putnam, 1910). Translation of *Entschung und Entwickelung der Kirchenverfassung und des Kirchenrechts in den zwei ersten Jahrhunderten* (Leipzig: Hinrichs, 1910)

Harris, Carl Vernon *Origen of Alexandria's Interpretation of the Teacher's Function in the Early Christian Hierarchy and Community* (New York; American Press, 1966)

Hart, Colin *The Ethics of Jesus* (Cambridge: Grove, 1997)

Harvey, William Wigan "Introduction" to *S. Irenaei episcopi Lugdenensis libros quinque adversus haereses* (Cantbridiae: Typis academicus, 1857)

Haymes, Brian "The Baptist and Pentecostal Churches" in Paul Avis (ed.) *The Christian Church: An Introduction to the Major Traditions* (London: SPCK, 2002) pp. [107]-131

Hays, Richard B. *The Moral Vision of the New Testament: Community, Cross, New Creation; A Contemporary Introduction to New Testament Ethics* (New York: HarperSanFrancisco, 1996)

Hazlett, Ian (ed.) *Early Christianity: Origin and Evolution to AD 600* (London: SPCK, 1991)

Hebblethwaite, Brian *Christian Ethics in the Modern Age* (Philadelphia: Westminster, 1982)

Hein, Kenneth *Eucharist and Excommunication: A Study in Early Christian Doctrine and Discipline* 2d ed. (Bern: Lang, 1975)

Heine, Ronald E. "Introduction" to *Origen: Homilies on Genesis and Exodus* (Washington, D.C.: Catholic University of America Press, 1982)

Heine, Suzanne *Women and Early Christianity: A Reappraisal* Translated by John Bowden (Minneapolis: Augsburg, 1988). Translation of *Frauen der frühen Christenheit* (Vandenhoeck & Ruprecht, 1986)

Helgeland, John "The Early Church and War: The Sociology of Idolatry" in Charles J. Reid (ed.) *Peace in a Nuclear Age: The Bishops' Pastoral Letter in Perspective* (Washington, D.C.: Catholic University of America Press, c1986) pp. 34-47

Helgeland, John, Robert J. Daly and J. Patout Burns *Christians and the Military: The Early Experience* edited by Robert J. Daley (Philadelphia: Fortress: 1985)

Henry, Carl F. *Christian Personal Ethics* (Grand Rapids, MI: Eerdmans, 1957)

Holloway, Zoe "A Conceptual Foundation for Using the Mosaic Law in Christian Ethics" (2006), 120 *The Churchman: A Journal of Anglican Theology* Part 1: pp.119-144; Part 2: pp. 213-230

Houlden, J. L. *Ethics and the New Testament* (London: Mowbray, 1973)

James, Montague R. (ed. and trans.) *Apocryphal New Testament* (Oxford: Clarendon, 1953)

Jersild, Paul T. *Making Moral Decisions: A Christian Approach to Personal and Social Ethics* (Minneapolis: Fortress, 1990)

Koester, Helmut *History and Literature of Early Christianity* (Philadelphia: Fortress; Berlin and New York: Walter De Gruyter, 1982) Translation by the author of his *Einfrührung in das Neue Testament* (Berlin and New York: Walter De Gruyter)

Lane Fox, Robin *Pagans and Christians* (New York: Knopf, 1987)

Layton, Bentley *The Gnostic Scriptures: A New Translation* (Garden City, N.Y.: Doubleday, 1987)

Lebreton, Jules, and Jacques Zeiller *The History of the Primitive Church* Translated by E. Messenger (New York; Macmillan, 1949)

Leyerle, Blake "Clement of Alexandria on the Importance of Table Etiquette" (1995) 3 *Journal of Early Christian Studies* pp. 123-141

Lienhard, Joseph T. introduction to *Origen: Homilies on Luke; Fragments on Luke* (Washington, D.C.: Catholic University of America Press, 1996)

Lillie, William *The Law of Christ: The Christian Ethic and Modern Problems* (Edinburgh: Saint Andrew Press, 1966)

Lillie, William *Studies in New Testament Ethics* (Edinburgh; London: Oliver and Boyd, 1961)

Lohse, Eduard *Theological Ethics of the New Testament* Translated by M. Eugene Boring (Minneapolis: Fortress, 1991). Translation of *Theologische Ethik des Neuen Testaments* (Stuttgart: W. Kohlhammner, 1988)

Longenecker, Richard N. *New Testament Social Ethics for Today* (Grand Rapids, MI: Eerdmans, 1984)

Mackey, James Patrick *Tradition and Change in the Church* (Dayton, Ohio: Pflaum Press, 1968)

Marrou, Henri Irénée *A History of Education in Antiquity* Translated by George Lamb (New York: Sheed and Ward, 1956). Translation of *Histoire de l'éducation dans l'antiquité* (Paris: Seuil, 1955)

Marxsen, Willi *New Testament Foundations for Christian Ethics* (Minneapolis: Fortress, 1993). Translated by O. C. Dean Jr. of *"Christliche" und Christliche Ethik in Neuen Testament* (Gütersloh: Gütersloher Verlaghaus Gerd Mohn)

McDonald, J. Ian H. *The Crucible of Christian Morality* (London; New York: Routledge, 1998)

McDonald, Lee M. *The Biblical Canon: Its Origin, Transmission, and Authority* (Peabody, MA: Hendrickson, 2007)

McDonald, Lee M. *The Formation of the Christian Biblical Canon* rev. ed. (Peabody, MA: Hendrickson, 1995)

Meeks, Wayne A. *The Moral World of the First Christians* (Philadelphia: Westminster, 1986)

Meeks, Wayne A. *The Origins of Christian Morality: The First Two Centuries* (New Haven, CT: Yale University Press, 1993)

Meeks, Wayne A. "Understanding Early Christian Ethics" (1986) 105 *Journal of Biblical Literature* pp. 3-11

Melton, Isaac (Father Andrew) "A Response to Harold O. J. Brown" in James S. Cutsinger (ed.) *Reclaiming the Great Tradition: Evangelicals, Catholics & Orthodox in Dialogue* (Downers Grove, Illinois: InterVarsity, 1997) pp. 87-99

Metzger, Bruce M. *The Canon of the New Testament: Its Origins, Development and Significance* (Oxford: Clarendon, 1987)

Metzger, Bruce M. *The Early Versions of the New Testament: Their Origins Transmission and Limitations* (Oxford: Clarendon, 1977)

Mikre-Sellassie, G. A. "The Bible and Its Canon in the Ethiopian Orthodox Church" (1993) 44 *Technical Papers for the Bible Translator* pp. 111-123

Milavec, Aaron *The Didache: Faith, Hope & Life of the Earliest Christian Communities, 50-70 C.E.* (New York; Mahwah, N.J.: Newman Press, 2003)

Mondésert, Claude "La tradition apostolique chez S. Justin (1979) 23 *l'Année canonique* pp. [145]-158

Moreschini, Claudio, and Enrico Norelli *Early Christian Greek and Latin Literature: A Literary History Vol. 1: From Paul to the Age of Constantine* (Peabody, MA: Hendrickson, 2005) Translation by Matthew J. O'Connell of *Storia della lettertura cristiana antica greca e latina Vol. 1: Da Paolo all'età constantiniana* (Brescia:Morcelliana Editrice of Brescia, 1995)

Munier, Charles "La tradition apostolique chez Tertullien (1979) 23 *l'Année canonique* pp. [175]-192

Murphy, Francis X. *Moral Teaching in the Primitive Church* (Glen Rock, N.J.: Paulist, 1968)

Nautin, Pierre *Lettres et écrivains des IIe et IIIe siècles* (Paris: Cerf, 1961)

Nautin. Pierre *Origène: sa vie et son oeuvre* (Paris: Beauchesne, 1977)

Neuhaus, Richard John "A New Thing: Ecumenism at the Threshold of the Third Millennium" in James S. Cutsinger (ed.) *Reclaiming the Great Tradition: Evangelicals, Catholics & Orthodox in Dialogue* (Downers Grove, Illinois: InterVarsity, 1997) pp. [47]-60

Ogletree, Thomas W. *The Use of the Bible in Christian Ethics* (Philadelphia: Fortress, 1983)

Osborn, Eric F. *Ethical Patterns in Early Christian Thought* (Cambridge: Cambridge University Press, 1976)

Pagels, Elaine *Beyond Belief: The Secret Gospel of Thomas* (New York: Random House, 2003)

Pamphilus of Caesarea, and Eusebius of Caesarea *Apologie pour Origène* Translated and edited by René Amacker and Éric Junod (Paris: Cerf, 2002) Translation of *Apologeticum sancti martyris pro Origene*

Piepcorn, Arthur C. "Theological Observer" (1972) 43 *Concordia Theological Monthly* pp. 449-453

Pinckaers, Servais *The Sources of Christian Ethics* (Washington, D.C.: Catholic University of American Press, 1995). Translated by Mary Thomas Noble of the 3rd edition of *Les sources de la morale chrétienne* (Fribourg: University Press, 1993)

Porter, Jean *Moral Actions and Christian Ethics* (Cambridge: Cambridge University Press, 1995)

Prestige, G. L. *Fathers and Heretics: Six Studies in Dogmatic Faith* (London: SPCK, 1940; reprinted 1954)

Prinzivalli, E. "Didaskalos" in *Encyclopedia of the Early Church* (New York: Oxford University Press, 1992) vol. 1 p. 235

Quasten, Johannes *Patrology* (Utrecht: Spectrum, 1950; reprinted Westminster, MD: Christian Classics 1986)

Rahner, Karl *Penance in the Early Church* Translated by Lionel Swain (New York: Crossroad, 1982). Translation of *Frühe Bussgeschichte in Einzslungtersuchungen* (Zurich: Benziger, 1971)

Ramsey, Boniface *Beginning to Read the Fathers* (New York; Mahwah, NJ: Paulist, 1985)

Rhyne, C(lyde) Thomas *Faith Establishes the Law* (Chico, Calif.: Scholars Press, 1981)

Richard, Lucien *Is There A Christian Ethics?* (New York: Paulist, 1988)

Riesenfeld, Harald *The Gospel Tradition* (Philadelphia: Fortress. 1970)

Riley, Gregory J. *One Jesus, Many Christs: How Jesus Inspired Not One True Christianity, But Many* (Minneapolis: Fortress, 2000)

Robinson, James M. (ed.) *The Nag Hammadi Library in English* (San Francisco: Harper & Row, 1978)

Rooney, Paul *Divine Command Morality* (Aldershot: Avebury, 1996)

Rordorf, Willy "An Aspect of the Judeo-Christian Ethic: The Two Ways" in Jonathan A Draper (ed.) *The Didache in Modern Research* (Leiden: E. J. Brill, 1996) pp. [148]-164

Rordorf, Willy "La tradition apostolique dans la Didachè" (1979) 23 *l'Année canonique* pp. [105]-114

Rordorf, Willy, and André Schneider *L'évolution du concept de tradition dans l'église ancienne* (Berne: P. Lang, 1982)

Roukema, Riemer *The Diversity of Laws in Origen's Commentary on Romans* (Amsterdam: Free University Press, 1988)

Rufinus *Sur la falsification des livres d'Origène* Translated and edited by René Amacker and Éric Junod (Paris: Cerf, 2002) Translation of *De adulteratione librorum Origenis*

Schlink, Edmund *Theology of the Lutheran Confessions* Translated by Paul F. Koehneke and J. A. Bouman (Philadelphia: Fortress, 1961)

Schneemelcher, Wilhelm (ed.) *New Testament Apocrypha* Translated and ed. by R. McL. Wilson (Cambridge: James Clarke; Louisville, Ky: Westminster/John Knox, 1991-92). Translation of *Neutestamentliche Apokryphen* (Tubingen: Mohr, 1989-90)

Schrage, Wolfgang *The Ethics of the New Testament* Translated by David W. Green (Philadelphia: Fortress, 1988). Translation of *Ethik des Neuen Testaments* (Gottingen: Vandenhoeck & Ruprecht, 1982)

Dillistone, F. W., G. W. H. Lampe, F. J. Taylor and D. E. M. Harrison *Scripture and Tradition: Essays by F. W. Dillistone, G. W. H. Lampe, F. J. Taylor and D. E. M. Harrison* (London: Lutterworth, 1955)

Sloyan, Gerard S. *Is Christ the End of the Law?* (Philadelphia: Fortress, 1978)

Smith, Morton *The Secret Gospel: The Discovery and Interpretation of the Secret Gospel according to Mark* (New York: Harper & Row, c1973)

Spanneut, Michel *Tertullien et les premiers moralistes africains* (Gembloux: J. Duculot; Paris: P. Lethielleux, 1969)

Spohn, William C. *What Are They Saying About Scripture and Ethics?* (New York: Paulist, 1984)

Spohn, William C. *What Are They Saying About Scripture and Ethics?* (New York and Mahwah, NJ: Paulist, 1995)

Stark, Rodney *The Rise of Christianity: A Sociologist Reconsiders History* (Princeton, N.J.: Princeton University Press. 1996)

Stendahl, Kirster "The Apocalypse of John and the Epistles of Paul in the Muratorian Fragment" in William Klassen and Grydon T. Snyder (eds) *Current Issues in New Testament Interpretation: Essays in honor of Otto A. Piper* (New York: Harper & Brothers, 1962) pp. 239-245

Stroker, William D. *Extracanonical Sayings of Jesus* (Atlanta, Ga: Scholars Press, 1989)

Stylianopoulos, Theodore "Tradition in the New Testament" (1970) 15 *Greek Orthodox Theological Review* pp. 7-21

Sundberg, Albert C. "The Making of the New Testament Canon" in Charles M. Laymon (ed.) *The Interpreter's One-Volume Commentary on the Bible* (Nashville and New York: Abingdon, 1971)

Sundberg, Albert C. *The Old Testament of the Early Church* (Cambridge, MA: Harvard University Press; London: Oxford University Press, 1964; reprinted New York; Kraus Reprint, 1969)

Swift, Louis J. "Search the Scriptures: Patristic Exegesis and the *Ius Belli*" in Charles J. Reid Jr. (ed.) *Peace in a Nuclear Age: The Bishops' Pastoral Letter in Perspective* (Washington, D.C. : Catholic University of America Press, c1986) pp. 48-68

Tavard, Georges Henri *Holy Writ or Holy Church: The Crisis of the Protestant Reformation* (New York: Harper and Brothers, 1959)

Theron, Daniel J. "The Most Probable Date of the First Epistle of Clement to the Corinthians (1989) 21 *Studia Patristica* pp. [106]-121

Tyson, Joseph B. *The New Testament and Early Christianity* (New York: Macmillan; London: Collier Macmillan, 1984)

Unnick, W. C. van *Tarsus or Jerusalem?: The City of Paul's Youth* (London: Epworth, 1962)

Verhey, Allen *The Great Reversal: Ethics and the New Testament* (Grand Rapids, MI: Eerdmans, 1984

Verhey, Allen *Remembering Jesus: Community, Scripture and the Moral Life* (Grand Rapids, MI: Eerdmans, 2002)

Veyne, Paul *A History of Private Life* vol. 1 *From Pagan Rome to Byzantium* Translated by Arthur Goldhammer (Cambridge, MA: Belknap Press of Harvard University Press, 1987). Translation of *Histoire de vie privée* t. 1 *De l'Empire romain à l'an mil* (Paris: Seuil, 1985)

Vincent of Lérins *Commonitorium*

Walsh, William J., and John P. Langan "Patristic Social Consciousness—The Church and the Poor" in John C. Haughey (ed.) *The Faith that Does Justice: Examining the Christian Sources for Social Change* (New York: Paulist, 1977) pp. 113-151

Webber, Robert E. *Ancient-Future Faith: Rethinking Evangelicalism for a Postmodern World* (Grand Rapids, MI: Baker, 1999)Wessely, Charles (ed. and trans.) «Les plus anciens monuments du Christianisme écrit sur papyrus" (1907), 4 *Patrologia orientalis*

Welborn, L. L. "On the Date of First Clement" (1984) 29 *Papers of the Chicago Society of Biblical Research* pp. 35-54

Westerholm, Stephen *Israel's Law and the Church's Faith: Paul and his Recent Interpreters* (Grand Rapids, MI: Eerdmans, 1988)

White, James R. *The King James Only Controversy: Can You Trust the Modern Translations?* (Minneapolis: Bethany, 1995)

White, Reginald E. O. *Christian Ethics: The Historical Development* (Atlanta: John Knox; London: Paternoster, 1981)

Whittaker, Molly *Jews and Christians: Greco-Roman Views* (Cambridge: Cambridge University Press, 1984)

Wilken, Robert L. *The Christians as the Romans Saw Them* 2d ed. (New Haven, CT: Yale University Press, 2003)

Wilken, Robert L. "The Lives of the Saints and the Pursuit of Virtue" in his *Remembering the Christian Past* (Grand Rapids, MI: Eerdmans, 1995) pp. 121-144. Originally published in Val Ambrose McInnes (ed.) *New Visions* (New York: 1993) pp. 55-76

Wilken, Robert L. "Memory and the Christian Intellectual Life" in his *Remembering the Christian Past* (Grand Rapids, MI: Eerdmans, 1995) pp. 165-180. Originally published in Frank F. Birtel (ed.) *Reasoned Faith* (New York: 1993) pp. 141-155

Wilken, Robert L. *The Spirit of Early Christian Thought: Seeking the Face of God* (New Haven, CT: Yale University Press, 2003)

Williams, Daniel H. *Retrieving the Tradition and Renewing Evangelicalism: A Primer for Suspicious Protestants* (Grand Rapids, MI; Cambridge, UK: Eerdmans, 1999)

Williams, Robert L. "Persecution" in *Encyclopedia of Early Christianity* (New York: Garland, 1990) pp. 712-715

Wilson, R. McL. "Ethics and the Gnostics" in Wolfgang Schrage (ed.) *Studien zum Text und zur Ethik des Neuen Testaments: Festschrift zum 80. Geburtstag von Heinrich Greeven* (Berlin: Walter De Gruyter, 1986)

Winger, Joseph M. *By What Law? The Meaning of Nomos in the Letters of Paul* (Atlanta: Scholars. 1992)

Winslow, Donald F, "Tradition" in *Encyclopedia of Early Christianity* (New York: Garland, 1990) p. 906

Wogaman, J. Philip *Christian Ethics: A Historical Introduction* (Louisville, Ky: Westminster/ John Knox, 1993)

Wogaman, J. Philip, and Douglas M. Strong *Readings in Christian Ethics: A Historical Sourcebook* (Louisville, Ky: Westminster John Knox Press, c1996)

Womer, Jan L. (ed. and trans.) *Morality and Ethics in Early Christianity* (Philadelphia: Fortress, 1987)

Woods, G. F. *A Defence of Theological Ethics* (Cambridge: University Press, 1966)

Yoder, John H. "War as a Moral Problem in the Early Church: The Historian's Hermeneutical Assumptions" in Harvey L. Dyck (ed.) *The Pacifist Impulse in Historical Perspective* (Toronto: University of Toronto Press, 1996)

Translations Used

ANF = *The Ante-Nicene Fathers; Translations of The Writings of the Fathers down to A.D. 325*, edited by Alexander Roberts and James Donaldson. American reprint ed. by A. Cleveland Coxe (Buffalo, NY: Christian Literature Publishing Co., 1885-96; continuously reprinted Grand Rapids, MI: Wm. B. Eerdmans; Peabody, MA: Hendrickson)

Abercius of Hierapolis [epitaph]

(1) in Quasten's *Patrology* (Westminster, Maryland: Christian Classics, 1950 reprinted 1986) vol. 1 p. 172 "All Rights Reserved" but no copyright holder indicated in book

(2) in Robert M Grant *Second-Century Christianity: A Collection of Fragments* at pages 101f at 102 line 19 (London; SPCK, 1946) no copyright information in book

Abercius Marcellus, Three Books to = *Against the Cataphrygians* ascribed to Asterius Urbanus in ANF 7.335-337

Abraham, Testament of [fragments] ANF 10:[185]-201

Against All Heresies (pseudo-Tertullian) ANF 3:649-654

Aleatoribus, De trans Scott T Carroll under title "An Early Church Sermon Against Gambling (CPL 60)" (1991), 8 *Second Century* 2,83 © The Second Century Journal Inc.

Apelles *On Genesis 3* [fragment] ANF 1:570f

Apelles *Syllogisms* fragment 3 in Robert M. Grant *Second-Century Christianity: A Collection of Fragments* pp. 84 to 88 at 85 (in fragment 3) (London; SPCK, 1946) no copyright information in book

Apollonius [*Against the Montanists*] [fragments] ANF 8:775f

Apostles, Epistle of Montague Rhodes James *The Apocryphal New Testament* pp. 485-503 (Oxford: Clarendon, 1953 reprinted 1963) no copyright information in book

Aristides *Apology* ANF 10:[263]-279

Ascension of Isaiah trans. C. Detlef G. Muller in Schneemelcher *New Testament Apocrypha* ET R. McL. Wilson revised ed. (Cambridge, UK: James Clarke & Co.; Louisville, Ky: Westminster/John Knox, 1991) vol. 2 pp. 605-619 © J. C. B. Mohr (Paul Siebeck) Tubingen 1990 ET © James Clarke & Co. Ltd, 1991

Athenagoras *A Presbeia for the Christians* ANF 2:129-148

Athenagoras *Treatise on the Resurrection of the Dead* ANF 2:149-162

Authoritative Teaching = Authenikos Logos Translated by George W. MacRae; Edited by Douglas M. Parrott at pp. [278]-283 of *The Nag Hammadi Library in English* edited by James M. Robinson (San Francisco: Harper & Row, 1981

Bardesan *De Fato = Book of the Laws of Regions*

(1) ANF 8:723-734
(2) Eusebius *La préparation évangélique* trans Edouard des Places (Paris: Cerf, 1980) © Editions du Cerf, 1980, 1987 Livre VI at VI.10.46 Sources chrétiennes 266

Barnabas, Letter of ANF 1:137-149

Baruch, Greek Apocalypse of trans. H. E. Gaylord Jr at vol. 1 pp. 662 to 679 at 668f, 672-675 and 679 of *The Old Testament Pseudepigrapha* ed. by James H. Charlesworth (Garden City: Doubleday, 1983-1985) © James H. Charlesworth 1983

Basilides *Exegetics = Commentary* Book 23 [fragment] Robert M Grant *Second-Century Christianity: A Collection of Fragments* (London: SPCK, 1946) pp. 18-21 at 20 no copyright information in book

British Museum Gospel = Unknown Gospel with Johannine Elements = Egerton 2 [fragment] published by H Idris Bell and T C Skeat at pp. [569]f of *The Apocryphal New Testament* trans Montague Rhodes James (Oxford: Clarendon, 1953 repr 1963). First published by Sir Harold Idris Bell and T C Skeat in *Fragments of an Unknown Gospel and Other Early Christian Papyri* (Oxford: 1935) (London: British Museum, 1935) no copyright information in book

Bruce Codex *Untitled Text* Chapter 16 at pp. 43f *The Books of Jeu and the Untitled Text in the Bruce Codex* at pp 43f trans Violet McDermot; ed. Carl Schmidt (Leiden: Brill, 1978) Series: Nag Hammadi Studies XII; Coptic Gnostic Library © E. J. Brill, Leiden, The Netherlands

Celsus *True Discourse* [fragments] trans. Joseph Hoffman under the name *On the True Doctrine* (New York: Oxford University Press 1987) © 1987 Oxford University Press, Inc.

1 Clement ANF 1:[5]-21, 10:[229]-248

2 Clement ANF 10:[251]-256

Clement of Alexandria *Eclogae propheticae* ANF 8:43-50

Clement of Alexandria *Exhortation to Endurance = To the Newly Baptized* in *Clement of Alexandria With an English Translation* by G W Butterworth (London: Wm Heinemann; New York: G P Putnam's Sons, 1919) pp. 370-377 with English and Greek on facing pages Loeb Classical Library. First printed 1919, reprinted 1939, 1953, 1960

Clement of Alexandria fragments ANF 2:571-586

Clement of Alexandria *Letters* [fragments] ANF 2:581 heading 10; 585 heading 12 fragments 6-8

Clement of Alexandria *On Slander* [fragments] ANF 2:580 Fragment 7

Clement of Alexandria *Paedagogus*

All but 2.10: ANF 2:209-296

2.10: Simon P. Wood *Clement of Alexandria: Christ the Educator* (New York: Fathers of the Church, 1954) pp. 164-178

Clement of Alexandria *Protrepticus* ANF 2:171-206

Clement of Alexandria *Quis Dives Salvetur* ANF 2:591-604

Clement of Alexandria *Stromata*

All but Book 3: ANF 2:299-567

Book 3: *Alexandrian Christianity: Selected Translations* by John Ernest Leonard Oulton and Henry Chadwick pp. 40-92 (London: SCM; Philadelphia: Westminster Press, 1954) no copyright information in book

Clement of Alexandria *Unidentified Fragments* ANF 2:580f, 585

3 Corinthians see *Paul, Acts of*

Cyprian *Letters* 1 to 5 and 7 to 43 (CSEL), ANF 5 under numbers 65, 60, 64, 61, 4 and 35, 2, 3, 8, 7, 36, 6, 5, 10, 9, 11-14, 20, 21, 16, 18f, 17, 22, 24, 23, 30 (same as CSEL), 25, 31, 26-29, 15, 32-34 and 37-42

Cyprian *On the Dress of Virgins* ANF 5:430-436

Dialogue of the Saviour trans. Harold W. Attridge at pp. 230-238 of James M. Robinson *The Nag Hammadi Library in English* (San Francisco, 1981) © 1978 E. J. Brill, Leiden, The Netherlands

Diatessaron ANF 10:43-129

Didache ANF 7:377-382

Didascalia apostolorum; The Syriac Version Translated and Accompanied by the Verona Latin Fragments by R. Hugh Connolly (Oxford: Clarendon, 1929) no copyright information in book

Diognetus, Letter to ANF 1:25-30

Dionysius of Alexandria *On Nature* [fragments] ANF 6:84-91

Dionysius of Alexandria *On Promises* [fragments] ANF 6:81-84

Dionysius of Corinth *Letter to the Roman Church* [fragments] ANF 8:765

Doctrina apostolorum (in Latin original) edited by Willy Rordorf and André Tuilier in *La Doctrine des Douze Apôtres = Didachè* (Paris: Editions du Cerf, 1978) pp. [207]-210 © Editions du Cerf, 1978

Egyptians, (Greek) Gospel of Vol. 1 Pages 209-213 trans Wilhelm Schneemelcher in his *New Testament Apocrypha* ET R. McL. Wilson revised ed. (Cambridge, UK: James Clarke & Co.; Louisville, Ky: Westminster/John Knox, 1991) © J. C. B. Mohr (Paul Siebeck) Tubingen 1990 ET © James Clarke & Co. Ltd, 1991

Elchasai, Book of [fragments] trans. Johannes Irmscher in Wilhelm Schneemelcher (ed.) *New Testament Apocrypha* English translation by R. McL. Wilson revised ed. (Cambridge, UK: James Clarke & Co.; Louisville, Ky: Westminster/John Knox, 1991) vol. 2 pp. 687-689 © J. C. B. Mohr (Paul Siebeck) Tubingen 1990 ET © James Clarke & Co. Ltd, 1991

3/5 Esdras (under name *2 Esdras*) in *Revised Standard Version of the Bible* at Apocrypha pp. 24 and 26 © Division of Christian Education of the National Council of Churches of Christ in the United States of America 1946, 1952, 1971 – 475 Riverside Drive, Room 872, New York, New York, 10115-0050

Exegesis on the Soul = Expository Treatise on the Soul trans. William C. Robinson Jr. pp. [180]-187 of *Nag Hammadi Library in English* (San Francisco, 1981) © 1978 E. J. Brill, Leiden, The Netherlands [fragment]

Galen in Walzer, Richard *Galen on Jews and Christians* References 1, 5 and 6 (Oxford: University Press, 1949) References 1, 5 and 6 no copyright information in book

Gnostic Apocalypse of Peter trans Roger A. Bullard under title *Apocalypse of Peter* at pp. 340 to 345 of James M. Robinson *The Nag Hammadi Library in English* (San Francisco, 1981) © 1978 E. J. Brill, Leiden, The Netherlands; not the same as *Peter, Revelation of* (Ethiopic Text I and Akhmim Fragment) below

Gospel of the Savior trans. Stephen Emmel in "The Recently Published *Gospel of the Savior* ("Unbekanntes Berliner Evangelium"): Righting the Order of Pages and Events" *Harvard Theological Review* 95 (2002) 45-72 as reprinted at pp. 53 to 56 of Bart

D. Ehrman *Lost Scriptures: Books That Did Not Make It into the New Testament* (Oxford: Oxford University Press, 2003) "Copyright of articles published in the Harvard Theological Review is held by President and Fellows of Harvard College" no copyright infringement

Gregory Thaumaturgus *Metaphrase of Ecclesiastes* ANF 6:9-17

Gregory Thaumaturgus *Oration and Panegyric to Origen = Prosphoneticus* ANF 6:21-39

Hebrews, Gospel of [fragments] trans Philipp Vielhauer and Georg Strecker at vol. 1 pp. 177f of Wilhelm Schneemelcher (ed). *New Testament Apocrypha* English translation by R. McL. Wilson revised ed. (Cambridge, UK: James Clarke & Co.; Louisville, Ky: Westminster/John Knox, 1991)

Hegesippus *Hypomnemata* [fragments] ANF 8:762-765

Herford, R. Travers *Christianity in Talmud and Midrash* (London: Williams & Norgate, 1903) no copyright information in book

Hermas, Shepherd of ANF 2:9-55

Hippolytus *Against Artemon* see *Little Labyrinth* [fragment] ANF 5:601f

Hippolytus *Against Noetus* see *Syntagma* ANF 5:223-231

Hippolytus *Apostolic Tradition* trans Burton Scott Easton (born 1877) *The Apostolic Tradition of Hippolytus* (New York: Macmillan; Cambridge, England: University Press, 1934) no copyright information in book

Hippolytus *Commentary on Canticles* in *Traités d'Hippolyte sur David et Goliath, sur le Cantique des cantiques et sur l'Antéchrist* as *Interpretatio Cantici canticorum Sur le Cantique des Cantiques et Sur l'Antéchrist* ed. by Gerard Garitte (Louvain: Secretariat du CorpusCSO, 1965) Series: Corpus scriptorum christianorum orientalium vol. 263f; Scriptores iberici t. 15f

Hippolytus *Commentary on Daniel* trans Maurice LeFèvre *Commentaire sur Daniel* (Paris: Cerf, 1947) Sources chrétiennes 14 no copyright information in book

Hippolytus *Homily on the Psalms* [fragments] "Homélie sur les Psaumes" Chapter 17 in Pierre Nautin *Dossier d'Hippolyte et de Meliton dans les florileges dogmatiques et chez les historiens modernes* (Paris: Cerf, 1953) pp. 166-183 at p. 178

Hippolytus *Little Labyrinth = Against the Heresy of Artemon* [fragments] ANF 5.601f

Hippolytus *On David and Goliath = Sermo de David et Goliath* in *Traités d'Hippolyte sur David et Goliath, sur le Cantique des cantiques et sur l'Antéchrist* ed. by Gerard Garitte (Louvain: Secretariat du CorpusCSO, 1965) Series: Corpus scriptorum christianorum orientalium vol. 263f; Scriptores iberici t. 15f

Hippolytus *On the Apocalypse* = *On the Resurrection* [fragments] in "Les fragments du De Apocalypsi d'Hippolyte" trans Pierre Prigent and Ralph Stehly (1973) 29 *Theologische Zeitschrift* 313 "Nachdruck verboten. Übersetzungsrecht vorbehalten"

Hippolytus *On the Blessings of Isaac and Jacob*}   *Hippolyte de Rome sur les*

Hippolytus *On the Blessings of Moses*   }   *bénédictions d'Isaac, de Jacob et de Moïse* trans Maurice Brière, Louis Mariès and B-Ch Mercier (1954) 27 *Patrologia orientalis* 1 pp. 148f + 155-157 no copyright information in item

Hippolytus *Oration on Daniel, Second* [fragments] ANF5:177-185

Hippolytus *Philosophumena* = *Refutation of All Heresies* 1-2 } ANF 5:9-153

Hippolytus *Philosophumena* = *Refutation of All Heresies* 4-10 }

Hippolytus *Syntagma* = *Against Thirty-two Heresies* = *Against All Heresies* ANF 5:223-231

Ignatius of Antioch *Letters* ANF 1:41-96

Irenaeus of Lyons *Against Heresies* ANF 1:315-567

Irenaeus of Lyons *The Blessings of Balaam* see Hippolytus

Irenaeus of Lyons *Demonstration of the Apostolic Preaching* trans Joseph P Smith under title *Proof of the Apostolic Preaching* Chapters 10, 18, 28, 87, 89, 95f + 98 (New York: Newman Press, 1952) Series: Ancient Christian Writers no. 16 © 1952 by Rev. Johannes Quasten and Rev. Joseph C. Plumpe

Chapter 10	Page 54
18	58
28	66
87	101
89	102
95	105
96	106
98	108

Irenaeus of Lyons *Letter to Victor on Florinus* [fragment] = *Epistula ad Victor de Florino* ANF 1:576 fragment 51

Isidore *Ethics* [fragment] Robert M Grant *Second-Century Christianity: A Collection of Fragments* (London: SPCK, 1946) pp. 22f no copyright information in book

Jacob, Testament of trans F. Stinespring at vol. 1 pp. [914]-918 of *The Old Testament Pseudepigrapha* ed by James H Charlesworth (Garden City: Doubleday, 1983-1985) © 1983 James H. Charlesworth

James, 1 Apocalypse of trans. William R. Schoedel in *The Nag Hammadi Library in English* edited by James M. Robinson (San Francisco: Harper & Row, 1981 c 1978) pp. [242]-248 at 243f and 248 © 1978 E. J. Brill, Leiden, The Netherlands

James, Ascents of reconstructed and trans. Robert E. Van Voorst at pp. 48-75 of his *The Ascents of James: History and Theology of a Jewish-Christian Community* (Atlanta, Ga: Scholars Press, 1989) at 52f, 55f, 57f, 65, 70 and 73 © 1989 Society of Biblical Literature

James, Protoevangelium of ANF 8:96-97

2 Jeou in *The Books of Jeu and the Untitled Text in the Bruce Codex* ed by Carl Schmidt trans by Violet MacDermot (Leiden: Brill, 1978) pp. 55, 57 + 63; Series: Nag Hammadi Studies XII; Coptic Gnostic Library © 1978 E. J. Brill, Leiden, The Netherlands

Job, Testament of trans R. P. Spittler in *The Old Testament Pseudepigrapha* ed by James H Charlesworth (Garden City: Doubleday, 1983-1985) vol. 1 pp [839]-868 © 1983 James H. Charlesworth

John, Acts of [fragments] trans Knut Schafendich in Wilhelm Schneemelcher (ed). *New Testament Apocrypha* English translation by R. McL. Wilson revised ed. (Cambridge, UK: James Clarke & Co.; Louisville, Ky: Westminster/John Knox, 1991) vol. 2 pp. 172-204 © J. C. B. Mohr (Paul Siebeck) Tubingen 1989, 1990 ET © James Clarke & Co. Ltd, 1991, 1992

John, Apocryphon of trans Frederick Wisse in *The Nag Hammadi Library in English* edited by James M. Robinson (San Francisco: Harper & Row, 1981 c 1978) © 1978 E. J. Brill, Leiden, The Netherlands pp. 99-116 [fragments]

Judas, Gospel of trans Randolphe Kasser, Marvin Meyer and Gregor Wurst at pp. 19 to 45 of *The Gospel of Judas from the Codex Tchacos* (Washington, DC: National Geographic, 2006) © 2006 National Geographic Society

Justin and Companions, Martyrdom of = *Acts of Justin and Companions* ANF 1.305f

Justin Martyr *1 Apology* ANF 1:163-187

Justin Martyr *2 Apology* ANF 1.188-193

Justin Martyr *Contra Marcionem* [fragment] *Eusebius History of the Church* trans Geoffrey Arthur Williamson (Minneapolis: Augsburg, 1975) pp 164f © G. A. Williamson 1985. For information about using or reproducing this item, contact Augsburg Publishing House, 426 South Fifth Street, Minneapolis, Minnesota, 55415

Justin Martyr *Dialogue with Trypho* ANF 1:194-270

Justinus *Baruch* ANF 5:69-73 except for one word (pederasty) from Robert McQueen Grant *Gnosticism: A Source Book of Heretical Writings from the Early Christian Period* (New York: Harper & Brothers, 1961) pp. 93-100 at p. 97 "For [copying] information address Harper & Brothers, 49 East 33rd Street, New York 16, N.Y."

Kerygmata Petrou reconstructed and translated by Georg Strecker in Wilhelm Schneemelcher (ed). *New Testament Apocrypha* English translation by R. McL. Wilson revised ed. (Cambridge, UK: James Clarke & Co.; Louisville, Ky: Westminster/John Knox, 1991) vol. 2 pp. 531-540 at p. 538 (11.27.3-28.3) and p. 539 (11.30.1) © J. C. B. Mohr (Paul Siebeck) Tubingen 1990 ET © James Clarke & Co. Ltd, 1991Schneemelcher NTA English trans R McL Wilson 1991

Krator = Monad: A Discourse of Hermes to Tat Robert McQueen Grant *Gnosticism: A Source Book of Heretical Writings from the Early Christian Period* (New York: Harper & Row, 1961) pp. 220-223 "For [copying] information address Harper & Brothers, 49 East 33rd Street, New York 16, N.Y."

Lucian of Samosata *The Passing of Perigrinus* in Austin M. Harmon *Lucian with an English Translation* (London: William Heinemann Ltd.; Cambridge, Mass.: Harvard University Press, 1936) vol. 5 pp. 2-51 with English and Greek on facing pages Loeb Classical Library. no copyright information in Volume 1 or Volume 5

Marcus Aurelius Antoninus *Meditations* 11.3 trans George Long (London; Glasgow: Collins Clear-Type Press [n.d.]) Translator died in 1879

Mary, Gospel of trans George W MacRae and R McL Wilson in *The Nag Hammadi Library in English* edited by James M. Robinson (San Francisco: Harper & Row, 1981 c 1978) pp. [471]-474 © 1978 E. J. Brill, Leiden, The Netherlands

Matthias, Traditions of Montague Rhodes James *The Apocryphal New Testament* (Oxford: Clarendon, 1953 reprinted 1963) pp. 12f no copyright information in book

Melito of Sardis *Book of Extracts = Prooemium Eklogôn* [fragment] ANF 8:759 fragment 4

Melito of Sardis *Discourse in the Presence of Antoninus Caesar = Oratio ad Antoninum Caesarem* [fragments] ANF 8:751-756

Melito of Sardis [unidentified homily] trans M. Van Esbroeck (1972) 90 *Analecta Bollandiana* pp. 72-89 as reproduced in *Melito of Sardis: On Pascha and Fragments*, texts and translations edited by Stuart George Hall at pp. 86-96 (Oxford: Clarendon, 1979) Series: Oxford Early Christian Texts © Oxford University Press 1979

Midrash in Herford, R. Travers *Christianity in Talmud and Midrash* (London: Williams & Norgate, 1903) no copyright information in book

Minucius Felix *Octavius* ANF 4:173-198

Mishna in Herford, R. Travers *Christianity in Talmud and Midrash* (London: Williams & Norgate, 1903) no copyright information in book

Muratorian Canon [fragment] ANF 5.603f

Nazareans, Gospel of [fragments] trans into German by Philipp Vielhauer and Georg Strecker in Wilhelm Schneemelcher (ed). *New Testament Apocrypha* English translation by R. McL. Wilson revised ed. (Cambridge, UK: James Clarke & Co.; Louisville, Ky: Westminster/ John Knox, 1991) vol. 1 pp. 160-164 © J. C. B. Mohr (Paul Siebeck) Tubingen 1990 ET © James Clarke & Co. Ltd, 1991Schneemelcher NTA English trans R McL Wilson 1991

Novatian two *Letters to Cyprian* ANF 5:307f (as number 30) and 306f (as number 29)

Novatian *On the Trinity* ANF 5:611

Oratio ad Graecos (pseudo-Justin)

(1) Greek Recension ANF 1.271f under name *Discourse to the Greeks*
(2) Syriac Recension = *Hypomnemata* = *Oratio ad Graecos* in William Cureton's *Spicilegium Syriacum* (London: Rivington, 1855)
(3) Ambrose ANF 8:739-741

Origen *Against Celsus* ANF 4:395-669

Origen *Commentary on Canticles* [fragments] in *Origen: The Song of Songs: Commentary and Homilies* trans and annotated by R. P. Lawson (New York; Ramsey, NJ: Newman Press, 1957) (Westminster, Md: Newman Press; London: Longmans, Green, 1957) pp. 21-263 at pp. 23 (Prologue 2), 76 (1.4), 88f (1.5), 130 (2.5), 133 (2.5), 138f (2.5), 145f (2.7), 158 (2.8), 164 (2.10), 176 (3.3), 204 (3.10), 235 (3.13) 242 (3[4].14), 251f (3[4].15) 256f (3[4].15) Series: Ancient Christian Writers 26 no indication of copyright holder

Origen *Commentary on 1 Corinthians* 14.34-35 [catena fragment]

(1) 10 *Journal of Theological Studies* 41-42 as quoted at pp. 28f of Roger Gryson *The Ministry of Women in the Early Church* trans Jean Laporte and Mary Louise Hall (Collegeville, Minnesota: Liturgical Press, 1976) © 1976 by The Order of St. Benedict, Inc., Collegeville, Minnesota Translation of *Le ministère des femmes dans l'Église ancienne* (Gembloux, Belgium: J. Duculot) original French pp. 56f © 1972 Editions J. Duculot, S.A., 18 rue Pierquin, 5800 Gembloux
(2) J. Kevin Coyle "The Fathers on Women and Women's Ordination" being pp. 117 to 167 at 139f of David M. Scholer (ed.) *Women in Early Christianity* (New York; London: Garland, 1993) Reprint of (1978) 9 *Église et théologie* 51-101 at 73f "Reprinted with permission of St. Paul University. Courtesy of *Église et théologie*

Origen *Commentary on Ephesians* trans Ronald E. Heine *The Commentaries of Origen and Jerome on St. Paul's Epistle to the Ephesians* (Oxford University Press, c2002) © 2002 Ronald E. Heine

Origen *Commentary on Genesis 1* in Eric Junod *Philocalie 21-27: Sur le libre arbitre* (Paris: Cerf, 1976) © Editions du Cerf 1976

Origen *Commentary on Genesis 3* [fragments in *Philocalia*] George Lewis *The Philocalia of Origen: A Compilation of Selected Passages from Origen's Works Made by St. Gregory of Nazianzus and St. Basil of Caesarea* (Edinburgh: T. & T. Clark, 1911)

Origen *Commentary on Isaiah*

(1) in Pamphilus and Eusebius *Apologie pour Origène* trans René Amacker and Eric Junod (Paris: Cerf, 2002) Extrait 137 pp. 220-223 © Editions du Cerf 2002

(2) selections in Richard Bartram Tollinton, ed. and trans., *Selections from the Commentaries and Homilies of Origen* (London: Society for Promoting Christian Knowledge, 1929) Selection LVII pp. 139-142 at 141 (Homily 6.1)

Origen *Commentary on John* [fragments]

(1) Books 1, 2, 4 [fragment], 5 [fragment], 6 and 10: ANF 10:297-408

(2) Ronald E Heine *Commentary on the Gospel of John Books 1-10* Fathers Of The Church 80 (Washington, D.C.: Catholic University of America Press, 1989) © Catholic University of America Press 1989

(3) trans Ronald E Heine *Commentary on the Gospel of John Books 13-32* Fathers of the Church vol. 89 (Washington, D.C.: Catholic University of America Press, 1993) © Catholic University of America Press 1993

Origen *Commentary on Luke* [fragments] trans Henri Crouzel, François Fournier and Pierre Périchon *Origène: Homélies sur S. Luc; Tomes sur Luc* (Paris: Cerf, 1962) reproduced from M. Rauer <u>GCS</u> 2nd ed. 1959 vol. 49; vol. 9 of *Origenes Werke* no copyright indicated in book

Origen *Commentary on Matthew* Books 1 and 2 [fragment], 10-14: ANF 10:413-512

Origen *Commentary on Matthew Commentariorum* in Richard B. Tollinton, ed. and trans., *Selections from the Commentaries and Homilies of Origen* (London: Society for Promoting Christian Knowledge, 1929) 28: pp. 111-114 (Selection XLVI) at 113 and 61: pp. 134-137 (Selection LV) at 136

Origen *Commentary on Philemon* in Pamphilus and Eusebius *Apologie pour Origène* trans René Amacker and Eric Junod (Paris: Cerf, 2002) Extrait 125 pp. 202-205 © Editions du Cerf 2002; *St. Pamphilus: Apology for Origen* trans Thomas P. Scheck (Washington, DC: Catholic University of America Press, 2010) © Catholic University of America Press 2010 p. 98

Origen *Commentary on Proverbs* fragments in Pamphilus and Eusebius *Apologie pour Origène* trans René Amacker and Eric Junod (Paris: Cerf, 2002) Extraits 186 and 188 © Editions du Cerf 2002 – both on reincarnation only

Origen *Commentary on Psalms* in Pamphilus and Eusebius *Apologie pour Origène* trans René Amacker and Eric Junod (Paris: Cerf, 2002) Extrait 148 pp. 202-205 © Editions du Cerf 2002

Origen *Commentary/Excerpt on Psalm 1* in Origen *Commentary/Excerpt on Psalm 1* George Lewis *The Philocalia of Origen: A Compilation of Selected Passages from Origen's Works Made by St. Gregory of Nazianzus and St. Basil of Caesarea* (Edinburgh: T. & T. Clark, 1911) pp. 32f; Marguerite Harl (ed.) *Origène Philocalie 1-20: Sur les écritures* (Paris: Cerf, 1983) Series: Sources chétiennes n° 302 pp. 240-259

Origen *Commentary on Psalm 4 = Commentaire sur le Psaume 4* [fragments in *Philocalia*] George Lewis *The Philocalia of Origen: A Compilation of Selected Passages from Origen's Works Made by St. Gregory of Nazianzus and St. Basil of Caesarea* (Edinburgh: T. & T. Clark, 1911)

Origen *Commentary on Psalms 26 to 150* in *Commentaire inédits des Psaumes: études sur les texts d'Origène contenus dans le Manuscrit vindobonensis 8* by René Cadiou (Paris: Les Belles letters, 1936) pp. [49]-67 Series: Collection d'études anciennes publiée sous le patronage de l'Association Guillaume Budé

Origen *Commentary on Psalm 50* George Lewis *The Philocalia of Origen: A Compilation of Selected Passages from Origen's Works Made by St. Gregory of Nazianzus and St. Basil of Caesarea* (Edinburgh: T. & T. Clark, 1911)

Origen *Commentary on Romans*

(1) trans. Thomas P. Scheck *Origen: Commentary on the Epistle to the Romans* 2 vols. (Washington, D.C.: Catholic University of America Press, Books 1-5 2001; Books 6-10 2002) © Catholic University of America Press 2001 and 2002. Through Rufinus' Latin. Nothing follows numbered subdivisions in the last column

(2) trans. Jean Scherer *Le Commentaire d'Origène sur l'Epître aux Romains 3.5 à 5.7 d'après les extraits du Papyrus no 88748 du Musée du Caire et les fragments de la Philocalie et du Vaticanus gr. 762* (Le Caire: Institut français d'archéologie orientale, 1957) Series: Institut français d'archéologie orientale. Bibliothèque d'étude t. 27. Critical edition of Volumes 5 and 6. Indicated in lists by "Scherer" follows numbering subdivisions in the last column

Origen *Commentary on the Song of Songs* in *Origen: The Song of Songs: Commentary and Homilies* trans R P Lawson (New York: Newman Press, 1957) (Westminster, Md: Newman Press; London: Longmans, Green, 1957) Series: Ancient Christian Writers 26 Chapter 8 p. 296 no indication in book of copyright holder

Origen *Commentary on 1 Thessalonians* [fragment] preserved in Jerome Epistle 119.9-119.10 in *Sancti Eusebii Hieronymi Opera* (Sect 1 Pars 2) Epistolarum Pars II: Epistolae LXXI-CXX recensvit Isidorus Hilburg (Vienna: F Tempsky; Leipsig: G Freytag, 1912; New

York; London: Johnson Reprint Corp., 1961) Johnson edition bears note: "Reprinted with the permission of the original publishers"

Origen *Commentary on Titus* in Pamphilus and Eusebius *Apologie pour Origène* trans René Amacker and Eric Junod (Paris: Cerf, 2002) Extraits 31, 33 and 35 (pp. 78f, 88f and 90f) © Editions du Cerf 2002; *St.Pamphilus: Apology for Origen* trans Thomas P. Scheck (Washington, DC: Catholic University of America Press, 2010) © Catholic University of America Press 2010 Extract 33 p. 59

Origen *De Principiis* ANF 4:239-382

Origen *Dialogue with Heraclides and the Bishops with Him*

(1) *Entretien d'Origène avec Heraclide* trans Jean Scherer (Paris: Cerf, 1960) © 1960 Editions du Cerf

(2) in *Origen: Treatise on the Passover; Dialogue of Origen with Heraclides and his Fellow Bishops on the Father, the Son and the Soul* trans Robert J Daly (New York; Mahwah, NJ: Paulist Press, 1992) Series: Ancient Christian Writers 54 pp. 57-78 at 64, 65 and 71 © 1992 by the New England Province of the Society of Jesus

Origen *Exhortation to Martyrdom = Exhortatio ad martyrium* in *Alexandrian Christianity: Selected Translations of Clement and Origen* by John Ernest Leonard Oulton and Henry Chadwick (London: SCM Press; Philadelphia: Westminster Press, 1954) pp. 388-429 Series: Library of Christian Classics II no copyright information in book

Origen *Homilies on Canticles* in *Origen: The Song of Songs: Commentary and Homilies* trans R P Lawson (New York: Newman Press, 1957) (Westminster, Md: Newman Press; London: Longmans, Green, 1957) Series: Ancient Christian Writers 26 Chapter 8 p. 296 no indication in book of copyright holder

Origen *Homilies on Exodus* in Ronald E. Heine *Origen: Homilies on Genesis and Exodus* (Washington, D.C.: Catholic University of America Press, 1982) © Catholic University of America Press 1982

Origen *Homilies on Ezekiel*

(1) *Homélies sur Ezéchiel* trans Marcel Borret (Paris: Cerf, 1986-90) Sources chrétiennes 352 © Editions du Cerf: vol. 1 © 1986, vol. 2 © 1990; a third part © 1989

(2) *Origen: Homilies1-14 on Ezekiel* trans Thomas P. Scheck (New York; Mahwah, NJ: Newman Press, 2010) Ancient Christian Writers series © 2010 Thomas P. Scheck

Origen *Homilies on Genesis* in Ronald E. Heine *Origen: Homilies on Genesis and Exodus* (Washington, D.C.: Catholic University of America Press, 1982) © Catholic University of America Press 1982

Origen *Homilies on Hebrews* [fragment] in Eusebius *History of the Church* trans G A Williamson (Minneapolis: Augsburg, 1975 © 1965) p. 266 © G. A. Williamson 1985. For information about using or reproducing this item, contact Augsburg Publishing House, 426 South Fifth Street, Minneapolis, Minnesota, 55415

Origen *Homilies on Isaiah* [fragments] in *Isaïe: Origène, Homélies traduites par Jacques Millet, Sermons d' Augustin, d'Eusèbe le Gallican, de saint Bernard, de Rupert de Deutz traduits par Jacqueline Legée et les Carmélites de Mazille* (n.p.: Desclée de Brower, 1983) Series: Les Pères dans la foi

Origen *Homilies on Jeremiah* [fragments]

(1) in *Origen: Homilies on Jeremiah, Homily on 1 Kings 28* trans John Clark Smith (Washington, DC: Catholic University of America Press, © 1998) Fathers of the Church v.20 © Catholic University of America Press, © 1998

(2) *Homélies sur Jérémie* trans Pierre Husson and Pierre Nautin (Paris: Cerf, 1976 and 1977) 2 vols.

Sources chrétiennes 232: t. 1 Homélies 1-9 © 1976 Editions du Cerf

Sources chrétiennes 238: t. 1 Homélies 12-20 © 1977 Editions du Cerf

Origen *Homilies on Joshua*

(1) trans. Barbara J. Bruce, ed. Cynthia White *Homilies on Joshua* (Washington, DC: Catholic University of America Press, © 2002) Fathers of the Church v. 105 © Catholic University of America Press 2002

(2) *Homélies sur Josué* trans Annie Jaubert (Paris: Cerf, 1960) no copyright information in book

Origen *Homilies on Judges*

(1) *Homélies sur les Juges* trans Pierre Messié, Louis Neyrand and Marcel Borret (Paris: Cerf, 1993) Sources chrétiennes 389 © 1993 Editions du Cerf

(2) trans. Elizabeth Ann Dively Lauro *Homilies on Judges* (Washington, DC: Catholic University of America Press, © 2010) Fathers of the Church v. 119 © Catholic University of America Press 2010

Origen *Homilies on Leviticus*

(1) *Homélies sur le Lévitique* trans Marcel Borret (Paris: Cerf, 1981) © 1981 Editions du Cerf

(2) *Homilies on Leviticus 1-16* trans Gary Wayne Barkley (Washington, DC: Catholic University of America Press, 1990) Fathers Of The Church no. 83 © 1990 Catholic University of America Press

Origen *Homilies on Luke*

(1) trans Henri Crouzel, François Fournier and Pierre Périchon *Origène: Homélies sur S. Luc; Tomes sur Luc* (Paris: Cerf, 1962) reproduced from M. Rauer <u>GCS</u> 2nd ed. 1959 vol. 49; vol. 9 of *Origenes Werke* no copyright indicated

(2) in *Homilies on Luke; Fragments on Luke* trans Joseph T Lienhard (Washington, DC: Catholic University of America Press, 1996) Fathers of the Church vol. 94 © 1996 Catholic University of America Press

Origen *Homilies on Numbers*

(1) "Homily XXVII on Numbers" in *Origen: An Exhortation to Martyrdom, Prayer, First Principles* trans Rowan A Greer (London: SPCK, 1979) © 1979 Missionary Society of St. Paul the Apostle in the State of New York

(2) *Homélies sur les Nombres* trans André Méhat (Paris: Cerf, 1951) Sources chrétiennes 29 no copyright information in book

(3) trans. Thomas P. Scheck; edited by Christopher A. Hall (Downers Grove, Ill.: IVP Academic, © 2009) Ancient Christian Texts series © 2009 Thomas P. Scheck, Christopher A. Hall, Gerald L. Bray, Thomas C. Oden, Michael Glerup and the Institute for Classical Christian Studies

Origen *Homilies on Psalm 36* in *Homélies sur les Psaumes 36 à 38* texte critique etabli par Emanuela Prinzivalli; trans Henri Crouzel and Luc Brésard (Paris: Cerf, 1995) Sources chrétiennes 441 © Editions du Cerf, 1995

Origen *Homilies on Psalm 37* in *Homelies sur les Psaumes 36 à 38* texte critique etabli par Emanuela Prinzivalli; trans Henri Crouzel and Luc Brésard (Paris: Cerf, 1995) Sources chrétiennes 441 © Editions du Cerf, 1995

Origen *Homilies on Psalm 38* in *Homelies sur les Psaumes 36 à 38* texte critique etabli par Emanuela Prinzivalli; trans Henri Crouzel and Luc Brésard (Paris: Cerf, 1995) Sources chrétiennes 441 © Editions du Cerf, 1995

Origen *Homilies on Psalms = Homélies sur les Psaumes* in *Commentaire inédits des Psaumes: études sur les texts d'Origène contenus dans le Manuscrit vindobonensis 8* by Rene Cadiou (Paris: Les Belles letters, 1936) pp. [49]-67 Series: Collection d'études anciennes publiée sous le patronage de l'Association Guillaume Budé

Origen *Homilies on Samuel* [fragments]

(1) All but Chapter 5 *Homélies sur Samuel* trans Pierre Nautin and Marie-Thérèse Nautin (Paris: Cerf, 1986) Sources chrétiennes 328 © 1986 Editions du Cerf

(2) Chapter t : *Origen: Homilies on Jeremiah, Homily on 1 Kings 28* trans John Clark Smith (Washington, DC: Catholic University of America Press, © 1998) Fathers of the Church v.20 © Catholic University of America Press, © 1998

Origen *Homily on Psalm 82* on Elchasites [fragment] Eusebius *History of the Church* 6.38 trans G A Williamson (Minneapolis: Augsburg, 1975 c1965) pp. 272f © G. A. Williamson 1985. For information about using or reproducing this item, contact Augsburg Publishing House, 426 South Fifth Street, Minneapolis, Minnesota, 55415

Origen *Letter to Alexander of Cappadocia and Jerusalem* in Eusebius *History of the Church* 6.38 trans G A Williamson (Minneapolis: Augsburg, 1975 c1965) 6.19.12-14 pp. 259f © G. A. Williamson 1985. For information about using or reproducing this item, contact Augsburg Publishing House, 426 South Fifth Street, Minneapolis, Minnesota, 55415

Origen *Letter to Firmilian of Cappadocia* [fragment] Pierre Nautin *Lettres et écrivains chrétiens des IIe et IIIe siècles* p. 250 (Paris: Cerf, 1961)

Origen *Letter to friends in Alexandria* reconstructed by Henri Crouzel then translated by Joseph D Gauthier in *The Heritage of the Early Church: Essays in Honor of the Very Rev. George Visilievich Florovsky* ed by David Neiman and Margaret Shatkin (Rome: Pont. Institutum Studiorum Orientalium, 1973) = (1973) 195 Orientalia Christiana Analecta pp. 135 to 150 at 138-140 and 142f

Origen *Letter to Gregory Thaumaturgus* ANF 4:393f and 10:295f

Origen *Letter to Julius Africanus* ANF 4:386-392

Origen *On First Principles* = *De principiis* ANF 4:239-382

Origen *On Prayer* trans Rowan A Greer in *Origen: An Exhortation to Martyrdom, Prayer, First Principles* (London: SPCK, 1979) © 1979 Missionary Society of St. Paul the Apostle in the State of New York

Origen *On the Pasch*

(1) trans Octave Guéraud and Pierre Nautin *Origène: Sur la pâque: traité inédit publié d'après un papyrus de Toura* (Paris: Beauchesne, 1979) pp. 215, 225, 227 and 229 Series: Christianisme antique; bibliothèque de recherches dirigé par P Nautin © 1979 Editions Beauchesne

(2) trans Robert J. Daley in *Origen: Treatise on the Passover and Dialogue of Origen with Heraclides and his Fellow Bishops on the Father, the Son and the Soul* trans Robert J Daly (New York; Mahwah, NJ: Paulist Press, 1992) Series: Ancient Christian Writers 54 © 1992 by the New England Province of the Society of Jesus pp. 27-56 at pp. 43, 44, 46, 47 and 48

(3) in *St. Pamphilus: Apology for Origen* trans Thomas P. Scheck (Washington, DC: Catholic University of America Press, 2010) © Catholic University of America Press 2010 Extract 128 p. 99

Origen *On the Resurrection* Pamphilus and Eusebius *Apologie pour Origène* trans René Amacker and Eric Junod (Paris: Cerf, 2002) Extrait 148 pp. 218f © Editions du Cerf 2002

Origen *Scholia on the Apocalypse* = *Scholies sur l'Apocalypse* in Césaire, saint, évêque d'Arles. 470?-542 *L'Apocalypse expliquée par Césaire d'Arles: Scholies attribuées à Origène* annotations by A.-C. Hamman (Paris: Desclée de Brouwer, 1989) Series: Les Pères dans la foi [37] pp. [167]-203

Origen *Selecta on Psalms* (Lommatzsch 12.160 to 162) [fragment] in R. B. Tollinton, ed. and trans., *Selections from the Commentaries and Homilies of Origen* (London: Society for Promoting Christian Knowledge, 1929) Selection C p. 267f

Origen *Selecta on Psalms* (Lommatzsch 13.82f) in R. B. Tollinton, ed. and trans., *Selections from the Commentaries and Homilies of Origen* (London: Society for Promoting Christian Knowledge, 1929) Selection XXI p. 47

Origen *Stromateis* Book 6 [fragment] in John M Hritzu *Jerome: Dogmatic and Polemical Works* (1965) Fathers of the Church 53 (Washington, D.C.: Catholic University of America Press, 1965 © 1965 Catholic University of America Press pp. 83f

Origen *Stromateis* [unidentified quotation] Pierre Nautin *Origène: sa vie et son oeuvre* (Paris: Beauchesne, 1977) pp. 298-300 © 1977 by Editions Beauchesne – cremation is the nearest topic

Papias *Expositions of the Oracles of the Lord* [fragments] ANF 1:153-155

De pascha computus = The Pseudo-Cyprianic De pascha comptus trans George Ogg (London: SPCK, 1955 the closing words of Chapter 23

Paul, Acts of

(1) ANF 8:489-492
(2) Montague Rhodes James *The Apocryphal New Testament* (Oxford: Clarendon, 1953 reprinted 1963) pp. 270-299 and 570-578 no copyright information in book

Periodoi Petrou 14 [fragment] George Lewis *The Philocalia of Origen: A Compilation of Selected Passages from Origen's Works Made by St. Gregory of Nazianzus and St. Basil of Caesarea* (Edinburgh: T. & T. Clark, 1911) Philocalia 23.22 pp. 195-197

Perpetua and Felicitas, Passion of ANF 3:[699]-706

Peter, Acts of [fragments] Montague Rhodes James *The Apocryphal New Testament* (Oxford: Clarendon, 1953 reprinted 1963) pp. 300-336 no copyright information in book

Peter *Letter to Philip* [fragments] trans Frederick Wisse in *The Nag Hammadi Library in English* ed. James M Robinson (San Francisco: Harper & Row, 1981) © 1978 E. J. Brill, Leiden, The Netherlands pp. 395 to398

Peter, Revelation of (Ethiopic Text I and Akhmim Fragment) in Montague Rhodes James *The Apocryphal New Testament* (Oxford: Clarendon, 1953 reprinted 1963) pp. 506-524 no copyright information in book not the same as *Gnostic Apocalypse of Peter* above

Philip, Gospel of trans Hans-Martin Schenke in Wilhelm Schneemelcher (ed.) *New Testament Apocrypha* ET R. McL. Wilson revised ed. (Cambridge, UK: James Clarke & Co.; Louisville, Ky: Westminster/John Knox, 1991) vol. 1 pp. 188-206 at 203 (verse 118) and

204 (verse 122b) © J. C. B. Mohr (Paul Siebeck) Tubingen 1990 ET © James Clarke & Co. Ltd, 1991

Pionius, Martyrdom of in Herbert Musurillo *The Acts of the Christian Martyrs* (Oxford: Clarendon, 1972) 9.3-5 (p. 147), 15.7 (p. 157) + 18.4 (p. 159) © Oxford University Press 1972

Pliny the Younger *Letter* 10.96 in Henry Melvill Gwatkin *Selections from Early Writers Illustrative of Church History to the Time of Constantine* (London: Macmillan, 1893 reprinted with additions and corrections 1914)

Poimandres in Robert McQueen Grant *Gnosticism: A Source Book of Heretical Writings from the Early Christian Period* (New York: Harper & Brothers, 1961) pp. 211-219 "For information [on copying] address Harper & Brothers, 49 East 33rd Street, New York 16, N.Y."

Polycarp *Letter to the Philippians* ANF 1:33-36

Polycarp, Martyrdom of ANF 1:39-44

Potamiaena and Basilides, Martyrdom of in Eusebius *Church History* 6.5 trans. Arthur Cushman McGiffert *Nicene and Post-Nicene Fathers 2d* vol. 1 p. 253 (New York: Christian Literature Co.; Oxford and London: Parker, 1890; reprinted Edinburgh: T & T Clark; Grand Rapids, MI: Eerdmans, 1997)

Ptolemy the Gnostic *Letter to Flora* in Karlfried Froehlich (ed. and trans.) *Biblical Interpretation in the Early Church* (Philadelphia: Fortress, 1985) pp. 37-43 © Fortress Press 1984

Rebirth, Concerning in Robert McQueen Grant *Gnosticism: A Source Book of Heretical Writings from the Early Christian Period* (New York: Harper & Row, 1961) pp. 226-233 "For information [on copying] address Harper & Brothers, 49 East 33rd Street, New York 16, N.Y."

Scillitan Martyrs, Acts of ANF 10{285]

Sextus, Sentences of trans Richard A Edwards and Robert A Wild *The Sentences of Sextus* (Chico, California: Scholars Press, 1981) Series: Texts and Translations 22; Early Christian Literature Series 5 © 1981 Society of Biblical Literature

Sibylline Oracles trans J J Collins in *The Old Testament Pseudepigrapha* vol. 1 Apocalyptic Literature and Testaments pp. [327]-472 ed. by James H Charlesworth (Garden City, NY: Doubleday, 1983) © James H. Charlesworth 1983

Silvanus, Teaching of trans Malcolm L Peel and Jan Vandee in *The Nag Hammadi Library in English* ed by James M Robinson (San Francisco: Harper & Row, 1981) pp 347-361 © 1978 E. J. Brill, Leiden, The Netherlands

Solomon, Odes of ed. and trans. by J. H. Bernard (Cambridge: Cambridge University Press, 1912; Nendeln, Liechtenstein: Kraus Reprint, 1967) reprinted with permission

Sophia of Jesus Christ in *The Nag Hammadi Library in English* edited by James M Robinson (San Francisco: Harper & Row, 1981) trans Douglas M. Parrott pp. 207-228 © 1978 E. J. Brill, Leiden, The Netherlands

Suetonius *Lives of the Caesars* Book 5 Paragraph 16 trans J. C. Rolphe (London: Heinemann; New York: Macmillan,1914) Volume 2 p. 111 no copyright indication in book

Tacitus *Annals* 15.44 trans John Church and William Jackson Brodribb *The Annals of Tacitus* (London: Macmillan, 1869 reprinted 1906) pp. 304f

Talmud in Herford, R. Travers *Christianity in Talmud and Midrash* (London: Williams & Norgate, 1903) no copyright information in book

Tatian *Address to the Greeks* ANF 2:65-83

Tatian *On Perfection According to the Saviour* ANF 2:82

Tertullian (pseudo-) *Against All Heresies* ANF 3:[649]-654

Tertullian *Ad Nationes = To the Nations* ANF 3:[109]-147

Tertullian *Against Hermogenes* ANF 3:[477]-502

Tertullian *Against Marcion* ANF 3:[271]-474

Tertullian *Against Praxeas* ANF 3:[597]-627

Tertullian *Against the Valentinians* ANF 3:[503]-520

Tertullian *Answer to the Jews* ANF3:[151]-173

Tertullian *Apologeticum* ANF 3:[17]-55

Tertullian *Exhortation to Chastity* ANF 4:50-58

Tertullian *On Baptism* ANF 3:[669]-679

Tertullian *On the Flesh of Christ* ANF 3:[521]-542

Tertullian *On Fasting* ANF 4:102-114

Tertullian *On Flight in Persecution* ANF 4:116-125

Tertullian *On Garlands = On Crowns = De corona* ANF 3:[93]-103

Tertullian *On Idolatry* ANF 3:[61]-76

Tertullian *On Modesty* ANF 4:74-101

Tertullian *On Monogamy* ANF 4:59-72

Tertullian *On Patience* ANF 3:[707]-717

Tertullian *On Prayer* ANF 3:[681]-691

Tertullian *On the Pallium* ANF 4:5-12

Tertullian *On Repentance = Penitence* ANF 3:[657]-666

Tertullian *On the Resurrection of the Flesh* ANF 3:[545]-594

Tertullian *On the Apparel of Women* ANF 4:14-25

Tertullian *On the Resurrection of the Flesh* ANF 3:[546]-594

Tertullian *On the Soul* ANF 3:[181]-235

Tertullian *On the Veiling of Virgins* ANF 4:27-37

Tertullian *De praescriptione haereticorum* ANF 3:243-265

Tertullian *Scorpiace* ANF 3:[633]-648

Tertullian *De spectaculis* ANF 3:[79]-91

Tertullian *Testimony of the Soul* ANF 3:[175]-179

Tertullian *To his Wife* ANF 4:39-49

Tertullian *To Scapula* ANF 3:[105]-108

Tertullian *To the Martyrs* ANF 3:[693]-696

Testimonies against the Jews (pseudo-Cyprian) ANF 5:507-557

Testimony of Truth [fragments] trans Søren Giverson and Birger A. Pearson in *The Nag Hammadi Library in English* edited by James M Robinson pp. [406]-416 (San Francisco: Harper & Row, 1981) © 1978 E. J. Brill, Leiden, The Netherlands

Theophilus of Antioch *To Autolycus* ANF 2:89-121

Thomas, Acts of Montague Rhodes James *The Apocryphal New Testament* pp. 365-438 (Oxford: Clarendon, 1953 reprinted 1963) no copyright information in book

Thomas, Gospel of (Gnostic) trans Beate Blatz in Wilhelm Schneemelcher (ed). *New Testament Apocrypha* English translation by R. McL. Wilson revised ed. (Cambridge, UK: James Clarke & Co.; Louisville, Ky: Westminster/John Knox, 1991) vol. 1 pp. 117-129 © J. C. B. Mohr (Paul Siebeck) Tubingen 1990 ET © James Clarke & Co. Ltd, 1991

Thomas the Contender trans John D Turner at pp. [188]-194 of *The Nag Hammadi Library in English* edited by James M Robinson (San Francisco: Harper & Row, 1981) © 1978 E. J. Brill, Leiden, The Netherlands

Tosephta in Herford, R. Travers *Christianity in Talmud and Midrash* (London: Williams & Norgate, 1903) no copyright information in book

Valentinus *On the Conversation of Friends* [fragments] in Robert M Grant *Second-Century Christianity: A Collection of Fragments* (London: SPCK, 1946) p. 73 no copyright information in book

Vienne and Lyons, Churches at *Letter to the Churches of Asia and Phrygia* ANF 8:778-784

Virginity, Two Letters on (pseudo-Clement) ANF 8:55-66

Wessely, Charles (ed.) *Les plus anciens monuments du Christianisme écrit sur papyrus* (1907) 4 *Patriologia orientalis*, reprinted 1946 pp. 151-158 Logia II and III no copyright holder indicated in volume

Xanthippe and Polyxena, Acts of ANF 10:[205]-217

Zephaniah, Apocalypse of trans O. S. Wintermute at vol. 1 pp [508] to 515 of *The Old Testament Pseudepigrapha* ed. by James H. Charlesworth (Garden City: Doubleday, 1983-1985) © James H. Charlesworth 1983

The twenty-seven books of the New Testament as commonly received © Division of Christian Education of the National Council of Churches of Christ in the United States of America 1946, 1952, 1971 – 475 Riverside Drive, Room 872, New York, New York, 10115-0050

Endnotes

Introduction

[1] Paul Avis "The Churches of the Anglican Communion" in his *The Christian Church: An Introduction to the Major Traditions* (London: SPCK, 2002) p. 141.

[2] Gregory J. Riley *One Jesus, Many Christs: How Jesus Inspired not One True Christianity, But Many* (Minneapolis: Fortress Press, 2000 c1997) pp. 8, 10f, and 13.

[3] Frederick Fyvie Bruce *The Spreading Flame: The Rise and Progress of Christianity from its First Beginnings to the Conversion of the English* (Greenwood, S.C.: Attic Press, 1978 c1958) p. 204.

[4] Frank Leslie Cross *The Early Christian Fathers* (London: Duckworth, 1960) p. 16.

[5] William Wigan Harvey's introduction to *S. Irenaei episcopi Lugdenensis libros quinque adversus haereses* (Cantbridiae: Typis academicus, 1857) vol. 1 p. clxiv.

[6] G. L. Prestige *Fathers and Heretics: Six Studies in Dogmatic Faith, with Prologue and Epilogue* (London: SPCK, 1940 reprinted 1954) pp. 23 and 33.

[7] Daniel H. Williams *Retrieving the Tradition and Renewing Evangelicalism: A Primer for Suspicious Protestants* (Grand Rapids, MI; Cambridge, UK: Eerdmans, 1999) p. 81.

[8] Colin Hart *The Ethics of Jesus* (Cambridge: Grove, 1997) pp. 3f.

[9] Williams, *Retrieving the Tradition and Renewing Evangelicalism* p. 82.

Chapter One: Terms, Values, and Approaches

[10] Or even in nonreligious academic treatments, e.g. Peter Singer *Practical Ethics* 2nd ed. (Cambridge: Cambridge University Press, 1993) p. 1.

[11] Paul Althaus *Gebot und Gesetz: Zum Thema "Gesetz und Evangelium": Beiträge zur Förderung christlicher Theologie* (Gütersloh: C. Bertelsman, 1952); Ernest De Witt Burton *A Critical and Exegetical Commentary on the Epistle to the Galatians* 1st ed. (Edinburgh: T. & T. Clark, 1921) pp. 447-60; Otto Kuss "Nomos Bei Paulus" (1966) 17 Münchener theologische Zeitschrift 173-227 at 221-223; Richard N. Longnecker *Paul, Apostle of Liberty* (New York: Harper & Row, 1964) at pp. 144-53; Heinrich Schlier *Ver Brief an de Galater* (Göttingen: Vandenhoeck & Ruprecht, 1962) at pp. 176-88; Wolfgang Schrage *Die konkreten Einzelgebote in der paulinischen Paränese: Ein Beitrag zur neutestamentliche Ethik* (Gütersloh: Gütersloher Verlagshaus Gerd Mohn, 1961) at pp. 232-33; Charles A. Anderson Scott *Christianity according to Saint Paul* (Cambridge University Press, 1927) at pp 42 and 45; and Peter Stuhlmacher *Gerechtigkeit Gottes bei Paulus* (Göttingen:

Vandenhoeck & Ruprecht, 1965), all as analyzed and paraphrased in C(lyde) Thomas Rhyne *Faith Establishes the Law* (Chico, Calif.: Scholars Press, 1981) at pp. 20f.

[12] Carl F. Henry *Christian Personal Ethics* (Grand Rapids, MI: Eerdmans, 1957) p. 193.

[13] James M. Gustafson *Can Ethics be Christian?* (Chicago: University of Chicago Press, 1975) p. 170.

[14] Eduard Lohse *Theological Ethics of the New Testament* trans. M. Eugene Boring (Minneapolis: Fortress, 1991). Translation of *Theologische Ethik des Neuen Testaments* (Stuttgart: W. Kohlhammner, 1988) p. 25.

[15] Paul Rooney *Divine Command Morality* (Aldershot: Avebury, 1996) p. 12.

[16] William Lillie *Studies in New Testament Ethics* (Edinburgh; London: Oliver and Boyd, 1961) p. 48; William Lillie *The Law of Christ: The Christian Ethic and Modern Problems* (Edinburgh: Saint Andrew Press, 1966) p. 12.

[17] R. J. Brooks *Ask the Bible* (New York: Gramercy, 1989) p. 52.

[18] Romans 13.5; 1 Corinthians 10.28.

[19] William Lillie *Studies in New Testament Ethics* p. 50.

[20] Jean Porter *Moral Actions and Christian Ethics* (Cambridge: Cambridge University Press, 1995) p. 42.

[21] Bruce C. Birch and Larry L. Rasmussen *Bible & Ethics in the Christian Life*. Rev. ed. (Minneapolis; Augsburg, 1989).

[22] Grand Rapids, MI; Cambridge, U.K.: Eerdmans, 2002, pp. 3-76. See also his *The Great Reversal: Ethics and the New Testament* (Grand Rapids, MI: Eerdmans, 1984)

[23] Roman Catholic Archbishop John R. Quinn of San Francisco "New Context for Contraceptive Teaching" (1980) 10 *Origins* pp 263-267, citing a Princeton University study, as reported in (1) Charles E. Curran *Moral Theology: A Continuing Journey* (Notre Dame, IN: University of Notre Dame Press, 1982) pp. 143f and 165 n. 6; and (2) idem *Tensions in Moral Theology* (Notre Dame, IN: University of Notre Dame Press, 1988) pp. 74 and 86.

[24] Allen Verhey *Remembering Jesus* pp. 6-8.

[25] Verhey *Remembering Jesus* p. 7

[26] Stanley J. Grenz *The Moral Quest: Foundations of Christian Ethics* (Downers Grove, Ill.: InterVarslty, 1997) p. 32.

[27] Richard N. Longenecker *New Testament Social Ethics for Today* (Grand Rapids, MI: Eerdmans, 1984) p. 8.

[28] Loc. cit.

[29] David Cook *The Moral Maze: A Way of Exploring Christian Ethics* (London: SPCK, 1983 repr. 1999) p. 72

[30] Loc. cit.

[31] Richard B. Hays *The Moral Vision of the New Testament: Community, Cross, New Creation: A Contemporary Introduction to New Testament Ethics* (New York: HarperSanFrancisco, 1996) p. 200.

[32] Richard B. Hays *The Moral Vision of the New Testament* p. 205 n. 34.

[33] Richard B. Hays *The Moral Vision of the New Testament* p. 201.

[34] Loc. cit.

[35] J. Ian H. McDonald *The Crucible of Christian Morality* (London; New York: Routledge, 1998) p.70.

[36] Waldo Beach and H, Richard Niebuhr *Christian Ethics: Sources of the Living Tradition* (New York: Ronald Press, 1955) p. 11.

[37] William Lillie *The Law of Christ* p. 14.

[38] Matthew 12.49f; Mark 3.33-35; Luke 8:21.

[39] Matthew 8.20; Luke 9.58.

[40] Matthew 5.41; Luke 7.14; Luke 8.54; John 11.43.

[41] Luke 2.21.

[42] Romans 2.25-29, 3.30; 1 Corinthians 7.18f; Galatians 2.3, 5.6 and 6.12f.

[43] Acts 15.1-29.

[44] E.g. Philippians 3.5.

[45] William Lillie *The Law of Christ* p. 20.

[46] Brian Hebblethwaite *Christian Ethics in the Modern Age* (Philadelphia: Westminster, 1982) p. 63.

[47] In the terms of Allen Verhey's *The Great Reversal*.

[48] See also 1 Corinthians 4.16; Philippians 3.17, 4.9; Origen *Homilies on Psalm 38* 2.1.

[49] Eduard Lohse *Theological Ethics of the New Testament* p. 26.

[50] In the terms of Allen Verhey's *The Great Reversal*.

[51] Lisa Sowle Cahill "Christian Character, Biblical Community and Human Values" pp. 3-17 at 10 of William P. Brown (ed.) *Character and Scripture: Moral Formation, Community and Biblical Interpretation* (Grand Rapids, MI; Cambridge, U.K.: William B. Eerdmans, 2002).

[52] Paul Rooney *Divine Command Morality* p. 1.

[53] J. L. Houlden *Ethics and the New Testament* (London and Oxford; Mowbray, 1973) pp. 70f and 114.

[54] Bruce D. Chilton and James I. H. MacDonald *Jesus and the Ethics of the Kingdom* (London: SPCK, 1987).

[55] Wolfgang Schrage *The Ethics of the New Testament* trans. David W. Green (Philadelphia: Fortress, 1988).

[56] Eduard Lohse *Theological Ethics of the New Testament* p. 42.

[57] Eduard Lohse *Theological Ethics of the New Testament* pp. 210f.

[58] Loc. Cit.

[59] J. L.Houlden *Ethics and the New Testament* p. 112.

[60] Sean Freyne "The Bible and Christian Morality" in *Introduction to Christian Ethics: A Reader* ed. Ronald P. Hamel and Kenneth R. Hynes (New York Paulist, 1989) pp. 9-32.

[61] J. L.Houlden *Ethics and the New Testament* p. 112.

[62] Richard N. Longenecker *New Testament Social Ethics for Today* p. 2.

[63] Gerard Stephen Sloyan *Is Christ the End of the Law?* (Philadelphia: Westminster, 1978) p. 67.

[64] Joseph Michael *Winger By What Law? The Meaning of Nomos in the Letters of Paul* (Atlanta: Scholars Press, 1992) p. 1. To the contrary, Origen in his *Commentary on the Epistle to the Romans* 3.6.1, 4.4.1-6, 5.1.24 and 5.6.2-4 maintained that by the word "law" Paul referred at various times in Romans to that of Moses, natural law, the "law of faith" and the "law of members" of the body, without Paul clearly specifying which system of law he meant.

[65] C. H. Dodd "Ennomos Khristou" in his *More New Testament Studies* (Grand Rapids, MI: Eerdmans, 1968) pp. [134]-148.

Chapter Two: Evidence for the Existence of an Early Christian Law

[66] Gerard Stephen Sloyan *Is Christ the End of the Law?* (Philadelphia: Westminster, 1978) p. 67.

[67] Wayne A. Meeks *The Origin of Christian Morality: The First Two Centuries* (New Haven and London: Yale University Press, 1993) p. 156.

[68] Richard N. Longenecker *New Testament Social Ethics for Today* (Grand Rapids, MI; Wm. B. Eerdmans, 1984) p. 2.

[69] Loc. cit.

[70] William Lillie *Studies in New Testament Ethics* (Edinburgh; London: Oliver and Boyd, 1961) p. 71.

[71] Hans Windisch *The Meaning of the Sermon on the Mount* (Philadelphia, 1951) as summarized by James M. Gustafson *Christ and the Moral Life* (New York: Harper & Row, 1968) pp. 215f.

[72] Galatians 5.16-26: 9 commanded acts and 18 prohibitions; Galatians 4-6.1: 15 prohibitions and 16 commands; Philippians 2.2-2.4, 2.14, 3.2-3.17, 4.2, 4.4-4.9: 23 positive injunctions and 3 prohibitions; Ephesians 4.2f: 4 duties; 4.22f: 2 duties; 4.25-32: 20 duties; 5.3-13: 17 duties; 5.15-22: 9 duties; 5.24f: 2 duties; 5:28: 1 duty; 5.33-6.9: 9 duties; 6.18: 3 duties; Colossians 2.16f, 3,12, 3.18-23, 4.2 and 4,5f: 17 duties; 1 Thessalonians 4.llf: 3

positive injunctions; 5.12: eight positive injunctions; 2 Thessalonians 3.11f and 3.14f: 4 forbidden acts; 1 Timothy 1.3f: 3 duties; 1.8-10: 8 prohibitions; 2.1: 4 duties; 2.8-12: 7 affirmative duties and 3 prohibitions; 4.7: 2 duties; 5.1-4: 7 duties; 5.14: 3 duties; 5.16; 1 duty; 6.9-11: 8 duties; 6.17f: 6 duties; 2 Timothy 2.22-2.25: 10 duties; 3.1-5: 19 duties; Titus 2.2-5: 16 duties; 3.1f: 7 duties; 3.9f: 5 duties.

[73] J. Ian H. McDonald *The Crucible of Christian Morality* (London; New York: Routledge, 1998) p. 136.

[74] Loc. cit.

[75] 1 Peter 2.1f; 2.11-14; 2.18-22; 3.1-17; 4.3-5; 4.7-5.9.

[76] 1 Peter 2.16.

[77] 1 Peter 4.6.

[78] 1 Peter 4.17.

[79] For a discussion of the date of *1 Clement*, see Daniel J. Theron "The Most Probable Date of the First Epistle of Clement to the Corinthians" (1989) 21 *Studia Patristica* pp. [106]-121. Less definite, but persuasive in freeing the date from being tied to the reign of the Emperor Domitian (A.D. 81 to 96) is L. L. Welborn "On the Date of First Clement" (1984) 29 *Papers of the Chicago Society of Biblical Research* pp. 35-54.

[80] Irenaeus *Against Heresies* 3.3.3 trans. A. Roberts and W. H. Rambaut at vol. 1 p. 416 of *The Ante-Nicene Fathers: Translations of the Writings of the Fathers down to A.D. 325* ed. Alexander Roberts and James Donaldson. American Reprint of the Edinburgh ed. by A. Cleveland Coxe (Buffalo, N.Y.: Christian Literature Publishing Co., 1885-96; continuously reprinted Edinburgh: T & T Clark; Grand Rapids, MI: Wm. B. Eerdmans) (hereinafter cited as ANF). ANF 1:416.

[81] .Loc. cit.

[82] ANF 1:[5]; ANF 10:[229].

[83] ANF 1:15; ANF 10:240.

[84] Translated by Alexander Roberts and James Donaldson at ANF 1:[5] and trans John Keith at ANF 10: 230.

[85] George E. Bebis "The Concept of Tradition in the Fathers of the Church" (1970) 15 *Greek Orthodox Theological Review* pp. 22-55 at p. 31.

[86] Servais Pinckaers *The Sources of Christian Ethics* (Washington, D.C.: Catholic University of American Press, 1995) p. 196. Trans. by Mary Thomas Noble of the 3rd edition of *Les sources de la morale chrétienne* (Fribourg: University Press, 1993).

[87] Daniel H. Williams *Retrieving the Tradition and Renewing Evangelicalism: A Primer for Suspicious Protestants* (Grand Rapids, MI; Cambridge, UK: Eerdmans, 1999) p. 67. To be precise, Williams is an ordained Baptist minister.

[88] Richard B. Hays *The Moral Vision of the New Testament: Community, Cross, New Creation: A Contemporary Introduction to New Testament Ethics* (New York: HarperSanFrancisco, 1996) p. 453. To be precise, Hays is an ordained United Methodist minister.

[89] Aaron Milavec *The Didache: Faith, Hope and Life of the Earliest Christian Communities, 50-70 C.E.* (New York; Mahwah, NJ: Newman Press, 2003)

[90] The final chapter (16) warns of the end of the world.

[91] Trans Isaac H. Hall and John T. Napier at ANF 7:379.

[92] Ignatius *To the Ephesians* 2.5; 4.3; 5.5; 6,5; 7.2; 8.3; 9,2; 10.10; 11.5; 13.1; 14.4; 15.4; 16.2; 17.1; 18.3; 19.2; 20.1; 21.1; *Magnesians* 1,1; 3.7; 4.2; 5.1; 6.5; 7.10; 8.4; 9.2; 10.6; 11.2; 12.2; 13.4; 14.2; *Trallians* 1.2; 2.4; 3.3; 4.2; 5.1; 6. 2; 7.1; 8.5; 9.1; 12.3; 13.2; *Romans* 3.1; 4.2; 6.4; 7.3; 9.1; *Philadelphians* 1.2; 2.2; 3.3; 4.1; 5.1; 6.5; 7.4; 8.1; 10.1; *Smyrnaeans* 4.2; 6.8; 7.4; 8.4; 9,2; 11.1; 12.1; *To Polycarp* 1.8; 2.6; 3.5; 4.10; 5.6; 6.13.

[93] Ignatius *To the Ephesians* 14 trans. Alexander Roberts and James Donaldson ANF 1:55.

[94] Ignatius *To the Trallians* 7 trans. Alexander Roberts and James Donaldson ANF 1:66.

[95] Polycarp *To the Philippians* 5 trans Alexander Roberts and James Donaldson ANF 1:34.

[96] Papias trans. Alexander Roberts and James Donaldson ANF l:l53 Fragment I.

[97] E.g. Athanasius *Easter Letter* of A.D. 367.

98 Justin *Dialogue with Trypho* 12 trans. Dods and Reith ANF 1:200; Justin *Dialogue with Trypho* 12 trans Dods and Reith ANF 1:203

99 Justin *Dialogue with Trypho* 14 trans Dods and Reith ANF 1:201.

100 Justin *Dialogue with Trypho* 11.

101 Justin *Dialogue with Trypho* 43 trans. Dods and Reith ANF 1:194.

102 Justin *Dialogue with Trypho* 20. See the conclusions of Winger and Dodd in Chapter 1 *supra*.

103 The French word for this sense of the word is "loi" as contrasted with the more comprehensive "droit".

104 Gerard Stephen Sloyan *Is Christ the End of the Law?* p. 120.

105 Justin Martyr *Dialogue with Trypho* 93 trans. Dods and Reith ANF 1:246.

106 Justin Martyr *First Apology* 10 trans. Dods and Reith ANF 1:165 (circa A.D. 150).

107 Justin Martyr *Dialogue with Trypho* 110 trans. Dods and Reith ANF 1:254.

108 Theophilus *To Autolycus* 2.27 trans. Marcus Dods ANF 2:105.

109 Theophilus *To Autolycus* 3.9 at ANF 2:113f.

110 Theophilus *To Autolycus* 3.9 at ANF 2:114.

111 Irenaeus *Against Heresies* 4.12.3 trans. A. Roberts and W. H. Rambaut ANF 1:476.

112 Irenaeus *Against Heresies* 4.13.4 at ANF 1:478.

113 Irenaeus *Against Heresies* 4.13.3.

114 Irenaeus *Against Heresies* 2.31.3, 2.32.1, 3.12.12, 4.12.5, 4.13.1, 4.13.3, 4.17.3.

115 Clement of Alexandria *Stromata* 2.7 trans. William Wilson ANF 2:355.

116 Clement of Alexandria *Stromata* 1.27 trans. William Wilson ANF 2:339.

117 Clement of Alexandria *Stromata* 2.23 at ANF 2:379.

118 Clement of Alexandria *Who Is the Rich Man that Shall be Saved?* trans. William Wilson ANF 2:599.

119 Origen *Contra Celsum* 8.30; idem *Homilies on Ezekiel* 1.11.

120 Tertulllan *De oratione* 22 trans. S. Thelwell ANF 3:688 (between A.D. 198 and 200).

121 Tertulllan *De virginibus velandis* 4 trans. S. Thelwell ANF 4:29 (before A.D. 207).

122 Tertulllan *De virginibus velandis* 8 trans. S. Thelwell ANF 4:32.

123 Tertulllan *De virginibus velandis* 16 trans. S. Thelwell ANF 4:36.

124 Tertullian *De poenitentiae* 2 trans. S. Thelwell ANF 3:658 (A.D. 203).

125 Tertullian *Adversus Marcionem* 4.9 trans. P. Holmes ANF 3:355f (between A.D. 207 and ca 212).

126 Tertullian *Adversus Marcionem* 4.25 trans. P. Holmes ANF 3:391.

127 Tertullian *Adversus Marcionem* 4.27 trans. P. Holmes ANF 3:394.

128 Tertullian *Scorpiace* 9 trans. S. Thelwell ANF 3:641 (A.D. 213).

129 Tertullian *Ad uxorem* 1.7 trans. S. Thelwell ANF 4:43 (between A.D. 200 and 206).

130 Tertullian *Ad uxorem* 2.2.

131 Tertullian *Ad uxorem* 2.3 trans. S. Thelwell ANF 4:45.

132 Tertullian *De pudicitia* 6 trans. S. Thelwall ANF 4:79 (after A.D. 217).

133 Loc. cit.

134 Loc. cit.

135 Tertullian *De idolatria* 24 trans. S. Thelwell ANF 3:76.

136 Acts 15.1-31.

137 I. e. cease to be Christians.

138 *Didascalia apostolorum* Chapters 10f.

139 See 1 Corinthians 6.1-6; 2 Corinthians 13.1f.

140 Irenaeus *Adversus Haereses* 4.12-17.

[141] *Didascalia apostolorum* Chapters 2, 4, 9, 19, 24, 26, as translated by R. Hugh Connolly in *Didascalia Apostolorum: The Syriac Version Translated and accompanied by the Verona Latin Fragments* (Oxford: Clarendon, 1929) at pp. 12, 14, 34, 98, 164, 202, 216, 218, 222, 224-226, 228, 230, 232f, 238, 240, 242, 248, 250, 252.

[142] Origen *De principiis* 3.1.20 trans. Frederick Crombie ANF 4:239.

[143] Homily 12.2 in *Homilies on Genesis and Exodus* trans. Ronald E. Heine (Washington, D.C.: Catholic University of America Press, 1982) p. 369 (all 3 quotations).

[144] Origen Homily 9.4 in *Homélies sur Josué* ed. Annie Jaubert (Paris: Cerf, 1960) Series: Sources chrétiennes 71 p. 252 my trans. of *legem spiritus* and *lex Evangelii*.

[145] Origen *Homilies on Joshua* 7.2 my trans. of *legis mystica praecepta*.

[146] Origen *Homilies on Joshua* 19.4.

[147] Matthew 5.21f, 27f, 31-39, 43f.

[148] Origen *Contra Celsum* 4.22 trans. Frederick Crombie ANF 4:506.

[149] Origen *Contra Celsum* 4.32 trans. Frederick Crombie ANF 4:511.

[150] Origen *Contra Celsum* 5.40 trans. Frederick Crombie ANF 4:561.

[151] Origen *Contra Celsum* 8.10 trans. Frederick Crombie ANF 4:643.

[152] Origen *Contra Celsum* 3.7; 3.8; 3.76; 4.72; 5.24; 5.33; 5.37; 6.24; 6.25; 6.26; 8.38.

[153] Origen *Homilies on Leviticus* 4.5 my trans. of *spirituali lege*; ibid. 11.3 my trans. of *spiritualem legem*.

[154] Origen *Homilies on Leviticus* 10.2 my trans. of *evangelicas leges*. See also Origen's *Exhortation to Martyrdom* 30 trans. Henry Chadwick in *Alexandrian Christianity: Selected Translations of Clement and Origen* by John Ernest Leonard Oulton and Henry Chadwick (London: SCM Press, 1954) p. 413.

[155] Origen *Homilies on Leviticus* 3.2 (*evangelicum praeceptum*), 4.9.2 (*divina praecepta*), 10.2 (*praeceptum Evangelii*).

[156] Origen *Homilies on Leviticus* 7.1.4 my trans. of *Novi Testamenti legibus*; identical trans. in *Homilies on Leviticus 1-16*, trans. Gary Wayne Barkley (Washington, D.C.: Catholic University of America Press, 1990) p. 130.

[157] Origen *Homilies on Leviticus* 15.2 my trans. of *lex Christi*; identical trans. at 15.1.2 in Gary Wayne Barkley p. 257.

[158] Origen *Homilies on Leviticus* 10.2 my trans. of *mandat*.

[159] Origen *Homilies on Leviticus* 4.9.2 my trans. of *implentes divina praecepta*; identical trans. in Gary Wayne Barkley p. 84.

[160] Origen *Homilies on Leviticus* 16.6.

[161] Origen *Homilies on Leviticus* 7.6.2 my trans. of *legem divinam* and *legis divinae*; identical trans. in Gary Wayne Barkley p. 148.

[162] Origen *Homilies on Leviticus* 7.1.

[163] Matthew 10.23.

[164] My trans. of *in legibus Christi* in Homily 9.1 of Origen *Homélies sur les Juges* ed. Pierre Messié, Louis Neyrand and Marcel Borret (Paris: Cerf, 1993) Series: Sources chrétiennes n° 389 p. 214.

[165] Origen *Homilies on Luke* 16.6.

[166] Origen *Homilies on Luke* 34.1.

[167] Loc. cit., in *Homélies sur S. Luc*, ed. Henri Crouzel, François Fournier and Pierre Périchon (Paris: Cerf, 1962) Series: Sources chrétiennes n° 87 p. [400] my trans. of *quodam compendio*.

[168] *Philocalia* 9.1f, reproduced as "Extrait du Commentaire sur l'Epître aux Romains" at pp. [350]-359 of *Origène Philocalie 1-20: Sur les écritures*, ed. Marguerite Harl (Paris: Cerf, 1983) Series: Sources chétiennes n° 302.

[169] As in Romans 2.14f; 3.21; 5.13; 7.7 and 7.14; Galatians 3.10; 3.19; 3.24-26; 4.21-33.

[170] E.g. Origen *Homilies on the Epistle to the Romans* Preface 8: "spiritual law", "law of the letter", "law of the flesh", "law of the members of the body", "law of the mind", "law of sin"; 4.4.2: law of Moses, natural law; 4.4.5: law of Moses, law of faith, law of God according to the inner man, law of the members of the body; 6.7.1-6: law of the members of the body, law of the mind, law of sin, law of God; 6.8.1-10: law of Moses; 6.13.2: law of the Spirit of Christ. The foregoing is the result of my research in Thomas P. Scheck's English rendering of Rufinus' translation: *Origen: Commentary on the Epistle to the Romans Books 1-5* (vol. 1) (Washington, D.C.: Catholic University Press, 2001). A slightly different list, also of a twelve meanings, appears at pp. 9f of Riemer Roukema's *The Diversity of Laws in Origen's Commentary on Romans* (Amsterdam: Free University Press, 1988) especially pp. 9f: "the law of Moses according to the letter", the law of Moses according to the spirit", "the natural law", "the history written by Moses", "the prophets", "the teaching of Christ", "the law of God", "the law of the mind", the law of the Spirit of life", "the law of the members", "the law of death" and "the law of sin".

[171] *Le Commentaire d'Origène sur Rom. III.5-V.7 d'après les extraits du Papyrus n° 88748 du Musée du Caire et les fragments de la Philocalie et du Vaticanus gr. 762* ed. by Jean Scherer (Le Caire: Institut français d'archéologie orientale, 1957) pp. 6f and 20f of 88748.

[172] Marguerite Harl in *Origène: Philocalie 1-20: Sur les écritures* pp. 362-364.

[173] See the conclusions of Winger and Dodd in Chapter 1 *supra*.

[174] Psalm 142.10 in *Commentaires inédits des Psaumes; étude sur les textes d'Origène contenus dans le Manuscrit Vindobonensis 8* par René Cadiou. (Paris: Société d'édition "Les Belles Lettres", 1936) Series: Association Guillaume Budé; Collection d'études anciennes, my trans The discrepancy in the numbering of this Psalm is because Origen followed the Septuagint numbering, while most Bibles today use the Jewish numbering.

[175] Ibid., Psalm 118.19. The discrepancy in the numbering of this Psalm is because Origen followed the Septuagint numbering, while most Bibles today use the Jewish numbering.

[176] *Gospel of Mary* 8.22 to 9.4 of the *Berlin Gnostic Codex 8502* trans. George W. MacRae and R. McL. Wilson in *The Nag Hammadi Library in English* ed. James M. Robinson (San Francisco: Harper & Row, 1978) p. 472.

[177] Epistula 73.20 trans. Ernest Wallis under title Epistle 72.20 ANF 5:384. Between A.D. 254 and 257.

[178] Epistula 15.1 trans. Ernest Wallis under title Epistle 10.1 ANF 5:291. Between A.D. December 249 and March 251.

[179] Loc. cit.

[180] Epistula 46.1. My trans. of *contra dei dispositionem, contra euangelicam legem, contra institutionis catholicae unitatem*. Between A.D. Spring 251 and Summer 253.

[181] My trans. from Chapter 14 of "Eine frühchristliche Schrift von den dreierlei Früchten des christlichen Lebens" in (1914), 15 *Zeitschrift fur die neutestamentliche Wissenschaft und die Kunde der altern Kirche* pp. 60-90, ed. and commentary by R. Reitzenstein.

[182] *Didache* 6.2.

[183] My trans. of *lex enim domini dura est et amara*.

[184] My trans. of *in his duobus mandatis omnia conclusa sint...ut credentes in regno atque praecepto diuino operis parcamus.*

[185] Eduard Lohse *Theological Ethics of the New Testament* (Minneapolis: Fortress, 1991) p. 199. Trans. by M. Eugene Boring of *Theologische Ethik des Neuen Testaments* (Stuttgart: W. Kohlhammer, 1988).

[186] Eduard Lohse *Theological Ethics of the New Testament* p. 219.

[187] Eduard Lohse *Theological Ethics of the New Testament* p. 31.

[188] Willi Marxsen *New Testament Foundations for Christian Ethics* (Minneapolis: Fortress, 1993) pp. xiif. Trans. by O. C. Dean Jr. of *"Christliche" und Christliche Ethik im Neuen Testament* (Gütersloh: Gütersloher Verlags Gerd Mohn).

[189] Willi Marxsen *New Testament Foundations for Christian Ethics* p. 51.

[190] J. Patout Burns "On Rebaptism: Social Organization in the Third Century Christian Church" (1993) 1 *Journal of Early Christian Studies* 367 at 381.

Chapter Three: The Place of Scripture in the Christian Life

[191] An earlier version of this chapter was published under title "The Insufficiency of Scripture" in (1998) 101 *Theology* pp. 345-353 in September/October 1998 by SPCK, London.

[192] Clement of Alexandria *Stromata* 1,28.177.2; 2.4,15.4; 6.10.81.2; 7.15.90.5.

[193] Origen *Commentary on John* 19.44; 32.215; *Commentary on Matthew* 12.1; *Homilies on Ezekiel* 2.2; *Homilies on Jeremiah* 12.7; *Homilies on Leviticus* 3.8; *Homilies on Luke* 1.1.

[194] *Didascalia apostolorum* 2.37.

[195] Dionysius of Alexandria *Third Letter on Baptism to Philemon* in Eusebius *The History of the Church* 7.7.3.

[196] *Clementine Homilies* 2.51; 3.50; 18.20 (2d half of 3rd century).

[197] Athanasius *Letters on the Opinions of Dionysius* (A.D. 350s).

[198] *Apostolic Constitutions* 2.36.9.

[199] trans. and ed. R. McL. Wilson (Oxford: Clarendon, 1972-74).

[200] Montague R. James *Apocryphal New Testament* (Oxford: Clarendon, 1953); James K. Elllott *Apocryphal New Testament* rev. ed. (Oxford: Oxford University Press, 1993).

[201] *New Testament Apocrypha* rev. ed. edited by Wilhelm Schneemelcher English trans. edited by R. McL. Wilson (Cambridge: James Clarke; Louisville, Ky: Westminster/John Knox 1991-92).

[202] San Francisco: Harper & Row, 1978; 3rd ed. New York: HarperSanFrancisco, 1990.

[203] Melito of Sardis *Extracts* in Eusebius *The History of the Church* 4.26.13f.

[204] Serapion of Antioch *The So-called Gospel of Peter* in Eusebius *History of the Church* 6.12.

[205] Sextus Julius Africanus *Letter to Origen* and Origen *Letter to Africanus*.

[206] Tertullian *De cultu feminarum* 1.3.

[207] Origen *Commentary on the Gospel of Matthew* 10.18; 14.21; 24.21. See also *De principiis* 4.1.11 and endnote 43 below.

[208] Origen *Commentary on the Gospel of John* 5.3.

[209] Origen *Commentary on the Gospel of John* 1.4; 1.5.

[210] Bentley Layton *The Gnostic Scriptures: A New Translation with Annotations and Introduction* (Garden City, N.Y.: Doubleday, 1987) p. xviii.

[211] Oxford; Clarendon, 1987.

[212] Bruce M. Metzger's *The Canon of the New Testament: Its Origins Development and Significance* (Oxford: Clarendon, 1987) pp. 11 to 24.

[213] Irenaeus *Demonstration of the Apostolic Preaching* 97.

[214] Irenaeus *Against Heresies* 5.35.1.

[215] Clement of Alexandria *Stromata* 1.5; 1.10; 2.5; 2.15; 2.16; 2.23; 4.11; 4.16; 5.3; 5.14; 6.6; 6.8; 6.11; 6.12; 6.14; *Paedagogus* 1.8; 1.9; 1.10; 1.13; 2.1-8; 2.10f; 3.3-4; 3.11.

[216] Tertullian *On Fasting* 7.

[217] Tertullian *Scorpiace* 8.

[218] Hippolytus *Commentary on Daniel* 1.12; 1.16; 1.18; 1.23; 2.29. The whole of Discourse 1 is an exegesis of the story of Susannah, which Hippolytus treats as an integral part of the Book of Daniel.

[219] Origen *Letter to Africanus*.

[220] Origen *Homilies on Jeremiah* 1.1.1; 2.1.1; 6.1.2; 6.2.2; 7.1.1; 7.3.3f; 8.1.3; 9.4.5; 10.6; 11.3.2; 12.13.1; 14.3.2; 16.7.1; 16.10.3; 20.7.3; 27.4.2; Origen *Homilies on Joshua* 9.10; Origen *Homilies on Leviticus* 1.1; Origen *Homilies on Luke* 3.4; 8.1; 21.6; Origen *Homilies on Numbers* 9.10; 18.1; 18.3; 20,2; 28.1; Origen *Homilies*

on Psalm 36 5.5; Origen *De oratione* 5.2; 11.1; 13.2f; 14.3f; Origen *De principiis* 2.1.5; 2.3.6; 4.1.33; Origen *Stromateis* Book 4.

221 Barsabas of Jerusalem *On Christ and the Churches* 24.

222 Alexander of Alexandria *Letter to Alexander of Constantinople* 5.

223 *De laude martyrii* 11 (3rd cent.); Cyprian *On the Mortality* 9; 10; 13; 23; Cyprian *On Works and Alms* 2; pseudo-Cyprian *Adversus Judaeos* 9 (3rd century); Novatian *De bono pudicitiae* 12f (shortly after A.D. 250).

224 Irenaeus *Against Heresies* 4.16.2.

225 Irenaeus *Demonstration of the Apostolic Preaching* 18.

226 *Barnabas* 16.5.

227 Clement of Alexandria *Eclogae propheticae* 53.

228 Tertullian *De idolatria* 4; Tertullian *De cultu feminarum* 1.3; Origen *De principiis* 1.3.3; 4.1.35.

229 Tertullian *De cultu feminarum* 1.3; Origen *Contra Celsum* 5.54.

230 Anatolius *Paschal Canons* in Eusebius *History of the Church* 7.32.19.

231 Irenaeus *Against Heresies* 4.20.2.

232 Clement of Alexandria *Stromata* 1.29; 2.1; 2.9; 2.12; 2.18; 4.9; 6.6; 6.15.

233 Origen *Commentary on Hosea* in *Philocalia* 8.3; Origen *Commentary on Matthew* 14.21; Origen *De principiis* 1.23; 2.1.5; 3.2.4; 4.1.11; Origen *Homilies on Ezekiel* 1.5.42-64; 8.3.32-34; Origen *Homilies on Joshua* 10.1; Origen *Homilies on Leviticus* 10.2; Origen *Homilies on Luke* 12.4; 35.3; Origen *Homilies on Numbers* 8.1; Origen *Homilies on Psalm 37* 1.1.

234 Origen *Commentary on Romans* 10.31.

235 *Easter Letter* of A.D. 367 trans. F. F. Bruce *The Canon of Scripture* (Downer's Grove, Ill.: InterVarsity Press, 1988) pp. 209f.

236 Loc. cit.

237 For example: Cyril of Jerusalem (died A.D. 386 or 387), Epiphanius of Salamis (died A.D. 403), Gregory Nazianzus (died A.D. 390), Augustine of Hippo and Jerome. See Bruce, *The Canon of Scripture* pp. 87-96 and pp. 210-214; Lee M. McDonald *The Formation of the Christian Biblical Canon* Rev. & expanded ed. (Peabody, Mass.: Hendrickson, 1995) pp. 193f and Appendixes B to D (pp. 268-276); Albert C. Sundberg *The Old Testament of the Early Church* (Cambridge MA: Harvard University Press; London: Oxford University Press, 1964; reprinted New York: Kraus Reprint, 1969), especially Table II (pp. 58f).

238 Rome (A.D. 382), Hippo (A.D. 393) and Carthage (A.D. 397). See Bruce *The Canon of Scripture* pp. 97 and 232; McDonald *The Formation of the Christian Biblical Canon* Appendix 1C (pp. 271-273); Sundberg, *The Old Testament of the Early Church* loc. cit.

239 Augustine *On Christian Doctrine* 2.12 (shortly after A.D. 396).

240 Except Gregory Nazianzus.

241 Bruce *The Canon of Scripture* pp. 78f; McDonald *The Formation of the Christian Biblical Canon* p. 268; Sundberg, *The Old Testament of the Early Church* pp. 58 and 140.

242 James Barr *Holy Scripture: Canon Authority Criticism* (Oxford: Clarendon, 1983) p. 59.

243 McDonald *The Formation of the Christian Biblical Canon* p. 131. See also p. 226. He reiterates this a number of times in his *The Biblical Canon: Its Origin, Transmission, and Authority* (Peabody, MA: Hendrickson, 2007)

244 McDonald *The Formation of the Christian Biblical Canon* p. 194.

245 Loc. cit.

246 Everett Kalin "Re-examining New Testament Canon History: 1. The Canon of Origen" (August 1990) 17 *Currents in Theology and Mission* pp. 274-282 at 279-281.

247 McDonald *The Formation of the Christian Biblical Canon* pp. 203-205.

248 Geoffrey Mark Hahneman *The Muratorian Fragment and the Development of the Canon* (Oxford: Clarendon, 1992).

249 McDonald *The Formation of the Christian Biblical Canon* p. 160.

250 McDonald *The Formation of the Christian Biblical Canon* pp. 209-220.

251 Eusebius *History of the Church* 6.13.6.

252 McDonald *The Biblical Canon* p. 378.

253 Melito of Sardis *Extracts* in Eusebius *History of the Church* 4.26.13f.

254 Irenaeus *Against Heresies* 3.11.8 trans. W. H. Rambaut ANF 1:428.

255 See the lists and catalogues Lee Martin McDonald *The Biblical Canon* pp. [439]-451, Albert C. Sundberg *The Old Testament of the Early Church* pp. 58f, and Bruce M. Metzger *The Canon of the New Testament* pp. [305]-315.

256 Lee M. McDonald *The Biblical Canon* pp. 353 and 362.

257 James Barr *Holy Scripture: Canon Authority Criticism* p. 25.

258 Revelation of John 1.3, 10-11; 22.7-9, 18-19.

259 McDonald *The Formation of the Christian Biblical Canon* p. 9 paraphrasing Kirster Stendahl "The Apocalypse of John and the Epistles of Paul in the Muratorian Fragment" in *Current Issues in New Testament Interpretation: Essays in Honor of Otto A. Piper* ed. William Klassen and Graydon T. Snyder (New York: Harper & Brothers, 1962) p. 240.

260 Bruce *The Canon of Scripture* pp. 104f.

261 Craig A. Evans *Noncanonical Writings and New Testament Interpretation* (Peabody, Mass.: Hendrickson, 1992) p. [189]; idem *Ancient Texts for New Testament Studies: A Guide to the Background Literature* (Peabody, Mass.: Hendrickson, 2005) p. [341]; Lee M. McDonald *The Biblical Canon* p. 210.

262 Bruce *The Canon of Scripture* p. 82.

263 H. Cunliffe-Jones "Scripture and Tradition in Orthodox Theology" in *Holy Book and Holy Tradition: International Colloquium held in the Faculty of Theology, University of Manchester* ed. F. F. Bruce and E. G. Ruff (Grand Rapids, Michigan: Eerdmans, 1968) p. 191.

264 Bruce *The Canon of Scripture* p. 215.

265 G. A. Mikre-Sellassie "The Bible and its Canon in the Ethiopian Orthodox Church" (*Technical Papers for The Bible Translator* vol. 44 no. 1 January 1993 pp. 111-123); Bruce M. Metzger *The Canon of the New Testament* pp. 226-228. For an outline of the differences between the Old and New Testaments in the Ethiopian Bible from that most used by Protestants, see J. M. Harden *An Introduction to Ethiopic Christian Literature* (London: SPCK; New York and Toronto: Macmillan, 1926), especially pp. 26, 37-40, 45f and 60.

266 Helmut Koester *History and Literature of Early Christianity* (Philadelphia: Fortress; Berlin and New York: Walter de Gruyter, 1982) pp. 32f. Translation by the author of his *Einführung in das Neue Testament* (Berlin and New York: : Walter de Gruyter, 1980) Chapters 7-12.

267 Evans *Noncanonical Writings* p. [189]; idem *Ancient Texts for New Testament Studies* p. [341].

268 Metzger, *The Canon of the New Testament* p. 247; Arthur Carl Piepcorn "Theological Observer" (1972) xliii *Concordia Theological Monthly* pp. 449-453 at p. 449 para. 4; Edmund Schlink *Theology of the Lutheran Confessions* trans. Paul F. Koehneke and J. A. Bouman (Philadelphia: Fortress Press, 1961) pp. 4f.

269 David W. T. Brattston "No Lutheran Bible" (July/August 2001) vol. 16 no. 5 *Canada Lutheran* p. 8. At a regional Church conference in Bridgewater, Nova Scotia, on 22 October 1988 the Presiding Bishop (national primate) of the Evangelical Lutheran Church in Canada stated that he was not aware of any authoritative Lutheran statement that delimited the canon or the scope of the terms "the Bible" and "the Holy Scriptures" in the *Book of Concord* and ELCIC's national and synodical constitutions.

270 Koester *History and Literature of Early Christianity* p. 11.

271 For an introduction to the "King James Only" debate, see James R. White *The King James Only Controversy: Can You Trust the Modern Translations?* (Minneapolis: Bethany House, 1995).

272 Graham Cole "Sola Scriptura: Some Historical and Contemporary Perspectives" (1990) 104 *Churchman; A Journal of Anglican* Theology pp. 20-34 at p. 27.

273 Lee M. McDonald *The Biblical Canon* pp. 9 and 427f.

192

[274] Bart D. Ehrman *The Orthodox Corruption of Scripture: The Effect of Early Christological Controversies on the Text of the New Testament* (New York; Oxford: Oxford University Press, 1993) p. 23.

[275] 1 Corinthians 16.21; Galatians 6.11; Colossians 4.18; 2 Thessalonians 3.17; Philemon 19.

[276] Revelation of John 22.18f.

[277] Dionysius of Corinth *Letter to the Roman Church* in Eusebius *The History of the Church* 4.23.

[278] Serapion of Antioch *The So-called Gospel of Peter* in Eusebius *The History of the Church* 6.12.6.

[279] Hippolytus *The Little Labyrinth* in Eusebius *History of the Church* 5.28.15-17.

[280] Tertullian *Praescriptio* 17.

[281] *Clementine Homilies* 2.38; 3.47.

[282] *Clementine Homilies* 2.39 trans. Thomas Smith ANF 8:223.

[283] Bart D. Ehrman *The Orthodox Corruption of Scripture: The Effect of Early Christological Controversies on the Text of the New Testament* (New York; Oxford: Oxford University Press, 1993).

[284] See W. C. van Unnick *Tarsus or Jerusalem: The City of Paul's Youth* trans. George Ogg (London; Epworth, 1962).

[285] Willi Marxsen *New Testament Foundations for Christian Ethics* (Minneapolis: Fortress, 1993) pp. 200 and 273. Trans. by O. C. Dean Jr. of *"Christliche" und Christliche Ethik im Neuen Testament* (Gütersloh: Gütersloher Verlagshaus Gerd Mohn); L. William Countryman *Dirt Greed and Sex: Sexual Ethics in the New Testament and Their Implications for Today* (Philadelphia: Fortress, 1988) p. 141.

[286] W. D. Davies "The Relevance of the Moral Teaching of the Early Church" in *Neotestamenica et Semitica: Studies in Honour of Matthew Black* (Edinburgh: T. & T. Clark, 1969) pp. 48f.

[287] Vincent of Lérins *Commonitorium* 2.

[288] Yves M.-J. Congar *Tradition and Traditions: An Historical and Theological Essay* (New York: Macmillan, 1967 c1966) p. 384, trans. by Michael Naseby and Thomas Rainborough of *La tradition et les traditions* (Paris: Arthème Fayard, 1960 and 1966).

[289] Congar *Tradition and Traditions* p. 421.

[290] This is a modification of the argument of Johann Eck of Ingolstadt in *De primatu Petri adversus Lutherum* (1521) as paraphrased by Georges Henri Tavard in his *Holy Writ or Holy Church: The Crisis of the Protestant Reformation* (New York: Harper and Brothers, 1959) pp. 119f.

[291] United Bible Societies *Scripture Language Report 2006* Statistical Summary.

[292] To find a copy, search the Internet or the catalogues of libraries of academic institutions under "Brenton, Lancelot Charles Lee".

[293] Liana Lupas, Curator of the Scripture Collection, American Bible Society, New York, telephone conversation and e-mail to the author, 10 August 2007. This total of 989 is based on Dr. Lupas' including 136 languages and dialects that were not included in the total of 853 in the Bible Societies' "Statistical Summary" because no complete book of the Bible had been translated into these 136 but only short excerpts such as the Decalogue or Lord's Prayer while the "Statistical Summary" counts only languages and dialects that possess one or more full books.

[294] United Bible Societies *Scripture Language Report 2006* Statistical Summary.

[295] This total of 2562 is based on Dr. Lupas' including 136 languages and dialects that were not included in the total of 2426 in the Bible Societies' "Statistical Summary" because no complete book of the Bible had been translated into these 136 but only short excerpts such as the Decalogue or Lord's Prayer while the "Statistical Summary" counts only languages and dialects that possess one or more full books.

[296] Using the lower total of 2426 in the United Bible Societies' "Statistical Summary", the percentages are still only 17.7 and 47 respectively.

[297] 1 Peter 1.25 paraphrasing Isaiah 40.8.

[298] Lee M. McDonald *The Biblical Canon* p. 426.

Chapter Four: The Apostolic Tradition on Ethics

[299] Harald Riesenfeld *The Gospel Tradition* (Philadelphia: Fortress Press, 1970) p. 1.

[300] Manfred Barthel *What the Bible Really Says* (New York; Avenel, NJ: Wings, 1982 repr. 1992) p. 300. Trans. and adaptation by Mark Howson of *Was Wirklich in der Bibel Steht* (Econ, 1980).

[301] Resolved in Clement of Alexandria *Excerpta ex Theodoto* 22: see David W. T. Brattston "Ancient Gnostic Heretics and Baptism for the Dead" www.irr.org/mit/brattston-article (Grand Rapids, MI: Institute for Religious Research, 2006).

[302] Craig A. Evans *Noncanonical Writings and New Testament Interpretation* (Peabody, Mass.: Hendrickson, 1992) p. 4.

[303] *Contra:* Lee Martin McDonald *The Biblical Canon: Its Origin, Transmission, and Authority* (Peabody, MA: Hendrickson, 2007) p. 331.

[304] Charles H. Cosgrove *Appealing to Scripture in Moral Debate: Five Hermeneutical Rules* (Grand Rapids, MI; Cambridge, UK: Eerdmans, 2002) pp.78f.

[305] Robert L. Wilken *The Christians as the Romans Saw Them* 2d ed. (New Haven and London: Yale University Press, 2003) p. 122.

[306] Henri Irénée Marrou *A History of Education in Antiquity* (New York: Sheed and Ward, 1956) p. 161, trans. by George Lamb of *Histoire de l'Éducation dans l'Antiquité* 3rd ed. (Paris: Seuil, 1955) as cited in Joseph B. Tyson *The New Testament and Early Christianity* (New York: Macmillan, 1984) p. 45.

[307] H. I. Marrou *A History of Education in Antiquity* trans. George Lamb p. 231.

[308] Paul Veyne "The Roman Empire" in *A History of Private Life: I. From Pagan Rome to Byzantium* trans. Arthur Goldhammer (Cambridge, MA, and London: Belknap Press of Harvard University Press, 1987) p. 177. Trans. of *Histoire de la vie privée: I. De l'Empire à l'an mil* (Paris: Seuil, 1985).

[309] Robert L. Wilken *The Christians as the Romans Saw Them* pp. 201f.

[310] McDonald *The Biblical Canon* p. 470.

[311] E. Flesseman-Van Leer *Tradition and Scripture in the Early Church* (Assen, Netherlands: Van Gorckum, c1954) p. 9.

[312] Tertullian *De praescriptione haereticorum* 28.

[313] Boniface Ramsey *Beginning to Read the Fathers* (New York; Mahwah, NJ: Paulist, 1985) p. 18.

[314] Boniface Ramsey *Beginning to Read the Fathers* p. 18.

[315] Craig A. Evans *Noncanonical Writings and New Testament Interpretation* pp. 5f.

[316] The ideas in this sentence are not original to me. They stuck in my mind some years ago but I have not been able to find their source again.

[317] Yves M.-J. Congar *Tradition and Traditions: An Historical and a Theological Essay* (New York: Macmillan, 1967) p. 351. Trans. by Michael Naseby and Thomas Rainborough of *Tradition et les Traditions* (Paris: Fayard, 1960 and 1966).

[318] Richard Patrick Crossland Hanson *Origen's Doctrine of Tradition* (London: SPCK, 1954) p. 181.

[319] Harold O. J. Brown "Proclamation & Preservation: The Necessity & Temptations of Church Tradition" in *Reclaiming the Great Tradition: Evangelicals, Catholics & Orthodox in Dialogue* ed. James S. Cutsinger (Downers Grove, Illinois: InterVarsity, 1997) pp. [69]-87 at 78f.

[320] Lee Martin McDonald *The Biblical Canon* p. 329.

[321] Harry Y. Gamble *The New Testament Canon: Its Making and Meaning* (Philadelphia: Fortress Press, 1985) p. 90; see also Richard John Neuhaus "A New Thing: Ecumenism at the Threshold of the Third Millennium" in *Reclaiming the Great Tradition: Evangelicals, Catholics & Orthodox in Dialogue* ed. James S. Cutsinger (Downers Grove, Illinois: InterVarsity, 1997) pp. [47]-60 at 55.

[322] Gamble *The New Testament Canon* p. 90.

[323] Stephen R. Holmes *Listening to the Past: The Place of Tradition in Theology* (Carlisle, Cumbria; Grand Rapids, MI: Baker Academic, 2002) p 7.

[324] Ibid. p. 6.

[325] Ibid. p. 7.

[326] Brian Haymes "The Baptist and Pentecostal Churches" in Paul Avis (ed.) *The Christian Church: An Introduction to the Major Traditions* (London: SPCK, 2002) pp.[107]-131 at 118.

[327] Loc. cit.; McDonald *The Biblical Canon* p. 428 and 471; remember that L. M. McDonald is president of a Baptist seminary.

[328] J. Ian H. McDonald *The Crucible of Christian Morality* (London; New York: Routledge, 1998) pp. 51f.

[329] Craig A. Evans *Noncanonical Writings and New Testament Interpretation* pp. 4 and [178]-188.

[330] William D. Stroker *Extracanonical Sayings of Jesus* (Atlanta, Ga: Scholars Press, 1989) pp.1f.

[331] Robert E. Webber *Ancient-Future Faith: Rethinking Evangelicalism for a Postmodern World* (Grand Rapids, MI: Baker, 1999) p. 28.

[332] Daniel H. Williams *Retrieving the Tradition and Renewing Evangelicalism: A Primer for Suspicious Protestants* (Grand Rapids, MI; Cambridge, UK: Eerdmans, 1999) pp. 26 and 218.

[333] Harold O. J. Brown "Proclamation & Preservation" pp. 83f.

[334] Brian S. Rosner *Paul, Scripture and Ethics: A Study of 1 Corinthians 5-7* (Leiden; New York; Köln: E. J. Brill, 1994) p. 192.

[335] Op. cit. p. 191.

[336] W. H. C. Frend *The Rise of Christianity* (Philadelphia: Fortress, 1984) p. 6.

[337] Tertullian *On the Apparel of Women* 1.3.

[338] See "The Problem of Forgery" in Chapter 3 above, and Bart D. Ehrman *The Orthodox Corruption of Scripture: The Effect of Early Christological Controversies on the Text of the New Testament* (New York; Oxford: Oxford University Press, 1993).

[339] *Letter of Artisteas* Sentences 310f.

[340] On the extent of the Samaritan canon, see Lee Martin McDonald *The Biblical Canon* pp. 137f.

[341] E. Flesseman-Van Leer *Tradition and Scripture in the Early Church* p. 34.

[342] Donald F. Winslow "Tradition" in *Encyclopedia of Early Christianity* ed. Everett Ferguson (New York and London: Garland, 1990) p. 906.

[343] Richard Patrick Crossland Hanson *Origen's Doctrine of Tradition* p. 31.

[344] Richard B. Hays *The Moral Vision of the New Testament: Community, Cross, New Creation: A Contemporary Introduction to New Testament Ethics* (New York: HarperSanFrancisco, 1996) p. 210.

[345] No instances of the noun "tradition" appear in the Gospels of Luke and John.

[346] Yves M.-J. Congar *Tradition and Traditions* p. 7. See also Theodore Stylianopoulos "Tradition in the New Testament" (1970) 15 *Greek Orthodox Theological Review* pp. 7-21 at p. 12, which cites Congar *loc. cit.*

[347] Readers who desire completeness of this word-study of the noun are referred to Matthew 15.2, Mark 7.3 and Mark 7.5, which refer to "the traditions" of the Jewish elders.

[348] Other uses of this verbal form are found elsewhere in the present New Testament but none of them is relevant to the present study. The sole exception is Lukan Acts 6.14, where Jewish opponents of Stephen the Martyr spoke of customs Moses had "handed on" to them.

[349] Marcel Simon "The Ancient Church and Rabbinical Tradition" in *Holy Book and Holy Tradition: International Colloquium Held in the Faculty of Theology, University of Manchester* (Grand Rapids, MI: Eerdmans, 1968) p. 97, paraphrasing Hans Lietzmann, *An die Korinther I-II (Handbuch zum Neuen Testament 9)²* (Tübingen: Mohr, 1949) p. 58.

[350] *1 Clement* 44 trans. Alexander Roberts and James Donaldson ANF 1:17, and John Keith ANF 10:242.

[351] *1 Clement* 7 trans. John Keith ANF 10:231 and trans. Kirsopp Lake *The Apostolic Fathers* (London: William Heinemann; Cambridge, MA: Harvard University Press, 1912) vol. 1 p. 19.

[352] Polycarp *Letter to the Philipians* 7 trans. Alexander Roberts and James Donaldson ANF 1:34.

[353] Papias *Expositions of the Oracles of the Lord* trans. Alexander Roberts and James Donaldson ANF 1:151 Frag. I.

[354] The story that Judas Iscariot was so obese that the loose flesh around his eyes prevented doctors from examining them probably dates from centuries after his time and is from a source other than Papias.

[355] Apolinarius of Hierapolis *Letter to Abircius Marcellus* in Eusebius *History of the Church* 5.16.3 trans. Arthur Cushman McGiffert under title *The Church History of Eusebius* in *Nicene and Post-Nicene Fathers, Second Series* (New York: Christian Literature Company; Oxford and London: Parker, 1890; repr. Edinburgh: T & T Clark; Grand Rapids, MI: Eerdmans, 1997) vol. 1 p. 230.

[356] Apolinarius of Hierapolis *Letter to Abircius Marcellus* in Eusebius *History of the Church* 5.16.7 trans. Arthur Cushman McGiffert NPNF 2d series p. 231.

[357] Irenaeus *Against Heresies* 1.10.1-3; 2.9.1; 3.1.1-4; 3.4.2; 4.33.8-9; 5.20.1f.

[358] Irenaeus *Against Heresies* 1.10.1 trans. Alexander Roberts ANF 1:330.

[359] See also Irenaeus *Demonstration of the Apostolic Preaching* 3, 5-7. For the "rule of faith" in other early authors, see Tertullian *De praescriptione haereticorum* 3, 13, Tertullian *Against Praxeas* 2, Tertullian *Against Marcion* 4.2.1, the "Preface" to Origen *De principiis*, Novatian *De trinitate* and--to a lesser extent--Clement of Alexandria *Stromata* 7.15f.

[360] Irenaeus *Against Heresies* 3.3.1 trans. W. H. Rambaut ANF 1:415.

[361] Loc. cit.

[362] Irenaeus *Against Heresies* 2.9.1 trans. Alexander Roberts ANF 1:369.

[363] Irenaeus *Letter to Florinus* in Eusebius *History of the Church* 5.20.4 trans. Arthur Cushman McGiffert NPNF 2d 1:238.

[364] Clement of Alexandria *Stromata* 1.1.11f trans. Wm Wilson ANF 2:301.

[365] Irenaeus *Against Heresies* 1.18.1

[366] Clement of Alexandria *Stromata* 7.16 trans. Wm Wilson ANF 2:551.

[367] Clement of Alexandria *Stromata* 7.16 trans. Wm Wilson ANF 2:553f.

[368] Clement of Alexandria *Stromata* 1.1.15 and 1.12.55.

[369] Clement of Alexandria *Stromata* 1.1.15, 4.1.3, 6.7.61 and 6.8.70.

[370] Clement of Alexandria *Stromata* 4.1.3.

[371] Clement of Alexandria *Stromata* 6.8.70.

[372] Clement of Alexandria *Stromata* 6.15.125.

[373] Clement of Alexandria *Stromata* 6.7.61.

[374] Clement of Alexandria *Stromata* 5.10.64.

[375] Clement of Alexandria *Stromata* 7.16.104 trans. Wm Wilson ANF 2:554.

[376] Clement of Alexandria *Stromata* 7.16.103 trans. Wm Wilson ANF 2:553f.

[377] Clement of Alexandria *Stromata* 6.15.124 trans. Wm Wilson ANF 2:509.

[378] Clement of Alexandria *Stromata* 7.17.

[379] Irenaeus *Against Heresies* 1.25.5.

[380] Clement of Alexandria *Stromata* 7.17.

[381] Bentley Layton *The Gnostic Scriptures: A New Translation with Annotations and Introduction* (Garden City, NY: Doubleday, 1987) p. xxii.

[382] Tatian *Address to the Greeks* 31 trans. J. E. Ryland ANF 2:77.

[383] Charles H. Cosgrove *Appealing to Scripture in Moral Debate* p. 7.

[384] Tertullian *The Chaplet, or De Corona* 3 trans. S. Thelwall ANF 3:94.

[385] Tertullian *The Chaplet, or De Corona* 4 trans. S. Thelwall ANF 3:95.

[386] Loc. cit.

[387] Tertullian *Against Marcion* 1.21 trans. Peter Holmes ANF 3:286.

[388] Tertullian *Against Marcion* 1.21.

[389] Tertullian *Against Marcion* 3.21 trans. Peter Holmes ANF 3:339.

[390] Tertullian *On the Flesh of Christ* 2 trans. Peter Holmes ANF 3:522.

[391] Loc. cit.

[392] Tertullian *On Modesty* 1 trans. S. Thelwall ANF 4:75.

[393] Tertullian *De praescriptione haereticorum* 21.

[394] Tertullian *De praescriptione haereticorum* 20.

[395] Tertullian *The Prescription against Heretics* 28 trans. Peter Holmes ANF 3:256.

[396] Johannes Quasten dates it before AD 207, and certainly pre-Montanist – *Patrology* (Westminster, Md.: Christian Classics, 1950 reprinted 1986) vol. 2 p. 307. Robert M. Grant in his revision of Edgar J. Goodspeed's *A History of Early Christian Literature* (Chicago: University of Chicago Press, 1966 reprinted Midway Reprint 1983) p. 163 dates it between AD 204 and 207. Eligius Dekkers and Aemelius Gaar in *Clavis Patrum Latinorum* 3rd ed. (Steenburgis: in Abbatia Sancti Petri, 1995) p. 7 entry 27 consider it Montanist. Claudio Moreschini and Enrico Norelli *Early Christian Greek and Latin Literature: A Literary History* trans. Matthew J. O'Connell (Peabody, Mass.: Hendrickson, 2005) vol. 1 p. 346 believe it is one of the latest of Tertullian's writings and undoubtedly Montanist.

[397] Tertullian *On the Veiling of Virgins* 1 trans. S. Thelwall ANF 4:27.

[398] I.e. puberty.

[399] 1 Corinthians 11.16.

[400] Tertullian *On the Veiling of Virgins* 2 trans. S. Thelwall ANF 4:28.

[401] Christians of this era used the term "Gentile" to denote anybody who was neither a Christian nor a Jew.

[402] *Epistle to Diognetus* 11 trans. Alexander Roberts and James Donaldson ANF 1:29.

[403] Edgar J. Goodspeed *A History of Early Christian Literature* rev. Robert M. Grant (Chicago: University of Chicago Press, 1966 repr. 1983) p. 143; Johannes Quasten *Patrology* (Westminster, MD: Christian Classics, 1950, repr. 1988) vol. 2 p. 163.

[404] Hippolytus *The Treatise on the Apostolic Tradition* 1.3 trans. Gregory Dix reissued Henry Chadwick (London: SPCK, 1968) p. 2.

[405] Hippolytus *Apostolic Tradition* 1.5 trans. Gregory Dix p. 2.

[406] Hippolytus *Little Labyrinth* or *Against the Heresy of Artemon* in Eusebius *History of the Church* 5.28.3-6.

[407] Hippolytus *Philosophumena* or *Refutation of All Heresies* 7.8 trans. J. H. MacMahon ANF 5:103.

[408] Ptolemy *Letter to Flora* 7.9.

[409] Elaine Pagels *The Gnostic Gospels* (New York: Random House, 1979) pp. 58f, 72.

[410] Clement of Alexandria *Stromata* 7.17.106.

[411] Irenaeus *Against Heresies* 1.25.5.

[412] G. W. H. Lampe "Scripture and Tradition: The Early Church" in *Scripture and Tradition: Essays* (London: Lutterworth, 1955) pp. 40f.

[413] Origen *De principiis*, esp. Preface 2, Preface 3, 2.11.3.

[414] Carl Vernon Harris *Origen of Alexandria's Interpretation of the Teacher's Function in the Early Christian Hierarchy and Community* (New York: American Press, 1966) pp. 19f, 122-124, 130f; Kenneth Hein *Eucharist and Excommunication: A Study in Early Christian Doctrine and Discipline* 2d ed. (Bern and Frankfort a.M.: Lang, 1975) p. 308; Ronald E. Heine "Introduction" to Origen *Homilies on Genesis and Exodus* (Washington, DC: Catholic University of America Press, 1982) pp. 33-38. For the inadequacies inherent in any translation from Greek to Latin, see Bonifatius Fischer "Limitations of Latin in Representing Greek" reprinted in Bruce M. Metzger *The Early Versions of the New Testament: Their Origins, Transmissions and Limitations* (Oxford: Clarendon, 1977) pp. 362-374.

[415] Richard Patrick Crossland Hanson *Origen's Doctrine of Tradition* pp. 40-47, 191; Ronald E. Heine "Introduction" to Origen *Homilies on Genesis and Exodus* p. 308.

[416] Gary Wayne Barkley "Introduction" to Origen *Homilies on Leviticus 1-16* (Washington, DC: Catholic University of America Press, 1990) p. 23; Henri Crouzel *Origen* trans. A. S. Worrall (Edinburgh: T. & T. Clark, 1989) pp. 42f, Trans. of *Origène* (1985); Ronald E. Heine "Introduction" to Origen *Homilies on Genesis and Exodus* pp. 38f; Joseph T. Lienhard "Introduction" to Origen *Homilies on Luke; Fragments on Luke* (Washington, DC: Catholic University of America Press, 1996) p. xxxvi.

[417] For a summary of the debate on the reliability of the Latin translations of Origen, see Ronald E. Heine "Introduction" to Origen *Homilies on Genesis and Exodus* pp. 30-32.

[418] Alexander of Jerusalem (or of Cappadocia) *Letter to Demetrius* in Eusebius *History of the Church* 6.19.17f.

[419] Jules Lebreton and Jacques Zeiller *The History of the Primitive Church* trans. E. Messenger (New York: Macmillan, 1949) vol. 2 p. 944 as paraphrased in Carl Vernon Harris *Origen of Alexandria's Interpretation of the Teacher's Function in the Early Christian Hierarchy and Community* p. 200.

[420] Cyprian *Epistula* 67.5 trans. Ernest Wallis as *Epistle* 67.5 (i.e same numbering) ANF 5:371.

[421] Cyprian *Epistula* 45.1 trans. Ernest Wallis as *Epistle* 41.1 ANF 5:320.

[422] Cyprian *Epistula* 45.3.

[423] Everett Ferguson "Dionysius of Alexandria" in *Encyclopedia of Early Christianity* (New York and London: Garland, 1990) pp. 266f.

[424] My translation of *nihil innoueter nisi quod traditum est* as Cyprian directly quoting Stephen of Rome in *Epistula* 74.1f.

[425] Cyprian *Epistula* 74.2.

[426] Firmilian *Epistula* 75.5f in the correspondence of Cyprian.

[427] Firmilian *Epistula* 75.19 in the correspondence of Cyprian.

[428] My trans. of *traditionem hanc humanum* in Firmilian *Epistula* 75.6 in the correspondence of Cyprian.

[429] Cyprian *Epistula* 63.14. trans. Ernest Wallis as *Epistle* 62.14 ANF 5:362.

[430] Loc. cit.

[431] My trans. of *qui mandatum dei reiciunt et traditionem suam statuere conantur* in Cyprian *Epistula* 43.6.

[432] Loc. cit.

[433] Cyprian *Epistula* 63.1 trans. Ernest Wallis as *Epistle* 62.1 ANF 5:359.

[434] Cyprian *Epistula* 63.19 trans. Ernest Wallis as *Epistle* 62.19 ANF 5:363.

[435] Cyprian *Epistula* 74.10 trans. Ernest Wallis as *Epistle* 73.10 ANF 5:389.

[436] Cyprian *Epistula* 46 trans. Ernest Wallis as *Epistle* 43 ANF 5:321.

[437] Cyprian *Epistula* 4.1 trans. Ernest Wallis as *Epistle* 61.1 ANF 5:357.

[438] Richard Patrick Crossland Hanson *Origen's Doctrine of Tradition* p. 181.

[439] *Martyrdom of Callistratus* 2, 10.

[440] Tertullian *Against Marcion* 4.5.

[441] E. Flesseman-Van Leer *Tradition and Scripture in the Early Church* p. 146.

[442] Robert E. Webber *Ancient-Future Faith* p. 186.

Chapter Five: The Decian Discontinuity

[443] Carl Vernon Harris *Origen of Alexandria's Interpretation of the Teacher's Function in the Early Christian Hierarchy and Community* (New York: American Press, 1966) p. 86, paraphrasing from Eugene De Faye *Origen and His Work* trans. Fred Rothwell (London: Allen & Unwin, 1926) p. 113.

[444] Charles Bigg *The Christian Platonists of Alexandria* (Oxford: Clarendon, 1886; rev. 1913 by F. E. Brightman; repr. 1968) p. 325 n. 2.

[445] Charles Bigg *The Christian Platonists of Alexandria* p. 331.

[446] Cyprian *On the Lapsed* 5 trans. Ernest Wallis ANF 5:438.

447 Origen *In Matthaeum commentariorum series 61* trans. R. B. Tollinton in *Selections from the Commentaries and Homilies of Origen* (London: SPCK, 1929) p. 136; also translated with identical wording at p. 171 of Carl Vernon Harris *Origen of Alexandria's Interpretation of the Teacher's Function in the Early Christian Hierarchy and Community*.

448 Origen *Homilies on Numbers* 2.1 3 trans. Arnold Ehrhardt *The Apostolic Succession in the First Two Centuries of the Church* (London: Lutterworth, 1953) pp. 151f (ellipses are the translator's), incorrectly ascribing the passage to Origen *Homilies on 1 Samuel* 1.7 ; Carl Vernon Harris at pp. 197 and 260 correctly attributes this passage to Origen *Homilies on Numbers* 2.1, as does Louis Doutreleau *Origène: Homélies sur les Nombres* (Paris: Cerf, 1996) vol. 1 pp. 56-59 lines 36-45 Sources chrétiennes n° 415.

449 Carl Vernon Harris *Origen of Alexandria's Interpretation of the Teacher's Function in the Early Christian Hierarchy and Community* p. 173 citing Origen *Homilies on Numbers* 20.4; André Méhat's *Homélies sur les Nombres* (Paris: Cerf, 1951) pp. 167f identifies the relevant passage as Origen *Homilies on Numbers* 9.1; Doutreleau's edition vol. 1 p. 232 identifies it as Origen *Homilies on Numbers* 9.1.7.

450 Carl Vernon Harris *Origen of Alexandria's Interpretation of the Teacher's Function in the Early Christian Hierarchy and Community* p. 217 citing Origen *In Matthaeum commentariorum series* 12.

451 Origen *In Matthaeum commentariorum series 61* trans. R. B. Tollinton in *Selections from the Commentaries and Homilies of Origen* p. 136; also translated with identical wording at p. 171 of Carl Vernon Harris *Origen of Alexandria's Interpretation of the Teacher's Function in the Early Christian Hierarchy and Community*.

452 Arnold Ehrhardt *The Apostolic Succession in the First Two Centuries of the Church* p. 144, citing Origen *Commentary on Matthew* 11.15.

453 Origen *Commentary on Romans* 1.2 trans. Arnold Ehrhardt *The Apostolic Succession in the First Two Centuries of the Church* p. 145.

454 Arnold Ehrhardt *The Apostolic Succession in the First Two Centuries of the Church* p. 145 citing Origen *Commentary on Romans* 2.11 (2.11.10).

455 Robert M. Grant *Augustus to Constantine: The Rise and Triumph of Christianity in the Roman World* (Louisville, Ky; London: Westminster John Knox, 2004) p. 175, citing Origen *Matthew Commentary 16.8*.

456 Origen *Homilies on 1 Samuel* 1.7.

457 Origen *Homilies on Leviticus* 5.8 my trans.

458 Robert M. Grant *Augustus to Constantine* p. 175, citing Origen *Homilies on Ezekiel* 3.3.

459 Origen *Homilies on Ezekiel* 9.2.39 to 49.

460 Origen *Homilies on Jeremiah* 11.3.2; Origen *In Matthaeum commentariorum series* 61.

461 Origen *Homilies on Joshua* 7.6 and 17.3.

462 Carl Vernon Harris *Origen of Alexandria's Interpretation of the Teacher's Function in the Early Christian Hierarchy and Community* p. 217; Harris' endnote (on p. 265) begins "Cf. *Hom. on Num.* XII.4", but in Méhat's and Doutreleau's editions 12.4 has no bearing on the subject matter. See instead Origen *Homilies on Numbers* 9.1 and 22.4.

463 Origen *Commentary on Matthew* 16.22 trans. Arnold Ehrhardt *The Apostolic Succession in the First Two Centuries of the Church* p. 149.

464 Arnold Ehrhardt *The Apostolic Succession in the First Two Centuries of the Church* p. 148, citing Origen but not identifying the work.

465 Origen *Homilies on Numbers* 22.4.

466 Karl Rahner *Penance in the Early Church* (New York: Crossroad, 1982) p. 288. Trans. by Lionel Swain of *Frühe Bussgeschichte in Einzslungterauchungen* (Zurich: Benziger, 1973). See also Origen *Homilies on Joshua* 7.6 and Kenneth Hein *Eucharist and Excommunication: A Study in Early Christian Doctrine and Discipline.* 2d ed. (Bern; Frankfurt a.M.: Lang, 1975) p. 330.

467 Cyprian *On the Lapsed* 6 trans. Ernest Wallis ANF 5:438.

468 *Didascalia apostolorum* 9.

[469] Loc. cit.

[470] Loc. cit.

[471] Loc. cit. in *Didascalia Apostolorum: The Syriac Version* 9 trans. R. Hugh Connolly (Oxford: Clarendon) p. 98-100.

[472] Hans von Campenhausen *Ecclesiastical Authority and Spiritual Power in the Church of the First Three Centuries* (London: Adam & Charles Black, 1969) p. 95f. Trans. by J. A. Baker of *Kirchliches Amt und Geistliche Vollmacht* (Tubingen: J. C. B. Mohr (Paul Siebeck), 1953).

[473] Hans von Campenhausen *Ecclesiastical Authority and Spiritual Power in the Church* p. 173.

[474] *Shepherd of Hermas* Vision 3.6.3, 3.12.3; Mandate 2.3; Similitudes 8.7.2, 8.7.5, 9.31.4, 9.32.2.

[475] *Shepherd of Hermas* Similitude 8.7.4.

[476] Loc. cit.

[477] *Shepherd of Hermas* Vision 3.5.1.

[478] *Shepherd of Hermas* Vision 3.9.10.

[479] *Shepherd of Hermas* Vision 3.9.7.

[480] *Shepherd of Hermas* Mandate 11.12.

[481] Hans von Campenhausen *Ecclesiastical Authority and Spiritual Power in the Church* p. 96.

[482] Arnold Ehrhardt *The Apostolic Succession in the First Two Centuries of the Church* p. 147.

[483] In *The Apocryphal New Testament* (Oxford: Clarendon, 1953) pp. 485-503.

[484] In *New Testament Apocrypha* rev. ed. by Wilhelm Schneenelcher; trans. R. McL. Wilson (Cambridge: James Clarke: Louisville, KY: Westminster/John Knox, 1991) vol. 1 pp. 252-278.

[485] Arnold Ehrhardt *The Apostolic Succession in the First Two Centuries of the Church* pp. 146-152.

[486] Arnold Ehrhardt *The Apostolic Succession in the First Two Centuries of the Church* p. 146.

[487] Loc. cit.

[488] *Shepherd of Hermas* Similitude 9.26.2.

[489] Irenaeus *Against Heresies* 4.26.3 trans. W. H. Rambaut ANF 1:497.

[490] Origen *Homilies on Numbers* 22.4.2 lines 165f my trans. of *ecclesiarum principes* in Doutreleau's edition vol. 3 p. 94.

[491] Cyprian *Epistulae* 5-43.

[492] Cyprian *Epistula* 33.1 trans. Ernest Wallis as *Epistle* 26.1 ANF 5:305.

[493] Cyprian *Epistula* 16.1 trans. Ernest Wallis as *Epistle* 9.1 ANF 5:289.

[494] William Hugh Clifford Frend *Saints and Sinners in the Early Church: Differing and Conflicting Traditions in the First Six Centuries* (Wilmington, Delaware: Michael Glazier, 1985) p. 99.

[495] *Against Celsus* 3.15 trans. Frederick Crombie ANF 4:470.

[496] Robert Lee Williams "Persecution" in *Encyclopedia of Early Christianity* ed. Everett Ferguson (New York: Garland, 1990) p. 715.

[497] Cyprian *On the Lapsed* 7f trans. Ernest Wallis ANF 5:439.

[498] Cyprian *On the Lapsed* 8.

[499] Cyprian *On the Lapsed* 9.

[500] Dionysius of Alexandria *Letter to Fabius, Bishop of Antioch* in Eusebius *History of the Church* 6.41.11f trans. J. D. F. Salmond ANF 6:98f.

[501] Rodney Stark *The Rise of Christianity: A Sociologist Reconsiders History* (Princeton, NJ: Princeton University Press, 1996) pp. 73 and 77, drawing on (i) E. R. Boak *A History of Rome to 565 A.D.* 3rd ed. (New York: Macmillan, 1947), (ii) E. R. Boak *Manpower Shortage and the Fall of the Roman Empire in the West* (Ann Arbor: University of Michigan Press, 1955), (iii) E. R. Boak "The Populations of Roman and Byzantine Karanis" (1955) 4 *Historia* pp. 157-162, (iv) William H. McNeill *Plagues and Peoples* (Garden City, NY:

Doubleday, 1976), and (v) J. C. Russell *Late Ancient and Medieval Populations* (Philadelphia: Transactions of the American Philosophical Society vol. 48 pt. 3, 1958).

[502] Rodney Stark *The Rise of Christianity* p. 73.

[503] Origen *Homilies on Joshua* 1.7.

[504] Cyprian *Epistula* 9.

[505] Cyprian *Epistula* 68.

[506] Cyprian *On the Lapsed* 22; Cyprian *Epistula* 59.17f.

[507] Cyprian *Epistula* 59.17 trans. Ernest Wallis as *Epistle* 54.17 ANF 5:345.

[508] Cyprian *Epistula* 3.

[509] Cyprian *Epistula* 59.2 trans. Ernest Wallis as *Epistle* 54.2 ANF 5:339.

[510] Cyprian *Epistula* 45.

[511] Cyprian *Epistulae* 44.1, 59.16.

[512] Cyprian *Epistulae* 44.2, 59.16.

[513] Cyprian *Epistula* 59.1, 59.10.

[514] Acts 25.16.

[515] Cyprian *Epistula* 45.2. See also Cyprian *Epistula* 59.10.

[516] Cyprian *Epistula* 59.5 trans. Robert Ernest Wallis as *Epistle* 54.5 ANF 5:340; Cyprian *Epistula* 72.1 trans. Robert Ernest Wallis as *Epistle* 71.1 ANF 5:378.

[517] Cyprian *Epistula* 59.14 trans. Robert Ernest Wallis as *Epistle* 54.14 ANF 5:344; Cyprian *Epistula* 73.2 trans. Robert Ernest Wallis as *Epistle* 72.2 ANF 5:380; Cyprian *On the Lapsed* 6 trans. Ernest Wallis ANF 5:438.

[518] Cyprian *Epistula* 66.8 trans. Robert Ernest Wallis as *Epistle* 68.8 ANF 5:374f.

[519] J. Patout Burns "On Rebaptism: Social Organization in the Third Century Church" (1993) 1 *Journal of Early Christian Studies* 386; Cyprian *Epistula* 55.17, 29, 60; Cyprian *On the Unity of the Catholic Church* 14.

[520] Cyprian *Epistula* 59.5 trans. Robert Ernest Wallis as *Epistle* 54.5 ANF 5:340.

[521] Cyprian *On Jealousy and Envy* 6; Cyprian *Epistula* 66.5.

[522] Cyprian *Epistula* 68. In the same vein, see his *Epistula* 59.

[523] Cyprian *Epistula* 3.1, 59.4 and 66.3.

[524] Cyprian *Epistula* 3.2, 59.4 and 66.3.

[525] Cyprian *Epistula* 3.1, 4.4, 43.7, 59.4 and 66.3. Only verse 12 is quoted in *Epistula* 43.7.

[526] Cyprian *Epistula* 59.16 trans. Ernest Wallis as *Epistle* 54.16 ANF 5:345.

[527] *Epistle of the Synod of Antioch* in Eusebius *History of the Church* 7.30.

[528] Phileas of Thmuis et al. *Epistle to Meletius* trans. S. D. F. Salmond ANF 6:162.

[529] Peter of Alexandria *Epistle to the Alexandrians*.

[530] Cyprian *Epistula* 71.4.

[531] Cyprian *Epistula* 71.3 trans. Robert Ernest Wallis as *Epistle* 70.3 ANF 5:377. See also Cyprian *Epistula* 74.9.

[532] Cyprian *Epistula* 73.13 trans. Robert Ernest Wallis as *Epistle* 72.13 ANF 5:382.

[533] Loc. cit.

[534] Cyprian *Epistula* 74.9.

[535] Firmilian *Epistula* 75.19 in the correspondence of Cyprian, trans. Robert Ernest Wallis as *Epistle* 74.19 ANF 5:395.

[536] Loc. cit.

[537] Libosus of Vaga in *Sententiae episcoporum de haereticus baptizandis* trans. Ernest Wallis as *Seventh Council of Carthage under Cyprian* ANF 5:569.

[538] Felix of Bussacene (or Byzacene) in *Sententiae episcoporum de haereticus baptizandis* trans. Ernest Wallis as *Seventh Council of Carthage under Cyprian* ANF 5:571.

539 Cyprian *Epistula* 74.9.

540 William H. Chalker *Science and Faith: Understanding Meaning, Method, and Truth* (Louisville, Ky; London: Westminster John Knox, 2006) *passim*.

541 Cyprian *Epistula* 74.10 trans. Robert Ernest Wallis as *Epistle* 73.10 ANF 5:389.

542 Cyprian *Epistula* 74.2.

543 Cyprian *Epistula* 74.10 trans. Robert Ernest Wallis as *Epistle* 73.10 ANF 5:389.

544 Cyprian *Epistula* 74.

545 Tertullian *Against Marcion* 4.5; E. Flesseman-Van Leer *Tradition and Scripture in the Early Church* (Assen, Netherlands; Van Gorckum, c1954) p. 146.

546 Cyprian *Epistula* 63.2 trans. Robert Ernest Wallis as *Epistle* 62.2 ANF 5:359.

547 Cyprian *Epistula* 63.

548 The Paschal Controversy of the late second century is not comparable to that over rebaptism because in the earlier dispute: (i) both sides knew of and tolerated the other's practice for forty years before the parties became disagreeable, (ii) no evidence has come down to use that either party used the New Testament to support its own observance or condemn that of its opponents, (iii) the Quartodecimans produced a number of attestations of their practice through an unbroken succession of bishops back to the immediate disciples of the apostles and purportedly to the apostles themselves, and (4) neither party raised the idea that the correct practice has been lost in some generations since the apostles and was later being restored by that party.

549 Robert Louis Wilken *The Spirit of Early Christian Thought: Seeking the Face of God* (New Haven, Conn.; London: Yale University Press, 2003) pp. 263f.

550 1 Corinthians 11.1 RSV.

551 Ignatius *Philadelphians* 7.2.

Chapter Six: Determining the Specifics of Early Christian Law

552 Origen *Commentary on Romans* 1.18.2; Richard B. Hays *The Moral Vision of the New Testament: Community, Cross, New Creation: A Contemporary Introduction to New Testament Ethics* (New York: HarperSanFrancisco, 1996) pp. 385-388 (on homosexuality).

553 Susanne Heine *Women and Early Christianity: A Reappraisal* (Minneapolis: Augsburg, 1988) p. 36. Trans by John Bowden of *Frauen der frühen Christenheit* (Vandenhoeck & Ruprecht, 1986).

554 Allen Verhey *The Great Reversal: Ethics and the New Testament* (Grand Rapids, MI: Eerdmans, 1984) p. 152.

555 Ibid., p. 170.

556 Ibid., p. 152.

557 See Chapter 1 supra.

558 Richard B. Hays *The Moral Vision of the New Testament* pp. 189-191.

559 Elaine Pagels *The Gnostic Gospels* (New York: Vintage Books, 1981 c1979) pp. 133-136.

560 See Daniel H. Williams *Retrieving the Tradition and Renewing Evangelicalism: A Primer for Suspicious Protestants* (Grand Rapids, MI; Cambridge, UK: Eerdmans, 1999) pp. 81f.

561 Hegesippus *Memoirs* in Eusebius *History of the Church* 3.32.7f, 4.22.2-5.

562 Richard Patrick Crossland Hanson *Origen's Doctrine of Tradition* (London: SPCK, 1954) p. 192.

563 R. P. C. Hanson *Origen's Doctrine of Tradition* p. 181.

564 Lee M. McDonald *The Formation of the Christian Biblical Canon* (Peabody, Mass.: Hendrickson, 1995) p. 253.

565 Lee M. McDonald *The Formation of the Christian Biblical Canon* p. 201.

566 Albert C. Sundberg Jr. "The Making of the New Testament Canon" in Charles M. Laymon *The Interpreter's One-Volume Commentary on the Bible* (Nashville: Abingdon, 1971) pp. 1216-1224 at 1222f.

567 Kenneth Hein *Eucharist and Excommunication: A Study in Early Christian Doctrine and Discipline* 2d ed. (Bern and Frankfurt a.M.: Lang, 1975) p. 411.

568 Lee Martin McDonald *The Biblical Canon: Its Origin, Transmission, and Authority* (Peabody, MA: Hendrickson, 2007) p. 200.

569 Irenaeus *Against Heresies* 3.2.2; Irenaeus *Letter to Florinus on the Sole Sovereignty of God*.

570 Irenaeus *Against Heresies* 3.31.

571 Irenaeus *Against Heresies* 4.26.2.

572 Clement of Alexandria *Stromata* 1.1.

573 Especially *De Principiis* 2.

574 See also Arnold Ehrhardt *The Apostolic Succession in the First Two Centuries of the Church* (London; Lutterworth, 1953) p. 140.

575 Fragment 71 of "Les fragments grec" of *Tomes sur Luc* in *Origène: Homélies sur S. Luc* ed. and trans. Henri Crouzel, Francois Fournier and Pierre Périchon (Paris: Cerf, 1962); reproduced from M. Rauer *Griechischen Christlichen Schriftsteller* 2d ed. 1959 vol. 49; vol. 9 of *Origenes Werke*.

576 Origen *Commentary on Matthew* 13.15 trans John Patrick ANF 10:413.

577 Joseph T. Lienhard's "Introduction" to *Origen: Homilies on Luke; Fragments on Luke* (Washington, D.C.: Catholic University of America Press, 1996) p. xx.

578 Matthew 8.19; 9.11; 12.38; 17.24; 19.16; 21.15; 22.16; 22.24; 22.36; 26.18; Mark 4.38; 5.35; 9.17; 9.38; 10.17; 10.20; 10.35; 12.14; 12.19; 12.32; 13.1; 14.14; Luke 3.12; 7.40; 8.49; 9.38; 10.25; 11.45; 12.13; 18.18; 19.39; 20.21; 20.28; 20.39; 21.7; 22.11; John 1.38; 8.4; 11.28; 20.16.

579 *Pastor of Hermas* Vision 3.5.1.

580 Arnold Ehrhardt *The Apostolic Succession in the First Two Centuries* p. 96.

581 *Pastor of Hermas* Similitude 9.15.4. Earlier, *Didache* 13.2 spoke of teachers as synonymous with prophets.

582 Acts 13.1.

583 1 Timothy 3.2; 4.11; 4.13; 5.17; 2 Timothy 2.24; 4.2; Titus 2.1.

584 Joseph T. Lienhard "Introduction" to *Origen: Homilies on Luke* p. xx.

585 Arnold Ehrhardt *The Apostolic Succession in the First Two Centuries* p. 84.

586 Arnold Ehrhardt *The Apostolic Succession in the First Two Centuries* p. 138. For more on the office of *didaskaloi*, see E. Prinzivalli article "Didaskalos" in *Encyclopedia of the Early Church* (New York: Oxford University Press, 1992) vol. 1 p. 235; G. L. Prestige *Fathers and Heretics* (London: S.P.C.K., 1940; repr. 1954) pp. 25f, 44f; Carl Vernon Harris *Origen of Alexandria's Interpretation of the Teacher's Function in the Early Christian Hierarchy and Community* (New York: American Press, 1966).

587 Tertullian *De praescriptione haereticorum* 20f and 36 (between AD 198 and 202).

588 Tertullian *De praescriptione haereticorum* 32.

589 Tertullian *Against Marcion* 4.5.

590 Tertullian *On Baptism* 6.

591 Tertullian *On Modesty* 21 trans. S. Thelwall ANF 4:74 (before AD 222).

592 Willi Marxsen *New Testament Foundations for Christian Ethics* (Minneapolis: Fortress, 1993) p. xiii. Trans. by O. C. Dean Jr. of *"Christliche" und Christliche Ethik in Neuen Testament* (Gütersloh: Gütersloher Verlaghaus Gerd Mohn).